OFFICE-HOLDERS IN MODERN BRITAIN

III

Officials of the Boards of Trade
1660–1870

OFFICE-HOLDERS
IN MODERN BRITAIN

III

Officials of the Boards of Trade
1660–1870

compiled by

J. C. SAINTY

UNIVERSITY OF LONDON
INSTITUTE OF HISTORICAL RESEARCH
THE ATHLONE PRESS
1974

Published by
THE ATHLONE PRESS
UNIVERSITY OF LONDON
at 4 *Gower Street, London* WC1

Distributed by
Tiptree Book Services Ltd
Tiptree, Essex

U.S.A. & Canada
Humanities Press Inc
New York

0 485 17143 0

Printed in Great Britain by
WESTERN PRINTING SERVICES LTD
BRISTOL

Contents

CONTENTS

Abbreviations

Add. Additional
app. appointed, appointment
Bart. Baronet
BM British Museum
c. circa
cr. created
d. death, died
dis. dismissed
ed. edited, edition
f., ff. folio, folios
HC House of Commons Paper
Hon. Honourable
Kal. Kalendar
kt., ktd. knight, knighted

MS, MSS manuscript, manuscripts
occ. occurrence, occurs
pd. paid
P.R.O. Public Record Office
pt. part
reapp. reappointed, reappointment
Rept. Report
res. resigned
ret. retired
succ. succeeded
TM Treasury Minute
v. vice
vac. vacated office, vacation of office

References

IN MANUSCRIPT

British Museum, London

Add. 9729, 9767–8, 38703	Blathwayt Papers.
Add. 15947	Prior Papers.
Add. 32716	Newcastle Papers.

Library of Congress, Washington

Journal (Plantations) 1670–2 and Journal (Trade and Plantations) 1672–4	Journals of the Councils of Foreign Plantations 1670–2 and Trade and Foreign Plantations 1672–4 (photographic copy in the possession of the Library of the Department of Trade and Industry, London).

Public Record Office, London

AO 1/2321/48	Declared Accounts: Treasury Solicitor.
BT 1	Board of Trade In Letters.
BT 3	Board of Trade Out Letters.
BT 5	Board of Trade Minutes.
BT 6/293	Appendix to the Report on the Board of Trade 1862.
BT 12	Board of Trade Commercial Department Out Letters.
BT 13	Board of Trade Establishment Department Correspondence and Papers.
BT 20	Board of Trade Establishment Department Out Letters.
C 66	Patent Rolls.
C 231/7	Crown Office Docquet Book 1660–78.
CO 1/14	Journal of the Council of Foreign Plantations 1660–4.
CO 388/75–84	Board of Trade Accounts and Establishments 1696–1782.
CO 389/5	Board of Trade Instructions, Petitions, Orders in Council, etc. 1670–4.
CO 389/36–9	Board of Trade Petitions, Orders in Council and Accounts 1696–1782.
CO 391/1–16	Board of Trade Journals 1675–1704.
Ind. 20442–20469	Board of Trade Registers and Indexes 1840–76.
MT 11	Board of Trade Railway Department Out Letters.
MT 13	Board of Trade Railway Department Minutes.
PC 2	Privy Council Registers.
PRO 30/8/184	Chatham Papers.
Prob 6	Prerogative Court of Canterbury Administration Act Books.
SP 29	State Papers: Charles II.
T 1	Treasury Papers

T 29	Treasury Minutes.
T 52	Warrants not relating to money.
T 53	Warrants relating to money.

IN PRINT

Andrews, *Committees*	C. M. Andrews, *British Committees, Commissions and Councils of Trade and Plantations, 1662–1675.* Baltimore 1908.
APC (Colonial)	*Acts of the Privy Council of England. Colonial Series.* 6 vols., 1613–1783. London 1908–12.
Chamberlayne, *Present State*	E. and J. Chamberlayne, *Angliae (Magnae Britanniae) Notitia; or the Present State of England (Great Britain).*
Court and City Reg.	*Court and City Register.*
CSPC (America & West Indies)	*Calendar of State Papers. Colonial Series (America and West Indies).* 39 vols., 1574–1738. London 1860–1969.
CSPD	*Calendar of State Papers Domestic.* 94 vols., 1547–1704. London 1856–1964.
CTB	*Calendar of Treasury Books.* 32 vols., 1660–1718. London 1904–69.
Gent. Mag.	*Gentleman's Magazine.*
Hist. Reg. Chron.	*Historical Register . . . Chronological Diary.*
JCTP	*Journal of the Commissioners for Trade and Plantations.* 14 vols., 1704–82. London 1920–38.
Royal Kal.	*Royal Kalendar.*
Staff Lists	*Staff Lists of the Board of Trade* (bound set in possession of the Library of the Department of Trade and Industry), vol. I. 1865–94.

Note on Editorial Method

This volume is designed to make available lists of the officials who served in the Boards of Trade between the Restoration in 1660 and the year 1870 which witnessed the introduction of the system of open competition for entrants into the Civil Service. The term Boards of Trade has been understood to cover all the institutional arrangements, whether they took the form of Councils or Committees of the Privy Council, which had charge of trade and foreign plantations, functions which were undertaken by separate bodies until 1672 but which were invariably linked thereafter. The material is presented in four parts: an introduction, lists of appointments, periodic lists of officials and an alphabetical list of officials. The purpose of the introduction is to provide a short account of the development of the Boards during the period in order that the various offices and grades may be related to their general context. The lists of appointments give the dates of appointments to these offices and grades. They are preceded by introductory notes which bring together such matters as the method of appointment, remuneration and the relevant statutes and minutes. The periodic lists enable the complete establishment to be seen at selected dates.

The alphabetical list is not intended to be a biographical index. Its purpose is confined simply to providing summarised accounts of the offices held by each individual serving the Boards during the period. No information has been included unless it is directly relevant to this purpose. Thus dates of death are included only if the individual was in office at his death. Appointments to offices elsewhere have been ignored unless they occasioned, or can reasonably be held to have occasioned, the departure of the official from the office. In general the accounts of the careers of the members of the successive Boards have been confined to providing the dates of their appointment. A terminal date is given only in the cases of salaried Commissioners and the President and Vice-President after 1786. Information concerning resignations and retirements is provided only for those holding 'permanent' offices. Where an individual held an additional office in the department such as a private secretaryship, which was not directly related to the ordinary course of promotion, the details of his period of service in this additional office have been placed in a separate paragraph. The accounts of the careers of those who were in office at the end of 1870 have not been continued beyond this point.

All references have been concentrated in the alphabetical list except in the case of the Commissioners where they are included in the relevant lists of appointments. Where printed calendars of manuscript material exist they have been used as authorities provided that the calendaring is sufficiently full. Peers and holders of courtesy titles have been indexed under their titles. In the case of changes of name or status, appropriate cross-references have been inserted. Unless otherwise noted, information concerning peers and baronets has been taken from the *Complete Peerage* (ed. G.E.C. 2nd ed. 13 vols. London 1910–59), the *Complete Baronetage* (ed. G.E.C. 5 vols. Exeter 1900–6) and Burke's *Peerage*.

Certain conventions have been adopted for dating appointments. The year is taken to have begun on 1 January throughout the period. Where offices were conferred by an instrument such as letters patent under the great seal, the date is that of the instrument. Where an appointment was by order in council or by minute of the Board, it is that of the order or minute. The task of determining the periods of service of 'political' officials presents considerable difficulty particularly in the nineteenth century when their appointments were frequently canvassed in newspapers and elsewhere several days before the date of their formal entry into office. For the sake of consistency the latter date has been adopted throughout the period. All officials are taken to have remained in office until the appointment of their successors unless there is clear evidence to support the selection of an earlier date. Where there is no indication of the date of appointment of an individual, his period of service is dated by reference to the time during which he received a salary or other remuneration or, failing this information, by reference to the earliest and latest date at which he is found occupying a particular office.

Introduction

COUNCILS OF TRADE AND PLANTATIONS 1660–74

Before the Restoration the responsibility for regulating trade and foreign plantations was entrusted to a series of different organisations.[1] In 1660 Charles II drew upon this earlier experience without reproducing exactly any of the previous expedients. In the first place he restored the Privy Council to its pre-eminent position as the ultimate authority in such questions. On 4 July 1660 a Committee of the Council for Foreign Plantations was established which, in one form or another, continued to exist until 1696.[2] Before the end of 1660 two standing Councils were appointed and given immediate responsibility for trade and for foreign plantations under the Committee's more general supervision. Both Councils were appointed by commission under the great seal and were composed of leading political figures and prominent merchants who served without salary. The Council of Trade consisted of sixty-two Commissioners and was given power to appoint a Secretary and other officials. An annual grant of £1000 was made available for their salaries and the incidental expenses of the Council.[3] Since the records of the Council have disappeared its history is largely obscure and, apart from its Secretary, the officials who served it are unknown.[4] The last clear indication of its activities occurs in 1664 but the fact that a journal of its proceedings between 1660 and 1668 was said once to have existed suggests that it continued, although probably in a moribund state, until the latter year.[5] In October 1668 the Council of Trade was reconstituted by commission under the great seal. The number of Commissioners, originally forty-one, was increased to forty-six in 1669.[6] As in the case of its predecessor the records of the Council are lost and, of its officials, the name of only its Secretary is known. The Council was dissolved in 1672.[7]

The Council of Foreign Plantations, appointed in 1660, was composed of forty-nine Commissioners and had power to employ subordinate officials, £300 being provided for their salaries and for incidental expenses.[8] The activities of this Council are a little better known than those of its counterpart since the journal of its proceedings for the years 1660–4 has survived.[9] However, of its officials, only the Secretary

---

[1] A general account of the Boards of Trade throughout the period covered by these lists is contained in H. Llewellyn Smith, *The Board of Trade* (London 1928). For the various administrative arrangements made between 1622 and 1675, see Andrews, *Committees*.

[2] *APC (Colonial) 1613–80*, 295, 321, 337–8, 433–4.

[3] Commission of 7 Nov. 1660 (C 66/2946); Andrews, *Committees*, 64–76, 80–5, 91–5.

[4] A petition of (?) May 1667 names Jane Woodcock, Thomas Guning, Thomas Gardener, William Briggs, Hugh Evington, Thomas Roe and Elizabeth Duncombe as 'attendants' of the Council but does not specify what posts they occupied in the office (SP 29/202 f. 190).

[5] *CTB*, i, 615; *APC (Colonial) 1613–80*, 435; Andrews, *Committees*, 75 n. 1; *CSPC (America & West Indies) 1697–8*, 188, 206; *JCTP 1704–9*, 396, 400.

[6] Commissions of 20 Oct. 1668 (C 66/3103) and 16 April 1669 (C 66/3106).

[7] Commission of 27 Sept. 1672 (C 66/3137).

[8] Commission of 1 Dec. 1660 (C 66/2946); Andrews, *Committees*, 64–79.

[9] CO 1/14.

is traceable. There is a suggestion that the Council had some sort of existence as late as 1667 but it is impossible to say how much longer it continued. In any event new arrangements were made in 1670 when a new Council was appointed by commission under the great seal consisting of the holders of the more important political offices *ex officio* and of named Commissioners, some of whom were accorded salaries. The salaried Commissioners, who were headed by a President, were originally nine; they were increased to ten in 1671. In addition certain other Commissioners were appointed to serve without salary. Provision was made for one of the salaried Commissioners to act as Secretary and for an Assistant. A sum of £1000 was made available for incidental expenses and the payment of the junior officials who consisted of three Clerks, a Messenger and a Doorkeeper.[10]

The year 1672 marked the end of the arrangement whereby trade and foreign plantations were dealt with concurrently by two parallel Councils. Henceforth these responsibilities were considered inseparable and, whatever the structure of the bodies exercising them, 'trade and foreign plantations' has continued to be the formal description of their spheres of activity. In institutional terms the fusion of the two functions was achieved by renewing, with appropriate amendments, the commission of 1670 constituting the Council of Foreign Plantations. The structure of its membership and staff underwent relatively little change. The second salaried Commissioner was given the title of Vice President and the officials of the Council consisted of a Secretary, three Clerks, a Messenger and a Doorkeeper.[11]

COMMITTEES OF THE PRIVY COUNCIL FOR TRADE AND PLANTATIONS 1675-96

The existence of the Council of 1672 was brought to a close in December 1674.[12] The business which it had undertaken was transferred in March of the following year to the Committee of the Privy Council for Trade and Plantations. As already noted this Committee had been established as the Committee for Foreign Plantations in 1660. It had continued to exist alongside the standing Councils, occasionally taking action in relation to matters within its jurisdiction. It was now reconstituted and given immediate responsibility for those questions with which the Councils had been concerned. It retained this position until 1696. The Committee was constituted as a select Committee of the Council from 1675 to 1688, as a Committee of the whole Council from 1688 to 1689 and again as a select Committee from 1689 to 1696. Its Members, commonly known as the Lords of Trade and Plantations, were unsalaried.[13]

[10] Commission of 30 July 1670 (C 231/7 p. 375). The full text of this commission has not survived but its main provisions are recited in that of 4 April 1671 (C 66/3125). See also Andrews, *Committees*, 96–106; R. P. Bieber, 'The British Plantation Councils of 1670–4', *Eng. Hist. Rev.*, xl (1925), 93–106. The MS Journal of the Council and that of the Council of Trade and Foreign Plantations 1672–4 are in the Library of Congress, Washington. I am very much indebted to Mr. K. A. Mallaber, Librarian of the Department of Trade and Industry, for making photographic copies of these Journals available to me.

[11] Commission of 27 Sept. 1672 (C 66/3137); Andrews, *Committees*, 106–12; K. H. D. Haley, *The 1st Earl of Shaftesbury* (Oxford 1968), 259–64. See also n. 10.

[12] Letters patent of 21 Dec. 1674 (C 66/3164).

[13] *APC (Colonial) 1613–80*, 619–20; W. T. Root, 'The Lords of Trade and Plantations', *American Hist. Rev.*, xxiii (1917), 20–41; R. P. Bieber, *The Lords of Trade and Plantations 1675–1696* (Allentown, Pa. 1919); G. A. Jacobsen, *William Blathwayt: a late 17th Century English Administrator* (New Haven 1932), 83–149.

At first no distinct establishment of officials was attached to the Committee, the necessary work being undertaken by certain of the existing staff of the Privy Council Office. Sir Robert Southwell, one of the Clerks of the Council, was selected to perform the duties of Secretary assisted by two Clerks who appear to have been Under Clerks of the Council.[14] In September 1675 Southwell obtained authority to employ an assistant and recruited William Blathwayt for this function.[15] In March 1676 the Clerks of the Privy Council were given the opportunity of serving as Secretary to the Committee for periods of six months in turn.[16] In June of the same year an establishment was authorised which provided an annual allowance for those Clerks of the Council who served as Secretary and salaries for Blathwayt as their Assistant and for two Clerks.[17] Shortly afterwards allowances were made available for the two Keepers of the Council Chamber and the Under Keeper of the Council Records in consideration of their additional labour in servicing the Committee.[18] Salaries were also provided for a Messenger and his assistant and a Cleaner.[19]

Apart from Southwell, who resigned his office in 1679, there is little evidence that any of the Clerks of the Council played an active part as Secretaries to the Committee. There seems little doubt that Blathwayt was the effective Secretary almost from the time of his entry into the office. Following the accession of William III his duties as Secretary at War and acting Secretary of State inevitably left him with less time to devote to the business of the Committee. In consequence Povey, his principal subordinate, was in 1692 formally authorised to act as Assistant Secretary in his absence.[20]

So far as the rest of the staff were concerned, few changes occurred in the arrangements made in 1676. In addition to the two ordinary Clerks an 'Extraordinary Clerk' was employed from 1677 to 1683 and when the establishment was renewed in 1685 the number of ordinary Clerks was increased to three at which level it remained until 1696.[21] However, since the journal of the Committee does not record changes that occurred in the staff of the office and the accounts do not usually specify the names of those receiving salaries, the identities and periods of service of the Clerks and other junior officials cannot be established precisely.[22]

COUNCIL OF TRADE AND PLANTATIONS 1696–1782

In 1696 the Committee of the Privy Council was dissolved and replaced by a Council or Board, appointed by letters patent under the great seal, which remained responsible

[14] *APC (Colonial) 1613–80*, 619–20; BM Add. MS 9767 pp. 14–16.
[15] CO 391/1 p. 39; BM Add. MS 9767 pp. 14–16.
[16] *APC (Colonial) 1613–80*, 664–5.
[17] BM Add. MS 9767 pp. 10–13.
[18] The Keepers of the Council Chamber were granted 2s a day each (ibid. pp. 22–3). Except for an interruption between 1684 and 1689 payment continued until 1696 (ibid. p. 113; BM Add. MS 9768 pp. 18–20, 21, 76). The allowances were continued after the abolition of the Committee (*CTB*, xv, 409; CO 389/36 pp. 153–7) and formed part of the remuneration of the Keepers until the early 19th century. The allowance to the Under Keeper of the Council Records, also 2s a day, was not continued after 1684 (BM Add. MS 9767 pp. 22–3, 31–2, 113).
[19] BM Add. MS 9767 pp. 22–3; ibid. 9768 p. 76.
[20] PC 2/74 p. 340.
[21] New establishments were authorised in 1679, 1685 and 1689 (BM Add. MS 9767 pp. 64–7, 115–22; ibid. 9768 pp. 3–10).
[22] The Journals of the Committee are in CO 391/1–8; the accounts in BM Add. MSS 9767–8.

for trade and plantation affairs until 1782.[23] The Board was composed of un-paid *ex officio* members who were not expected to attend regularly and of a body of salaried Commissioners who undertook the business. The number of salaried Commissioners was fixed in principle at eight. The senior such Commissioner, usually known as the First Lord of Trade, presided. The First Lord was almost invariably a member of the House of Lords; the other Commissioners were usually selected from the House of Commons. The functions of the Board tended to be of an advisory nature, executive authority in colonial matters being vested in the Secretary of State who had charge of the Southern Department. As a result of the efforts of Halifax as First Lord the Board was given increased responsibilities in colonial matters in 1752. However, when Halifax left office in 1761, the most important of these, the right to nominate colonial officials, was withdrawn. In 1766 the function of corresponding with colonial Governors, which had also been conferred on the Board in 1752, was removed from it.[24] In January 1768 the general responsibility for colonial matters was transferred from the office of the Secretary of State for the Southern Department to the newly created office of third Secretary of State. In July of the same year the office of First Lord of Trade was abolished and the Board was placed under the immediate direction of the Secretary of State for the Colonies. In 1779 this arrangement was discontinued and the office of First Lord was revived. The Board was abolished in 1782.[25]

The composition and remuneration of the Board's staff, which was subject to the approval of the Treasury, was fixed by letters of privy seal, renewable following the issue of successive letters patent appointing the Commissioners. In the original establishment provision was made for a Secretary, a Deputy Secretary, four Clerks, two Office Keepers, two Messengers and a Necessary Woman at a total cost of £1090 a year.[26] In 1700 the office of one of the Messengers was suppressed and a fifth clerkship created. A sixth Clerk was appointed in 1701.[27] A comprehensive revision of the establishment was made in 1708 when provision was made for a Secretary, a Deputy Secretary, seven Clerks, two Office Keepers, a Messenger and a Necessary Woman at a total cost of £1150 a year.[28] From 1718 a Counsel, who did not form part of the ordinary establishment, was permanently attached to the Board for consultation on routine legal questions.[29] In 1724 the Treasury authorised the appoint-ment of a Porter on condition that the office of one of the Office Keepers was abolished on the next vacancy. This occurred in 1728.[30] In 1730 the Treasury sanctioned the

[23] For the origins of the 1696 Board, see Jacobsen, *William Blathwayt*, 297–354; R. M. Lees, 'Parliament and the Proposals for a Council of Trade 1695–6', *Eng. Hist. Rev.*, liv (1939), 38–66; P. Laslett, 'John Locke, the Great Recoinage, and the Origins of the Board of Trade 1695–8', *William and Mary Quarterly*, xiv (1957), 370–402. For general accounts of its activities, see M. P. Clarke, 'The Board of Trade at Work', *American Hist. Rev.*, xvii (1911–12), 17–43; A. H. Basye, *The Lords Commissioners of Trade and Plantations 1748–1782* (New Haven 1925); M. A. Thomson, *The Sec-retaries of State 1681–1782* (London 1932), 44–64; M. M. Spector, *The American Department of British Government 1768–1782* (New York 1940) 11–21.

[24] *APC (Colonial) 1745–66*, 153–7; *APC (Colonial) 1766–83*, 3–4.

[25] The services of the Board were dispensed with 2 May 1782 (*JCTP 1776–82*, 472). It was finally abolished by act 11 July 1782 (22 Geo. III, c 82).

[26] CO 389/36 pp. 35–8. The Secretary was responsible for paying the salaries of the officials of the Board from money received quarterly at the Exchequer.

[27] Ibid. pp. 106–7, 136–8.   [28] *JCTP 1704–9*, 451.

[29] *CSPC (America & West Indies) 1717–18*, 198; *JCTP 1715–18*, 369.

[30] *JCTP 1723–8*, 106, 425.

creation of the office of Solicitor and Clerk of Reports, the function of which was to relieve the Secretary of the task of making reports and thus to enable him to concentrate on the general business of the Board.[31] No changes were made in the structure of the office between 1730 and 1764. In the latter year a major revision of the establishment took place. Authority was given for the appointment of two additional Clerks and a sum of £715 was made available for a general increase in salaries.[32] From this date until the abolition of the Board the establishment was fixed in principle at a Secretary, a Deputy Secretary, a Solicitor and Clerk of Reports, nine Clerks, an Office Keeper, a Messenger and Porter and a Necessary Woman.[33]

In addition to their salaries the officials of the Board enjoyed certain fees. At first these were exacted without specific authority but in 1731 an official table of fees was authorised by order in council. The receipts from this source were divided up amongst the officials in fixed proportions.[34] In 1704 those officials whose salaries were less than £100 successfully petitioned to have their taxes reimbursed. As a result an arrangement was made whereby the taxes of the Deputy Secretary and all those ranking below him were charged to the incidental expenses of the office.[35]

With the exception of the offices of Secretary and Counsel, to which nominations were made by the crown, the right of appointment was vested in the Board.[36] Under an arrangement which is traceable to the year 1703 nominations to vacancies were made by the salaried Commissioners in rotation, the First Lord enjoying the privilege of nominating to the first vacancy which occurred after his appointment.[37] At the time of the revision of the establishment in 1764 provision was made for each candidate nominated for a clerkship to undergo an examination in order that his fitness for office might be assessed by the Board.[38]

In a single instance an Office Keeper was appointed a Clerk;[39] otherwise the clerical and subordinate grades of the office remained distinct. Amongst the Clerks the rule was for promotion to be governed by seniority although the Board reserved to itself the freedom, rarely exercised, to vary this arrangement if it thought fit.[40] The Clerks

---

[31] *CSPC (America & West Indies) 1730*, 231–2; *JCTP 1729–34*, 139.

[32] The total cost of the establishment was thus raised to £2265. This sum includes £400 for the salaries of the Deputy Secretary and the Solicitor and Clerk of Reports which had previously been carried on the incidental account. At the same time provision was made for £365 to be paid as pensions to retired officials. As these pensions fell in the sums in question were to be applied to augment the salaries of the Solicitor and Clerk of Reports and the Clerks (*JCTP 1764–7*, 89–91).

[33] By 1782 the number of Clerks had been reduced to seven, the vacancies that occurred in 1777 and 1781 not having been filled. The offices of Messenger and Porter were held by the same person from 1756.

[34] *CSPC (America & West Indies) 1731*, 109; *APC (Colonial) 1720–45*, 319–21; *JCTP 1729–34*, 232, 288. For the receipts from fees in 1782, see T 1/579 Schedule 3.

[35] CO 388/75 no. 84; CO 389/36 pp. 169–70.

[36] Appointments of officials are not regularly recorded in the Journal of the Board until 1714. The Journal has been published verbatim for the years 1704 to 1782. For the period 1696 to 1704 the MS Journal (CO 391/9–16) has been consulted. Supplementary material on establishment matters exists in two series of documents: Petitions, Orders in Council, etc., Board of Trade Accounts 1696–1782 (CO 389/36–9) and Accounts and Establishments of the Board of Trade 1696–1782 (CO 388/75–84).

[37] CO 391/16 p. 111; *JCTP 1764–7*, 89–90; *JCTP 1776–82*, 257. In 1772 the Board agreed to make an appointment 'at the humble request' of the Secretary (*JCTP 1768–75*, 330).

[38] *JCTP 1764–7*, 91, 117, 120, 168. There is, however, no evidence that any candidate was subjected to examination after the appointment of Wilks in 1766.

[39] Campion (1735).   [40] *JCTP 1704–9*, 451.

gradually rose up the list and in due course became entitled to the higher salaries attached to the more senior clerkships. The highest post ordinarily available to the Clerks was that of Deputy Secretary to which the longest serving Clerk was usually held to be entitled when a vacancy occurred.[41] The right of the Deputy Secretary to be appointed Secretary was never admitted although such a promotion did occur on one occasion.[42] Secretaries were usually selected from amongst the officials of the Board but appointments were made without reference to seniority.[43] Similarly the office of Solicitor and Clerk of Reports remained outside the ordinary course of promotion.[44]

In practice all the officials of the Board, from the Secretary to the Necessary Woman, enjoyed a secure tenure, holding their offices until death or voluntary retirement.[45] Apart from the cases of Wheelock and Drift, who were removed for political reasons in 1714, the Board appears to have dismissed officials only when they were found guilty of misconduct.[46] From 1714 arrangements were made in appropriate cases for officials to receive allowances on retirement. In some cases provision was made for these allowances by means of abatements in the salaries of those serving on the establishment.[47] When, however, the Deputy Secretary and four Clerks were retired by the Board at the time of the reorganisation of 1764, separate allowances were granted to them.[48]

COMMITTEE OF THE PRIVY COUNCIL FOR TRADE AND PLANTATIONS 1784-6

In 1782 the Commissioners of Trade were abolished by act which provided that a committee of the Privy Council might take over the business done by them and all the authority and jurisdiction which had been vested in them.[49] In 1784 the necessity of considering a representation from the West India planters occasioned the appoint-

---

[41] CSPC (America & West Indies) 1734-5, 404; JCTP 1735-41, 13.

[42] W. Popple, jun. was promoted from Deputy Secretary to Secretary in 1707. On his death in 1722 the Board failed to secure the secretaryship for Wheelock, the then Deputy Secretary (CSPC (America & West Indies) 1722-3, 42-3; JCTP 1718-22, 350, 359).

[43] Hill (1737) was appointed from outside the office; A. Popple (1722) from a junior clerkship; J. Pownall (1753) and Cumberland (1776) from the office of Solicitor and Clerk of Reports.

[44] Three Clerks, J. Pownall (1745), Sedgwick (1753) and Goddard (1779), and one former Clerk, Bradbury (1763) were appointed to this post; otherwise appointments were made from outside the office.

[45] It was the regular practice for the office of Counsel to the Board to be held by an M.P. The security enjoyed by the Secretary was probably due in part to the fact that the office never became parliamentary in character. The only Secretary to sit in the Commons was J. Pownall (1775-6).

[46] For Wheelock, see JCTP 1709-15, 551; CSPC (America & West Indies) 1722-3, 42-3. Drift, a Tory closely connected with Matthew Prior, failed to retain office after the accession of George I when he was replaced by Wheelock (BM Add. MS 15947 f. 1; JCTP 1709-15, 575). Other dismissals included four Clerks: Hoskins and Spencer (1727), Bradley (1741) and Lewis (1770) and two Office Keepers: Armitage (1745) and Terrie (1767). Three Clerks: Gedney (1732), Davis (1777) and Hughes (1781) were temporarily suspended for misconduct (JCTP 1729-34, 311; JCTP 1776-82, 79, 265).

[47] See the cases of the Clerks, Carroll (1714) and Gedney (1738) (JCTP 1709-15, 575; JCTP 1735-41, 243; JCTP 1742-9, 268-9), the Office Keeper, Willis (1758) (JCTP 1754-8, 437) and the Necessary Woman, Wright (1777) (JCTP 1776-82, 2).

[48] The individuals in question were Rogers, Cranwell, Peacock, Green and Cuckow (JCTP 1764-7, 89). In 1777 Palmer was allowed to retire from a clerkship on full salary (JCTP 1776-82, 125).

[49] 22 Geo. III, c 82.

ment of such a committee. At first this body was of a temporary character. Its Members were unpaid and no separate establishment was provided for it.[50] The necessary work was undertaken by the two active Clerks of the Privy Council, certain subordinate officials of the Council Office, the Under Secretary of the Plantation Department of the Home Office and one of the Clerks of the Home Office who was also a Clerk Extraordinary of the Privy Council. These officials received bounties for their additional work in this connection.[51]

COMMITTEE OF THE PRIVY COUNCIL FOR TRADE AND PLANTATIONS 1786–1871

In 1786 the Committee of 1784 was replaced by a permanent Committee of the Privy Council which provided the formal structure of the Board thereafter. The new Committee was composed of a President and a Vice President who became the political heads of the department, the holders of certain offices *ex officio* and an unfixed number of nominated Members. Apart from the President and Vice President who were later accorded salaries, Members received no remuneration.[52] Some of them attended meetings of the Board in the years immediately following its appointment but their position became increasingly nominal and with three exceptions no new appointments were made after 1823. From the early nineteenth century it was unusual for the Board to be attended by any Members apart from the President and Vice President in whom all effective authority came to be concentrated. During the same period the functions of the Board changed considerably. Having begun as a group of Privy Counsellors whose task was to consider and recommend policies relating to trade and the colonies, it was gradually transformed into a predominantly administrative body whose duties were confined to commercial matters.[53] This tendency became more marked as the century progressed and the Board was given responsibility for collecting statistics and for regulating railways, the merchant marine, harbours, industrial design and joint stock companies.[54]

The Board of 1786 was provided with a permanent establishment.[55] Specific

[50] PC 2/129 p. 56; A. L. Lingelbach, 'The Inception of the Board of Trade', *American Hist. Rev.*, xxx (1924–5), 705–10.

[51] BT 5/1 p. 1; BT 5/2 pp. 258–60. For the Plantation Department, see HC 309 pp. 25–6 (1806) vii, 25–6; R. R. Nelson, *The Home Office 1782–1801* (Durham, N.C. 1969), 132–4.

[52] PC 2/231 pp. 403–4; A. L. Lingelbach, 'The Inception of the Board of Trade', *American Hist. Rev.*, xxx (1924–5), 711–27.

[53] G. A. Cockcroft, *The Public Life of George Chalmers* (New York 1939), 118–23. For the attempt to revive the functions of the Board in relation to colonial matters, see HC 543, pt. i p. 428 (1847–8) xviii, 492; W. P. Morrell, *British Colonial Policy in the Age of Peel and Russell* (Oxford 1930), 204–5; C. J. M. Ward, 'The Retirement of a Titan: James Stephen, 1847–50', *Journal of Modern History*, xxxi (1959), 197–205; A. Todd, *Parliamentary Government in England*, 2nd ed. (London 1887–9), ii, 639, 790–1.

[54] R. Prouty, *The Transformation of the Board of Trade* (London 1957); L. Brown, *The Board of Trade and the Free-Trade Movement 1830–42* (Oxford 1958); H. Parris, *Government and the Railways in 19th Century Britain* (London 1965). The Board also had general responsibility for the schools of industrial design and the Department of Practical Art (1837–57), the offices of Registrar of Designs (1839) and Registrar of Joint Stock Companies (1844). Responsibility for the office of Registrar of Seamen (1835) was transferred to it from the Admiralty in 1850. The staffs attached to these bodies remained distinct from the establishment of the Board of Trade and have not been included in these lists.

[55] Decisions relating to establishment matters were recorded in a series of minute books which was apparently discontinued in 1853 (BT 5/65, 11 Feb. 1857). The period covered by the minute

allowances were made available for the two active Clerks of the Privy Council who were to act as its Secretaries, assisted by the Under Secretary of the Plantations Department who was appointed an additional Clerk of the Privy Council for the purpose. Provision was also made for a Chief Clerk, six other Clerks, an Office Keeper, a Necessary Woman or Housekeeper and three Messengers. In the following year the establishment was increased by the addition of a Law Clerk and a Porter.[56] It was the practice for there to be one Supernumerary Clerk from 1786; a second was appointed in 1802.[57] In 1805 the number of established Clerks was raised to seven and a general increase of salaries took place.[58] In 1810 Cotterell, the Clerk of the Privy Council who had undertaken the bulk of the secretarial duties, resigned and one of the Clerks of the Board was appointed Assistant Secretary.[59] Thereafter the connection of the Clerks of the Council with the Board was largely nominal and the Assistant Secretary became in effect the senior permanent official. In 1812 the practice of appointing Supernumerary Clerks ceased, the number of established Clerks was raised to eight and a further general increase of salaries took place.[60] Until 1853 the promotion of Clerks was governed almost exclusively by the principle of seniority. There was, however, no expectation of advancement beyond the clerical grade and the appointment of T. Lack as Assistant Secretary in 1810 remained an isolated case. The Clerks and other officials enjoyed permanent tenure and were granted retiring allowances in appropriate cases.

Until 1817 neither the President nor the Vice President received salaries as such although it was usual for them to hold concurrently some other office to which remuneration was attached. In that year a salary was made available for the Vice President, a course that was followed in the case of the President in 1826.[61] In 1821 the Board was given statutory responsibility for corn returns. This gave rise to the creation of a distinct Corn Department, consisting of a Receiver, whose title was changed to Comptroller in 1827, a Deputy or Principal Clerk and one other Clerk.[62]

In 1822 the office was reorganised. The post of Assistant Secretary was separated from the clerkship with which it had previously been associated and made a distinct appointment and the ordinary establishment was divided into one First Class, three Second Class and three Third Class Clerks. New salary scales were introduced which

books in the P.R.O. extends from 1784 to 1838 (BT 5/1-46). The later volumes, which remained at the Board of Trade, have now disappeared. A collection of unbound minutes beginning in 1839 exists in the P.R.O. (BT 5/47 onwards) but is very imperfect. It is evident that a substantial amount of material concerning the establishment, particularly for the latter part of the 19th century, has been destroyed. The information contained in the minutes may be supplemented principally from the following sources: BT 3 (Out Letters 1786-1863), BT 12 (Commercial Department Out Letters from 1864), BT 13 (Establishment Department Correspondence and Papers from 1865) and BT 20 (Establishment Department Out Letters from 1865).

[56] BT 5/4 pp. 4, 11-15, 211, 319. The salaries of the officials of the Board were carried on the civil list until 1808 when it was provided that they should be met from the fee fund of the Council Office (BT 5/18 pp. 251-2). Following the Civil List Act 1816 (56 Geo. III, c 46) estimates of the amount of the deficiency of the fee fund were laid before the House of Commons and the sums voted annually. It was not until 1837 that the estimates presented and the sums voted were described as being for the Council Office and Board of Trade. Separate estimates for the two departments were presented from 1859 (BT 3/55 no. 130).

[57] BT 5/9 p. 90; BT 5/13 pp. 146-7.　　[58] BT 5/15 pp. 315-22.
[59] BT 5/20 pp. 88, 90, 95.　　[60] BT 5/21 pp. 349-51.
[61] 57 Geo. III, c 66; 7 Geo. IV, c 32.
[62] 1 & 2 Geo. IV, c 87, s 4; BT 5/29 pp. 381-4. A second Clerk was appointed to the Corn Department in the following year.

were also applied to the Corn Department.[63] In 1823 the office of Law Clerk was abolished, an additional Clerk was appointed and a salary was made available for the Private Secretary to the President.[64] In 1825 the office of Chief Clerk was discontinued and the sum thus saved was used to increase the remuneration of the Assistant Secretary and to pay part of the salary of the Counsel to the Colonial Office who henceforth acted as Law Clerk to the Board.[65] In 1829 the first class clerkship was abolished and a second office of Assistant Secretary created.[66] Thereafter the permanent establishment was headed by two Joint Assistant Secretaries or, as they came increasingly to be called, Joint Secretaries. These offices were permanent and non-parliamentary in character. At the same time the terms Senior and Junior Clerk began to be used to describe the holders of second and third class clerkships.

In 1832 the first step was taken in the creation of a Statistical Department. Treasury authority was given for the temporary employment of G. R. Porter for the purpose of arranging and making abstracts from parliamentary returns, assisted by one of the Junior Clerks in the office. In 1834 Porter was given an established post as Superintendent of the Statistical Department. Later in the same year three established Clerks were assigned to the department. In 1838 their number was increased to five.[67] In 1836 a vacancy occurred in one of the joint secretaryships and it was laid down that one of these offices should henceforth be held by a person with legal qualifications. At the same time the arrangement whereby the Counsel to the Colonial Office acted as Law Clerk to the Board was discontinued and his responsibilities were transferred to the Secretary in question.[68]

In 1840 the responsibilities conferred upon the Board in connection with railways necessitated the creation of a new sub-department to deal with them.[69] As constituted in that year the Railway Department consisted of a Superintendent, a Law and Corresponding Clerk, a Junior Clerk and an Inspector General.[70] A Registrar was appointed in 1842.[71] In 1844 railway business, which had previously come before the Board in the ordinary way, was transferred to a new Railway Board composed of the President or Vice President of the Board of Trade, the former Superintendent (now known as the Senior Member), the Inspector General or the newly appointed Assistant Inspector General and two Joint Secretaries. One of these Secretaries, known as the Law Secretary, was the former Law and Corresponding Clerk; the other, known as the General Secretary, was a new appointment. The Railway Board was abolished in the following year and railway business was again brought before the Board of Trade. The office of one of the Secretaries was discontinued but otherwise the number and standing of the officials of the department remained unaffected by this change.[72]

In 1846 railway business was transferred to the Commissioners of Railways, a statutory body independent of the Board of Trade. Provision was made for five Commissioners, of whom the President and two others were salaried. In fact only

[63] BT 5/29 pp. 438–44; BT 5/30 pp. 82–4, 393, 406.
[64] BT 5/31 pp. 227–9, 337–8.   [65] BT 5/34 pp. 67–70.   [66] BT 5/38 pp. 260–2.
[67] BT 5/40 pp. 506–7; BT 5/41 pp. 543–5; BT 5/42 p. 267; BT 5/45 pp. 283–5, 290, 412–13.
[68] BT 5/43 pp. 248–9, 284.
[69] For the Railway Department generally, see Parris, *Government and the Railways*; *Rept. of Select Committee on Miscellaneous Expenditure 1848* (HC 543 pt. i, pp. 162–88 (1847–8) xviii, pt. i, 227–52).
[70] BT 3/29 pp. 535–8; BT 1/365, Treasury to Board of Trade, 20 Aug. 1840; BT 3/29 pp. 666–70; BT 5/48, 2 Dec. 1840.
[71] BT 5/50, 5 Jan. 1842; BT 5/51, 7 Jan. 1843.
[72] BT 5/52, 6 Aug. 1844; BT 5/53, 10 and 22 July 1845.

four Commissioners were appointed and by the end of 1848 the number had been reduced to three, of whom the President and one of the others were respectively President and Vice President of the Board of Trade itself. The Commissioners were abolished in 1851 when railway business was once again transferred to the Board.[73] The officials serving the Commissioners consisted of a Secretary, an Assistant Secretary, a Registrar, a Statistical and Topographical Assistant who also acted as Private Secretary to the President, a Legal Assistant, three Inspectors of Railways, an Office Keeper, three Messengers and a Porter.[74] At first there were only three established Clerks who were assisted by two or three temporary Clerks. However, in 1848 the establishment was expanded to include two Senior, two Junior and two Supernumerary Clerks. The Supernumerary Clerks were absorbed into the Junior grade in 1851.[75] In 1850 the office of Statistical and Topographical Assistant was abolished and that of one of the Inspectors of Railways left vacant.[76] On the abolition of the Commissioners in 1851 their former officials were transferred to the Board of Trade, remaining distinct from the ordinary establishment but placed under the immediate direction of Booth, one of the Joint Secretaries.[77]

In 1850 the Board was required by act to undertake the general superintendence of matters relating to the merchant marine.[78] For this purpose a distinct department of the Board was created, known sometimes as the 'Naval' but more usually as the Marine Department. It consisted of a Secretary, two Clerks, two Professional Members and an Accountant.[79]

During the period when the Board's functions were being extended to include responsibility for statistics, railways and the merchant marine, its original advisory functions continued to be carried out by a group of officials under its immediate direction. In order to distinguish these officials from those in the new sub-departments, they were known collectively as the General Department. Since 1829 the department had undergone little change. In 1842 a reorganisation took place. The new posts of Registrar and Librarian were created and an arrangement was made for two of the Clerks to be particularly attached to the Joint Secretaries to act as Private Secretaries. The establishment of the General Department was fixed at two Joint Secretaries, a Registrar, a Librarian, four Senior and four Junior Clerks, Private Secretaries to the President and Vice President, together with an Office Keeper and other subordinate officials. At the same time the establishment of the Corn Department was increased by the addition of a Clerk to consist of a Comptroller, a Deputy and three Clerks. Changes were also made in the Statistical Department. One of the Clerks was promoted to be Assistant to the Superintendent and a new agricultural branch was created and placed in the charge of a Clerk of superior standing who soon acquired the title of Assistant as well. As settled in 1842 the establishment of the Statistical Department comprised a Superintendent, two Assistants and four Clerks.[80]

---

[73] 9 & 10 Vict., c 105; 14 & 15 Vict., c 64; Parris, *Government and the Railways*, 103–6. Between 1846 and 1851 the Railway Department was formally distinct from the Board of Trade. However, in the interests of continuity, its officials have been included in the lists.

[74] MT 13/7 pp. 561–3.

[75] MT 13/6 pp. 1–2, 53, 65; MT 13/7 pp. 561–3; MT 13/8 p. 191; MT 13/15 pp. 419–20.

[76] MT 13/12 pp. 89, 98.   [77] BT 3/41 pp. 368–9.

[78] 13 & 14 Vict., c 93; Prouty, *Transformation of the Board of Trade*, 30–98; J. H. Wilde, 'The creation of the Marine Department of the Board of Trade', *Journal of Transport History*, ii (1955–6), 193–206.

[79] BT 5/59, 23 Dec. 1850; BT 3/45 pp. 1–5.   [80] BT 5/50, 5 Jan. and 13 July 1842.

In 1845 a new post of Legal Assistant was created and given the function of assisting the Legal Joint Secretary but this post was not filled on the resignation of its holder in 1850.[81] In 1846 a Précis Writer was appointed whose office was united with that of Librarian in 1849.[82] In 1851 the organisation of the office was made more flexible by the amalgamation of the clerical staffs of the General and Statistical Departments.[83]

While the last measure made some contribution to the better functioning of the department, there could be little doubt that there was room for a comprehensive investigation of the establishment in its widest sense. This need was recognised in December 1852 when, on the initiative of the Treasury, a committee of enquiry was set up.[84] The committee was composed of Sir Charles Trevelyan, Assistant Secretary of the Treasury, Sir Stafford Northcote, an M.P. and former official of the Board and Booth, one of the Joint Secretaries. Their report,[85] which was made in March 1853, began by pointing out that the department had originally been designed for consultative and not executive functions and that its structure was ill-adapted to perform the important new tasks which had been entrusted to it in the last twenty years. As need arose new officials and sub-departments had been attached to it. The establishment had never been reorganised to deal with the business in the most efficient manner. In order to rectify the deficiencies of the existing system the committee laid down four principles: the subordination of all parts of the work to a single authority, the proper division of work, uniformity in the transaction of business and, so far as possible, a clear distinction between intellectual and mechanical work. Proceeding on these principles, the committee recommended that the discrepancies which existed in the transaction of business should be abolished and proposed a recasting of the whole establishment. This involved the replacing of the Joint Secretaries by a single Secretary who would be responsible to the President for all the work of the department and the division of the office into three branches designated the General, Railway and Marine Departments, each of which was to be placed in the immediate charge of an Assistant Secretary. In addition to the Assistant Secretaries it was proposed that certain other officials should be appointed to act under the Secretary. These included the Inspectors of Railways, the Professional Members of the Marine Department, the Legal Assistant, the Accountant and the Registrar. The Inspectors of Railways and the Professional Members of the Marine Department were to be relieved of routine departmental work in order that they might concentrate on the particular duties for which their skills fitted them. The post of Legal Assistant, which had been vacant since 1850, was to be revived and filled by the former Legal Assistant to the Railway Department, thus rendering unnecessary the requirement that one of the Joint Secretaries should be legally qualified. Similarly the services of the Accountant, who had previously been attached exclusively to the Marine Department, were to be made available to the Board generally. The offices of Registrar, Librarian and Précis Writer were to be combined and their holder given important new functions. He was to be responsible for maintaining a uniform system of keeping the minutes of each department as well as making up serviceable indexes of

[81] BT 5/53, 22 March 1845; BT 3/43 pp. 257–60.
[82] BT 5/55, 29 Aug. 1846; BT 3/38 pp. 155–6.
[83] BT 3/41 pp. 89–93.
[84] BT 3/43 p. 264.
[85] [Cd. 1713] pp. 129–55 HC (1854) xxvii, 161–87.

current business. The whole establishment of Clerks was to be placed under the direction of the Registrar who was to be responsible to the Secretary for their regular attendance and the satisfactory discharge of their duties. The separate existence of the Corn Department was to be brought to an end.

In order to implement the principle of the division of labour the committee proposed that the Clerks should be divided into two classes. Work of an intellectual character should be entrusted to Clerks 'drawn from those ranks of society which usually furnish the supply of persons for the higher appointments in the Government Offices' while the more mechanical duties should be undertaken by Copyists drawn 'from among persons of a humbler sphere, who have not had the advantage of a liberal education, and who do not look to rise above the rank of persons of their own class employed in private establishments'. Candidates for entry into both classes were to undergo examinations appropriate to their rank and Clerks on the superior establishment were to be placed on probation for three months before being confirmed in office. The superior establishment itself was to be divided into senior and junior grades. The committee stressed the need to replace the existing system whereby Clerks were promoted largely by reference to length of service with one in which merit was the sole criterion of advancement. The career structure of the office was to be made more attractive to Clerks by holding out to them the possibility of promotion to the highest posts including that of Secretary which, with a single exception, had hitherto been filled from outside the office. The Copyists were to be distinct from the superior establishment but, in cases of special merit, they should be enabled to receive higher salaries. Finally the committee recommended that there should be a single Office Keeper and a unified corps of Messengers at the disposal of the department.

The recommendations of the committee of 1853 have been set out at some length both on account of their intrinsic interest and because they provide a framework against which to measure the developments that took place in the following years. Not all the changes proposed were implemented at once. The substitution of a single Secretary for the two Joint Secretaries was delayed until 1867. The separate existence of the Corn Department was not finally brought to a close until 1865. No appointment was made to the office of Assistant Secretary for the General Department with which it had been proposed that the post of Superintendent of the Statistical Department should be combined. Nevertheless the Board agreed in principle to the recommendations of the committee with only minor modifications and set about carrying them into effect as soon as possible. The various component parts of the old establishment were consolidated to consist of two Joint Secretaries, two Assistant Secretaries for the Railway and Marine Departments, a Registrar, an Accountant, three Inspectors of Railways and two Professional Members of the Marine Department. The Senior Clerks from the former establishment, henceforth known as Old Senior Clerks, were allowed to retain their positions and salaries on the understanding that they would not be replaced while six fresh appointments were made to the new grade of Senior Clerk envisaged by the committee. The Board agreed to make no appointment to the grade of Junior Clerk until the existing number of eleven had been reduced to eight as proposed by the committee. The Board also began the process of recruiting individuals for the new class of Copyists.[86] In 1855 arrangements were made for

[86] [Cd. 1713] pp. 156–80 HC (1854) xxvii, 188–212; *Royal Kal.* (1854), 160.

candidates for clerkships in the department to be examined by the Civil Service Commissioners.[87]

In 1854 the Board was given responsibility for meteorological observations, a development that gave rise to the creation of the office of Chief of the Meteorological Department. In the same year a Surveyor General of Steam Ships was appointed in accordance with the terms of the Merchant Shipping Act.[88] This act also authorised the employment of Nautical Assessors of whom one was appointed in 1857 and a second in 1862.[89]

Comprehensive though the reorganisation of 1853 had been, it soon became apparent that the size of the clerical establishment which had then been envisaged was inadequate to cope effectively with the range of responsibilities entrusted to the Board and the growing amount of work which they entailed. This was particularly the case with the Marine Department following the passage of the Merchant Shipping Act. The result was that the Clerks generally were overburdened. Responsible work was entrusted to the Supplementary Clerks, as the Copyists had come to be known, thus blurring the distinction between the two establishments on which the committee had insisted. In 1853 a permanent complement of twenty-six Clerks, composed of fourteen Senior and Junior Clerks and twelve Supplementaries, had been considered sufficient. In 1856 there were no fewer than sixty-four Clerks in continuous employment of whom twenty-seven were Supplementaries and ten were borrowed from the office of the Registrar of Seamen or hired from law stationers.

In these circumstances the Treasury agreed that the establishment should be revised in the light of developments since 1853. It accepted the proposal that the position of the Senior Clerks should be strengthened by allowing them properly qualified assistants drawn from the ranks of the existing Junior Clerks. It agreed that, within the supplementary establishment, Clerks who were doing work of a responsible character should be promoted to the higher grade. Finally the Treasury sanctioned the appointment of enough Junior Supplementary Clerks to render unnecessary the employment of Clerks borrowed or hired from elsewhere. As recast in 1857 the establishment was fixed at sixty-five Clerks. The superior class was composed of twenty-eight who were divided into six First Class, eight Second Class and fourteen Third Class Clerks. The supplementary class was composed of thirty-seven of whom twelve were Senior and twenty-five were Junior Clerks. At the same time adjustments were made in the salaries of the Registrar, Accountant, Legal Assistant and the professional officers of the Board.[90]

Such was the increasing burden of work, however, that in 1859 the Board was forced to apply again to the Treasury for a revision of the establishment. It pointed out that, although the arrangements made in 1857 were intended to enable it to dispense with the services of temporary Clerks, it had in fact been obliged to obtain help from this quarter in spite of the enlargement of the establishment. A permanent addition of twelve to the clerical staff was now essential. Furthermore, experience had shown that it was impossible to adhere to the firm division of function between the Clerks on the superior and inferior establishments envisaged in 1853. Of the thirty-two Clerks in the latter class only seven were in fact employed in purely mechanical

[87] BT 3/49 no. 471.
[88] BT 3/47 pp. 474–87; Prouty, *Transformation of the Board of Trade*, 51–5, 59–62.
[89] BT 5/65, 28 July 1857; BT 5/70, 30 Oct. 1862.
[90] BT 3/51 no. 19; BT 5/65, 30 April 1857.

tasks such as copying. In the circumstances it was impractical to insist on the distinction and the Board proposed that, for the future, all new appointments should be made to the grade of Junior Supplementary Clerk. Vacancies on the superior establishment should be filled, wherever possible, from this class. The grade of Senior Supplementary Clerk should be reserved for those who had given long and meritorious service in the junior grade and any Clerk so promoted should lose all claim to further advancement in the office.[91]

The Treasury countered these proposals with a completely different plan. The supplementary class should be abolished in its existing form and replaced by a fluctuating number of temporary Clerks paid on a weekly basis who after not less than twenty years' service might be promoted to be Supplementary Clerks with a permanent tenure. The Board declined to accept this suggestion in advance of a comprehensive review of the position of Supplementary Clerks throughout the government service.[92] Such a review was undertaken by a committee appointed by the Treasury which reported in 1860.[93] No action was taken on its recommendation to establish a central copying agency for government departments.

In the meantime there was evidence of considerable dissatisfaction with the manner in which the office was organised, which culminated in petitions from the First Class and Supplementary Clerks drawing attention to their grievances. In November 1861 Emerson Tennent, one of the Joint Secretaries, was appointed by the President to investigate the matter. His report, of which no copy appears to have survived, was made in March 1862.[94] In January of the following year the Treasury decided that a committee should be appointed to make a full-scale enquiry into the establishment.

The committee, whose members were G. A. Hamilton, the Assistant Secretary of the Treasury, G. Arbuthnot, the Auditor of the Civil List and Booth, one of the Joint Secretaries of the Board, reported in July 1863.[95] In the first place they directed their attention to the position of the Secretaries. In 1853 it had been proposed that the number of Secretaries should be reduced from two to one when a vacancy occurred. The committee, however, were of the opinion that there should continue to be two Joint Secretaries at the head of the Board's permanent staff. The situation was complicated by the special position of Farrer, the Assistant Secretary in charge of the Marine Department. The Marine Department now accounted for at least half of the total work of the Board and it was strongly urged that Farrer should at once be promoted to the position of third Joint Secretary. It was pointed out that Booth, the Joint Secretary who was nominally Farrer's superior, had little time to devote to the affairs of the Marine Department particularly since the discontinuance in 1860 of the office of Assistant Secretary for the Railway Department for which he was also responsible. The committee found themselves unable to make a recommendation on this point. Eventually the proposal was rejected by Gladstone, the Chancellor of the Exchequer. Farrer was, however, given an increased salary and the title of Marine Secretary on a temporary basis with the promise that he would succeed to one of the joint secretaryships when a vacancy occurred.

[91] BT 3/55 no. 179.
[92] ibid. no. 299.
[93] HC 251 pp. 1–12 (1865) xxx, 219–30.
[94] A number of memoranda and other material associated with this enquiry are to be found in a volume entitled 'Appendix to the Report on the Board of Trade 1862' (BT 6/293).
[95] The report and other related material are to be found in T 1/6433B/13012.

Turning to the clerical organisation the committee recommended the discontinuance of the First Class Clerks and their replacement by a new grade known as Assistants. These were to be four in number and to be attached to the General or Commercial, Statistical, Railway and Marine Departments. The Clerks were to be divided into sixteen Seniors and twenty-six Juniors, to be reduced to twenty-four as vacancies occurred. On the subject of the supplementary establishment the committee reiterated the views which the Treasury had expressed in 1859. The grade of Junior Supplementary Clerk should be abolished as soon as practicable, its occupants being transferred either to the superior establishment as Junior Clerks or promoted to the grade of Senior Supplementary Clerk. No new supplementaries should be appointed. As suggested in 1859 they should be replaced by a varying number of Temporary Clerks, engaged to undertake purely mechanical work and paid on a weekly basis who might, in appropriate cases, be given permanent positions after not less than twenty years' service.

The committee recommended the abolition of the office of Registrar whose holder had since 1853 been in immediate charge of the clerical establishment. Experience had shown that his position was anomalous and tended to blur the proper lines of authority in the department. The post of Librarian with which it had been combined was, however, to be continued. The position of Draftsman for the Railway Department, which had previously been held by a First Class Clerk, was to be made a distinct office. The committee recommended that the abolition of the Corn Department, which had been proposed in 1853, should take place as soon as possible and the office of Comptroller of Corn Returns combined with that of Superintendent of the Statistical Department. Finally improvements were recommended in the salaries of the other officials attached to the Board.

So far as possible the recommendations of the committee were carried into effect at once.[96] The recruitment of Temporary Clerks began in November 1863[97] and the process of abolishing the grade of Junior Supplementary Clerk was completed in the following year.[98] The Corn Department was finally wound up in 1865 when the Superintendent of the Statistical Department was appointed Comptroller of Corn Returns.[99] In the same year the retirement of Booth made possible the promotion of Farrer to the position of full Joint Secretary.[100]

In 1865 the Chief of the Meteorological Department died. No successor was appointed and the work was continued on an interim basis while the future of the office was considered. In the event the responsibility for meteorological observations was transferred to the Royal Society.[101] A number of measures enacted in the parliamentary sesssion of 1866 imposed new functions on the Board.[102] In particular the Standard of Weights, Measures and Coinage Act transferred responsibility for weights and measures from the Exchequer. Three officials in the service of the Comptroller General were incorporated into the establishment to form a new Standard Department.[103]

---

[96] BT 3/64 no. 379.

[97] Temporary Clerks are not included in these lists. For the regulations governing their appointment, see BT 3/64 no. 577.

[98] BT 5/72, 27 Aug. 1864.

[99] BT 13/1, Board of Trade to Treasury, 23 Nov. 1864; Ind. 20470 no. 4.

[100] BT 5/73, 30 Sept. 1865. [101] HC 47 pp. 7, 15 (1867) xxxix, 219, 227.

[102] ibid., 213–14. [103] 29 & 30 Vict., c 82; BT 5/74, 20 Aug. 1866.

By 1866 the burden of work undertaken by the Board had again increased to the point where a further comprehensive enquiry into the establishment was felt necessary. The Treasury appointed G. W. Hunt, its Financial Secretary, and Cave, the Vice President of the Board, to undertake the investigation. Their report,[104] which was made in November 1866, began by reviewing the new responsibilities which had been placed upon the Board since 1863 and the existing arrangements for the conduct of business. Its first recommendation was the abolition of the office of Vice President, which had become an anomalous feature of the department, and the substitution for it of the post of Parliamentary Secretary, whose holder was to be directly subordinate to the President and to be given definite duties. Associated with this recommendation was the proposal that, as soon as a vacancy occurred, the two Joint Secretaries should be replaced by a single Permanent Secretary. The report went on to propose that the work of the Board should be divided into six departments with the titles of Commercial, Railway, Harbour,[105] Marine, Statistical and Financial Departments. The last two were to be presided over by the Superintendent of the Statistical Department and the Accountant respectively. The first four were to be entrusted to the immediate supervision of four Assistant Secretaries, of whom those in charge of the Railway and Harbour Departments were to have legal qualifications. The office of Assistant Secretary for the Commercial Department was to be combined with that of Warden of the Standards. The office of Assistant, which had been created in 1863, was to be gradually abolished as vacancies occurred. The report proposed that the number of Senior Clerks should be fixed at sixteen and that there should be up to thirty-five Juniors. It found that, although the rigid distinction between intellectual and mechanical work which had been recommended by the committee of 1863, had been more strictly observed than similar recommendations made in the past, there were still cases in which Temporary Clerks were performing duties which were more responsible than those of some of the established Clerks. It was recommended that in these cases the Temporary Clerks should not be debarred from obtaining appointments to the establishment. Amongst other recommendations of the report were the appointment of an additional Inspector of Railways and the revival of the office of Registrar although with a status inferior to that which it had previously enjoyed.

The Board accepted the substance of the recommendations contained in the report. Certain modifications were, however, made. It was found that not all of the existing Senior Clerks were capable of undertaking the increased responsibilities which were to be attached to their grade. Three were therefore retired and two others were allowed to remain at a reduced salary, their places being taken by Clerks promoted from the junior grade. The Board was unwilling at once to amalgamate the office of Warden of the Standards with that of Assistant Secretary for the Commercial Department and the former remained a distinct post until after the end of the period. However, Emerson Tennent agreed to retire from the office of Joint Secretary and the Board was thus enabled to implement the recommendation that the whole establishment should be placed under a single Permanent Secretary.[106]

[104] HC 47 pp. 3–13 (1867) xxxix, 215–26.

[105] Responsibility for harbours had been transferred from the Admiralty to the Board in 1863 by 25 & 26 Vict., c 69 (BT 3/62 no. 676).

[106] HC 47 pp. 15–19 (1867) xxxix, 227–31. The new arrangements were carried into effect by minute of 2 Jan. 1867 (BT 5/75).

On the resignation of Cave in 1868 the office of Vice President was abolished and a Parliamentary Secretary appointed.[107] A new office of Translator was created in the same year,[108] but no other changes were made in the establishment before the end of the year 1870 which witnessed the introduction of the system of open competition for entry into the Civil Service and which marks the terminal point for the period covered by these lists.

[107] 30 & 31 Vict., c 72; BT 5/76, 14 Dec. 1868.
[108] BT 5/76, 9 Jan. 1868.

Lists of Appointments

COUNCILS OF TRADE 1660–72

Commissioners 1660–72

Two Councils of Trade were appointed by Charles II. Appointments were made by commission under the great seal. In both cases the Commissioners served without salary. The first Council, appointed in 1660, consisted of sixty-two Commissioners.[1] After 1664 its activities appear to have diminished although it may have continued to exist in some form until 1668. In the latter year it was replaced by a new Council consisting of forty-two Commissioners.[2] The membership was increased to forty-six in 1669.[3] The second Council ceased to exist in 1672 when responsibility for questions of trade was transferred to the newly constituted Council of Trade and Foreign Plantations.[4]

LIST OF APPOINTMENTS

1660	7 Nov.	Hyde, Lord; Southampton, Earl of; Albemarle, Duke of; Manchester, Earl of; Pembroke, Earl of; Marlborough, Earl of; Portland, Earl of; Norwich, Earl of; Sandwich, Earl of; Robartes, Lord; Brouncker, Viscount; Willoughby of Parham, Lord; Colepepper, Lord; Berkeley of Stratton, Lord; Holles, Hon. D.; Carteret, Sir G.; Nicholas, Sir E.; Morrice, Sir W.; Annesley, A.; Cooper, Sir A. A.; Coventry, Hon. W.; Freeman, Sir R.; Crow, Sir S.; Abdy, Sir R.; Harbord, Sir C.; Wolstenholme, Sir J.; O'Neill, D.; Ingram, Sir T.; Crispe, Sir N.; Thompson, Sir W.; Ford, Sir R.; Chamberlain, Sir T.; Riccard, Sir A.; Downing, Sir G.; Shaw, Sir J.; Ashe, Sir J.; Draxe, Sir J.; Hyde, H.; Waller, E.; Povey, T.; Slingsby, H.; Dunkley, W.; Digges, E.; Noel, M.; Allen, W.; Ingram, A.; Boone, C.; Richbell, R.; Chiverton, R.; King, R.; Williams, W.; Torriano, G.; Fisher, W.; Parker, J.; Tyte, T.; Jolliffe, W.; Walker, W.; Miro, S.; Kendall, T.; Colleton, J.; Lidcot, G.; Lewis, J. (C 66/2946).
1668	20 Oct.	York, Duke of; Rupert, Prince; Bridgeman, Sir O.; Robartes, Lord; Buckingham, Duke of; Albemarle, Duke of; Ormond, Duke of; Bridgwater, Earl of; Ossory, Earl of; Anglesey, Earl

[1] Commission of 7 Nov. 1660 (C 66/2946).
[2] Commission of 20 Oct. 1668 (C 66/3103).
[3] Commission of 16 April 1669 (C 66/3106).
[4] Commission of 27 Sept. 1672 (C 66/3137).

of; Carlisle, Earl of; Craven, Earl of; Lauderdale, Earl of; Arlington, Lord; Berkeley of Stratton, Lord; Holles, Lord; Ashley, Lord; Clifford, Sir T.; Carteret, Sir G.; Trevor, Sir J.; Morrice, Sir W.; Coventry, Hon. Sir W.; Osborne, Sir T.; Littleton, Sir T.; Blount, Sir H.; Downing, Sir G.; Riccard, Sir A.; Thompson, Sir W.; Titus, S.; Garroway, W.; Slingsby, H.; Grey, Hon. T.; Birch, J.; Love, W.; Worsley, B.; Buckworth, J.; Papillon, T.; Page, J.; Child, J.; Tyte, T.; Albin, B.; Shorter, J. (C 66/3103).

1669   16 April   York, Duke of; Rupert, Prince; Bridgeman, Sir O.; Robartes, Lord; Buckingham, Duke of; Albemarle, Duke of; Ormond, Duke of; Devonshire, Earl of; Bridgwater, Earl of; Sandwich, Earl of; Ossory, Earl of; Anglesey, Earl of; Carlisle, Earl of; Craven, Earl of; Lauderdale, Earl of; Halifax, Viscount; Arlington, Lord; Berkeley, Lord; Berkeley of Stratton, Lord; Holles, Lord; Ashley, Lord; Clifford, Sir T.; Carteret, Sir G.; Trevor, Sir J.; Morrice, Sir W.; Coventry, Hon. Sir W.; Osborne, Sir T.; Littleton, Sir T.; Blount, Sir H.; Downing, Sir G.; Riccard, Sir A.; Thompson, Sir W.; Titus, S.; Garroway, W.; Slingsby, H.; Grey, Hon. T.; Birch, J.; Love, W.; Worsley, B.; Buckworth, J.; Papillon, T.; Page, J.; Child, J.; Tyte, T.; Albin, B.; Shorter, J. (C 66/3106).

Secretary 1660–72

Both in 1660 and in 1668 the Councils of Trade were empowered to appoint a Secretary and other officials, allowances of up to £1000 a year payable at the Exchequer being provided for their salaries and for incidental expenses.[1] In neither case is the amount of the Secretary's salary known.

LIST OF APPOINTMENTS

1660	Nov.	Duke, G.
1668	22 Oct.	du Moulin, P.

[1] Commissions of 7 Nov. 1660 (C 66/2946) and 20 Oct. 1668 (C 66/3103); letters patent of 7 March 1661 (C 66/2961); *The Rawdon Papers*, ed. J. Bramhall (London 1819), 237–8.

COUNCILS OF PLANTATIONS 1660–72

Commissioners 1660–72

Two Councils of Foreign Plantations were appointed by Charles II. Appointments were made by commission under the great seal. The first Council, appointed in 1660, consisted of forty-nine Commissioners who were unsalaried.[1] After 1664 its activities appear to have diminished although it may have continued to exist in some form until 1670. In the latter year it was replaced by a new Council consisting partly of *ex officio* Commissioners, the Lord Chancellor or Lord Keeper, the Lord Treasurer or Commissioners of the Treasury, the Chancellor of the Exchequer and the Secretaries of State, and partly of nominated Commissioners who were accorded salaries, payable at the Exchequer. The first paid Commissioner was designated President and received £700. The remaining nine received £500.[2] In the course of 1671 a tenth salaried Commissioner was appointed and seven unpaid nominated Commissioners were added.[3] The Council was reconstituted in 1672 as the Council of Trade and Foreign Plantations.[4]

In the following list *ex officio* Commissioners are omitted. The names of salaried Commissioners are preceded by an asterisk.

LIST OF APPOINTMENTS

1660	1 Dec	Hyde, Lord; Southampton, Earl of; Manchester, Earl of; Lincoln, Earl of; Clare, Earl of; Marlborough, Earl of; Portland, Earl of; Saye and Sele, Viscount; Dacre, Lord; Windsor, Lord; Willoughby of Parham, Lord; Robartes, Lord; Berkeley of Stratton, Lord; Carteret, Sir G.; Holles, Hon. D.; Nicholas, Sir E.; Morrice, Sir W.; Annesley, A.; Cooper, Sir A. A.; Doyle, R.; Willoughby, W.; Coventry, Hon. W.; Berkeley, Sir W.; Leere, Sir P.; Minnes, Sir J.; Crispe, Sir N.; Riccard, Sir A.; Draxe, Sir J.; Shaw, Sir J.; O'Neill, D.; Denham, J.; Waller, E.; Vernon, E.; Venables, R.; Pym, C.; Povey, T.; Limbrey, J.; Digges, E.; Colleton, J.; Waldrond, E.; Noel, M.; Williams, W.; Kendall, T.; Lewis, J.; Middleton, T.; Jeffreys, J.; Glascock, W.; Watts, W.; Howe, A. (C 66/2946).
1670	30 July	*Sandwich, Earl of (*President*); *Gorges, Lord; *Alington, Lord; *Grey, Hon. T.; *Brouncker, Hon. H.; *Winch, Sir

---

[1] Commission of 1 Dec. 1660 (C 66/2946).

[2] Commission of 30 July 1670 (C 231/7 p. 375). The full text of this commission has not survived but its main provisions are recited in that of 4 April 1671 (C 66/3125). The salaries were granted by letters patent of 11 Jan. 1671 and made payable from 24 June 1670 (C 66/3121).

[3] Commissions of 4 April, 19 June and 15 Aug. 1671 (C 66/3125). Colepepper subsequently received payment as if he had been a salaried Commissioner since 1670 (*CTB*, iv, 14).

[4] Commission of 27 Sept. 1672 (C 66/3137).

H.; *Finch, Sir J.; *Waller, E.; *Slingsby, H.; *Titus, S. (C 231/7 p. 375).

1671   4 April   York, Duke of; Rupert, Prince; Buckingham, Duke of; Ormond, Duke of; Lauderdale, Earl of; Colepepper, Lord; Carteret, Sir G.; *Evelyn, J. (C 66/3125).

1671   19 June[1]   Temple, Sir R. (C 66/3125).

Secretary 1660–72

In 1660 the Council of Foreign Plantations was empowered to appoint officials, an allowance of £300 payable at the Exchequer being provided for their salaries and for incidental expenses.[2] The amount of the Secretary's salary is unknown. When the Council was reconstituted in 1670 the Secretary was appointed by the crown, the office being conferred upon one of the paid Commissioners. The Secretary, who also acted as Treasurer of the Council, received a salary of £500 as an ordinary paid Commissioner.[3]

LIST OF APPOINTMENTS

1660   10 Dec.   Frowde, P.
1670   30 July   Slingsby, H.

Assistant 1670–2

Between 1670 and 1672 the Council of Foreign Plantations employed an Assistant with a salary of £300 payable at the Exchequer.[4]

APPOINTMENT

1670   Worsley, B.

Clerks 1670–2

The employment of Clerks by the Council of Foreign Plantations was envisaged in 1660.[5] Before 1670 nothing is known of the size of the clerical establishment or of the identity of those who composed it. Between 1670 and 1672 the Clerks appear to have been three in number. During this period the Secretary was allowed £400 a year for Clerks and incidental expenses.[6] The size of individual salaries is unknown.

---

[1] This commission was renewed in different terms on 15 Aug. 1671 (C 66/3125; Journal (Plantations) 1670–2, 47).

[2] Commission of 1 Dec. 1660 (C 66/2946); CSPC (*America & West Indies*) 1574–1660, 494.

[3] Commission of 30 July 1670 (C 231/7 p. 375); letters patent of 11 Jan. 1671 (C 66/3121).

[4] *CSPD 1670*, 538–9; letters patent of 11 Jan. 1671 (C 66/3121).

[5] Commission of 1 Dec. 1660 (C 66/2946).

[6] Journal (Plantations) 1670–2, 53, 90–5.

LIST OF APPOINTMENTS

1670	12 Aug.	Collins, J.
1670	12 Aug.	Frowde, C.
1671	6 March	Barber, R.

Messenger 1670–2

Between 1670 and 1672 the Council of Foreign Plantations employed a Messenger at £30 a year.[1]

APPOINTMENT

1670	12 Aug.	Sampson, J.

Doorkeeper 1670–2

Between 1670 and 1672 the Council of Foreign Plantations employed a Doorkeeper at £25 a year.[2]

APPOINTMENT

1670	12 Aug.	Roe, T.

[1] Journal (Plantations) 1670–2, 4, 53, 90–5.
[2] Journal (Plantations) 1670–2, 3–4, 53, 90–5.

COUNCIL OF TRADE AND PLANTATIONS
1672–4

Commissioners 1672–4

The Council of Trade and Foreign Plantations was appointed by commission under the great seal. Its membership fell into three groups. In the first place there were the *ex officio* Commissioners who consisted of the Lord Chancellor or Lord Keeper, the Lord Treasurer or Commissioners of the Treasury, the Chancellor of the Exchequer and the Secretaries of State. Secondly there were nine unpaid Commissioners. Finally there was a group of paid Commissioners who received their salaries at the Exchequer. The first paid Commissioner was designated President with a salary of £800 and the second Vice President with a salary of £600. The remaining nine Commissioners received £500.[1] The Council was dissolved in 1674.[2]

In the following list *ex officio* Commissioners are omitted. The names of the salaried Commissioners are preceded by an asterisk.

LIST OF APPOINTMENTS

1672	27 Sept.	*Shaftesbury, Earl of (*President*); *Colepepper, Lord (*Vice President*); *Gorges, Lord; *Alington, Lord; *Brouncker, Hon. H.; *Winch, Sir H.; *Finch, Sir J.; *Waller, E.; *Slingsby, H.; *Titus, S.; *Evelyn, J.; York, Duke of; Rupert, Prince; Buckingham, Duke of; Lauderdale, Duke of; Ormond, Duke of; Halifax, Viscount; Carteret, Sir G.; Osborne, Sir T.; Long, Sir R. (C 66/3137).
1672	7 Dec.	*Hickman, Sir W. (v. Finch) (C 231/7 p. 428).

Secretary 1672–4

The Secretary of the Council of 1672, who also acted as its Treasurer, was appointed by the crown. The appointment of Worsley was contained in the commission appointing the Council; that of Locke was made by warrant under sign manual. The salary attached to the office was £500.[3]

LIST OF APPOINTMENTS

1672	27 Sept.	Worsley, B.
1673	14 Oct.	Locke, J.

---

[1] Commission of 27 Sept. 1672 (C 66/3127).   [2] Letters patent of 21 Dec. 1674 (C 66/3164).
[3] Commission of 27 Sept. 1672 (C 66/3137); *CSPD 1673*, 578; *CSPC (America & West Indies) 1669–74*, 527–8, 531. There is no evidence to support Locke's statement, made in 1690 (*CSPD 1689–90*, 455), that his salary had been £600.

Clerks 1672–4

The Council of 1672 was served by three Clerks. The usual salary was £100. Frowde received £150 as 'Chief Clerk' until his resignation in 1673.[1]

LIST OF APPOINTMENTS

1672	24 Oct.	Frowde, C.	1673	27 Oct.	Wilson, G.
1672		Swan, W.	1674	20 March	Richards, J.
1672		Pottle, W.			

Messenger 1672–4

The Council of 1672 was served by a Messenger with a salary of £30.[2]

APPOINTMENT

1672   Sampson, J.

Doorkeeper 1672–4

The Council of 1672 was served by a Doorkeeper with a salary of £30.[3]

APPOINTMENT

1672   Roe, T.

[1] Journal (Trade and Plantations) 1672–4, 2, 10, 83; CO 389/5 pp. 117–19; CTB, v, 308.
[2] Journal (Trade and Plantations) 1672–4, 10.
[3] ibid.

COMMITTEES OF THE PRIVY COUNCIL FOR TRADE AND PLANTATIONS 1675–96

Members 1675–96

From 1675 to 1696 the Board of Trade took the form of successive Committees of the Privy Council which had immediate responsibility for trade and plantation affairs and whose Members, often known as the Lords of Trade and Plantations, served without salary. As constituted in 1675 the Committee was select in character and provision was made for nine of its Members 'to have immediate care and intendency' of the business.[1] In 1679 the Committee was reappointed following the remodelling of the Privy Council.[2] It was revived at the accession of James II in 1685.[3] In 1688 trade and plantation affairs were entrusted to a Committee of the whole Council.[4] In the following year it was reconstituted as a select Committee which undertook the business until 1696.[5]

At no time during the period was attendance at the Committee restricted to those who had been specifically nominated to serve upon it. Other Privy Counsellors frequently attended and took part in its business.[6]

LIST OF APPOINTMENTS

1675	12 March	Danby, Earl of	1675	12 March	Williamson, Sir J.
1675	12 March	Anglesey, Earl of	1675	12 March	Duncombe, Sir J.
1675	12 March	Lauderdale, Duke of	1675	12 March	Carr, Sir R.
1675	12 March	Ormond, Duke of	1675	12 March	Seymour, E.
1675	12 March	Worcester, Marquess of	1676	20 Oct.	London, Bishop of
			1677	22 Dec.	Northampton, Earl of
1675	12 March	Ossory, Earl of	1678	26 July	Berkeley, Lord
1675	12 March	Arlington, Earl of	1678	13 Dec.	Ailesbury, Earl of
1675	12 March	Bridgwater, Earl of			
1675	12 March	Essex, Earl of	1679	22 April	Finch, Lord
1675	12 March	Carlisle, Earl of	1679	22 April	Shaftesbury, Earl of
1675	12 March	Craven, Earl of	1679	22 April	Anglesey, Earl of
1675	12 March	Fauconberg, Viscount	1679	22 April	Albemarle, Duke of
1675	12 March	Halifax, Viscount	1679	22 April	Lauderdale, Duke of
1675	12 March	Berkeley of Stratton, Lord	1679	22 April	Ormond, Duke of
			1679	22 April	Winchester, Marquess of
1675	12 March	Holles, Lord			
1675	12 March	Savile, H.	1679	22 April	Worcester, Marquess of
1675	12 March	Coventry, Hon. H.			

[1] PC 2/64 p. 395. The nine Members were Anglesey, Bridgwater, Carlisle, Craven, Fauconberg, Halifax, Berkeley of Stratton, Savile and Duncombe.
[2] PC 2/68 p. 6.   [3] PC 2/71 p. 17.   [4] PC 2/72 p. 585.   [5] PC 2/73 p. 8.
[6] R. P. Bieber, *The Lords of Trade and Plantations 1675–1696* (Allentown, Pa. 1919), 47–8, 91–2.

1679	22 April	Arlington, Earl of	1681	23 Feb.	Ailesbury, Earl of
1679	22 April	Bridgwater, Earl of	1681	9 March	Craven, Earl of
1679	22 April	Sunderland, Earl of	1685	30 Oct.	Berkeley, Earl of
1679	22 April	Essex, Earl of			
1679	22 April	Fauconberg, Viscount	1689	16 Feb.	Danby, Earl of
1679	22 April	Halifax, Viscount	1689	16 Feb.	Halifax, Marquess of
1679	22 April	London, Bishop of	1689	16 Feb.	Devonshire, Earl of
1679	22 April	Russell, Lord	1689	16 Feb.	Shrewsbury, Earl of
1679	22 April	Cavendish, Lord	1689	16 Feb.	Bath, Earl of
1679	22 April	Coventry, Hon. H.	1689	16 Feb.	Nottingham, Earl of
1679	22 April	Ernle, Sir J.	1689	16 Feb.	Fauconberg, Viscount
1679	22 April	Temple, Sir W.	1689	16 Feb.	Mordaunt, Viscount
1679	22 April	Powle, H.	1689	16 Feb.	London, Bishop of
1679	27 June	Robartes, Lord	1689	16 Feb.	Capel, Hon. Sir H.
1679	27 June	Holles, Lord	1689	16 Feb.	Powle, H.
1679	26 Nov.	Hyde, Hon. L.	1689	16 Feb.	Russell, E.
1680	14 Feb.	Jenkins, Sir L.	1689	26 Feb.	Lumley, Viscount
1680	29 June	Clarendon, Earl of	1690	20 Nov.	Godolphin, Lord
1680	20 Oct.	Carr, Sir R.	1691	14 May	Bridgwater, Earl of
1681	23 Feb.	Chesterfield, Earl of			

Secretary 1675–96 and Assistant Secretary 1692–6

In March 1675 it was ordered that Sir Robert Southwell, one of the four Clerks in Ordinary of the Privy Council, should 'constantly attend' the Committee for Trade and Plantations as its Secretary.[1] In 1676 it was provided that such of the Clerks of the Council who wished should have the opportunity of undertaking the duties of Secretary, serving for periods of six months in turn. At the same time £400 a year was made available for their remuneration.[2] How far the Clerks of the Privy Council, apart from Southwell who resigned his office in 1679, played an active part as Secretaries is uncertain. Payments were made to them by name for successive periods of six months until 1685 after which they were made simply 'To the Clerk of the Council in Waiting' each quarter. It seems clear that, from this date at least, the £400 was treated simply as an additional salary to be divided equally amongst the four Clerks without regard to their attendance on the Committee.[3]

There seems little doubt that the actual duties of Secretary were undertaken almost from the first by Blathwayt who had entered the office in September 1675. In May 1676 he was, in consideration of the fact that he had been approved by the King as 'assistant to the clerks of the council in the business of trade and plantations' called

[1] APC (Colonial) 1613–80, 619–20. For the secretarial arrangements generally, see G. A. Jacobsen, William Blathwayt: a late 17th Century English Administrator (New Haven 1932), 84–95.

[2] APC (Colonial) 1613–80, 664–5; BM Add. MS 9767 pp. 10–13.

[3] Apart from Southwell the recorded recipients of this allowance were Sir Philip Lloyd, Sir Thomas Doleman and Francis Gwyn (BM Add. MS 9767). In 1697 the Clerks of the Council succeeded in having additional salaries of £100 attached to their offices in place of the allowances which ceased on the dissolution of the Committee in the previous year (APC (Colonial) 1680–1720, 313; CO 389/36 pp. 35–8). These additional salaries continued to form part of their remuneration until the early 19th century.

in to give his attendance at the Committee. Thereafter his industry and continuous attendance ensured that the direction of the Committee's affairs passed effectively into his hands. His salary was fixed at £150 and raised to £250 in the following year.[1] He was himself appointed a Clerk of the Council in Extraordinary in 1678 and a Clerk in Ordinary in 1686.[2]

Although Blathwayt retained his position until 1696 his additional responsibilities as Secretary at War (1683) and as acting Secretary of State during the reign of William III restricted the amount of time that he could devote to the office. As a result much of the business devolved upon his principal subordinate, Povey. Povey's position was regularised in 1692 when he was appointed a Clerk of the Council in Extraordinary with special instructions 'to assist the Clerks of the Council at the Committee of Trade and Plantations' in the absence of Blathwayt. Povey continued to act as Assistant Secretary until 1696.[3]

LISTS OF APPOINTMENTS

SECRETARY

1675   Sept.   Blathwayt, W.

ASSISTANT SECRETARY

1692   1 March   Povey, J.

Clerks 1675–96

Two Clerks, who were apparently Under Clerks of the Privy Council, served the Board from 1675 until March 1676, each with salaries of £50.[4] The first establishment of the office dated April 1676 made provision for two Clerks with the same salaries.[5] An 'Extraordinary Clerk' was also employed at the same salary from 1677 to 1683.[6] In 1685 a new establishment made provision for three Clerks, all with salaries of £50.[7] This arrangement continued in operation until 1696. The Journal of the Committee does not record the appointment of Clerks and the accounts specify the names of those who received salaries in only one case. It is, therefore, impossible to provide a satisfactory account of these officials. Apart from those who served between 1675 and 1676 the name of only one other Clerk is known.

LIST OF APPOINTMENTS

1675   March   Madox, P.
1675   March   Sergeant, B.
c. 1684   Povey, J.

---

[1] CO 391/1 p. 118; BM Add. MS 9767 pp. 10–13, 37–9; *APC (Colonial) 1613–80*, 743–4.
[2] PC 2/66 p. 370; PC 2/71 p. 325.   [3] PC 2/74 p. 340; *CTB*, xii, 222.
[4] BM Add. MS 9767, pp. 14–16.
[5] ibid. pp. 10–13.   [6] ibid. pp. 41, 104.   [7] ibid. pp. 115–22.

COUNCIL OF TRADE AND PLANTATIONS
1696–1782

Commissioners 1696–1782

The Council of Trade and Foreign Plantations of 1696 was appointed by the crown by commission under the great seal. It was composed of various unsalaried *ex officio* Commissioners who were not expected to attend the Board regularly and a certain number of paid Commissioners to whom the conduct of business was entrusted. Originally the *ex officio* Commissioners consisted of the holders of the offices of Lord Chancellor or Lord Keeper, Lord President of the Council, Lord Privy Seal, Lord Treasurer or First Lord of the Treasury, Lord Admiral or First Lord of the Admiralty, Secretary of State and Chancellor of the Exchequer. To these were added the Bishop of London in 1702 and the Surveyor and Auditor General of Plantations in 1721.[1]

The number of paid Commissioners was fixed in principle at eight although it fell to seven between 1707 and 1712 and between 1768 and 1779. The senior such Commissioner, usually known as the First Lord, presided. This office was discontinued between 1768 and 1779 when the Secretary of State for the Colonies, an *ex officio* Commissioner, presided.[2] The Council was dismissed by the King on 2 May 1782, being abolished by act later in the same year.[3]

The salaries of the Commissioners were fixed at £1000 each payable at the Exchequer.[4] Under an arrangement which cannot be dated precisely the First Lord was accorded an additional salary from the secret service money. The earliest First Lord who is known to have enjoyed such a salary was Monson (1737–48) who received £500 a year. His successor, Halifax, received the same until about 1752 when the amount was raised to £1500.[5] In 1761 regular provision was made for the First Lord to be paid an additional salary of £1000 at the Exchequer. Payment of this salary was suspended between 1768 and 1779 during the period when the Board was presided over by the Secretary of State for the Colonies, who received no remuneration for his services in this respect.[6]

In the following list *ex officio* Commissioners are omitted.

---

[1] Commissions of 15 May 1696 (C 66/3386), 19 June 1702 (C 66/3430), 14 Oct. 1721 (C 66/3546). The office of Surveyor and Auditor General of Plantations, created in 1680, was held during the relevant period by Horatio Walpole (later Lord Walpole of Wolterton) 1717–57 and Hon. (later Lord) Robert Cholmondeley 1757–1804 (C. M. Andrews, *Materials for American History to 1783* (Washington 1912–14), ii, 144–8).

[2] The Secretaries of State presided as follows: Earl of Hillsborough 12 July 1768–15 Aug. 1772; Lord Dartmouth 15 Aug. 1772–10 Nov. 1775; Lord George Germain 10 Nov. 1775–15 Nov. 1779.

[3] *JCTP 1776–82*, 472; 22 Geo. III, c 82.

[4] CO 389/36 pp. 35–8.

[5] BM Add. MS 32716 ff. 337–8; A. H. Basye, *The Lords Commissioners of Trade and Plantations 1748–1782* (New Haven 1925), 34, 70 n. 97; M. A. Thomson, *The Secretaries of State 1681–1782* (Oxford 1932), 170–1; L. B. Namier, *The Structure of Politics at the Accession of George III*, 2nd ed. (London 1960), 227–8.

[6] T 52/52 p. 153; T 53/48 pp. 7, 16; T 52/55 pp. 49, 54–5, 311–12; T 52/57 pp. 312–13; T 52/58 pp. 360–1, 416; T 52/68 p. 176; T 52/69 p. 248.

LIST OF APPOINTMENTS

1696	15 May	Bridgwater, Earl of; Tankerville, Earl of; Meadows, Sir P.; Blathwayt, W.; Pollexfen, J.; Locke, J.; Hill, A.; Methuen, J. (C 66/3386).
1697	6 July	Bridgwater, Earl of; Tankerville, Earl of; Meadows, Sir P.; Blathwayt, W.; Pollexfen, J.; Locke, J.; Hill, A.; Stepney, G. (C 66/3397).
1699	9 June	Stamford, Earl of; Lexington, Lord; Meadows, Sir P.; Blathwayt, W.; Pollexfen, J.; Locke, J.; Hill, A.; Stepney, G. (C 66/3413).
1700	11 July	Stamford, Earl of; Lexington, Lord; Meadows, Sir P.; Blathwayt, W.; Pollexfen, J.; Hill, A.; Stepney, G.; Prior, M. (C 66/3416).
1702	8 Jan.	Stamford, Earl of; Lexington, Lord; Meadows, Sir P.; Blathwayt, W.; Pollexfen, J.; Stepney, G.; Prior, M.; Cecil, Hon. R. (C 66/3422).
1702	19 June	Weymouth, Viscount; Dartmouth, Lord; Meadows, Sir P.; Blathwayt, W.; Pollexfen, J.; Stepney, G.; Prior, M.; Cecil, Hon. R. (C 66/3430).
1707	25 April	Stamford, Earl of; Dartmouth, Lord; Herbert of Chirbury, Lord; Meadows, Sir P.; Stepney, G.; Pulteney, J.; Monckton, R. (C 66/3461).
1708	4 May	Stamford, Earl of; Dartmouth, Lord; Herbert of Chirbury, Lord; Meadows, Sir P.; Pulteney, J.; Monckton, R.; Turner, Sir C. (C 66/3463).
1710	12 May	Stamford, Earl of; Dartmouth, Lord; Meadows, Sir P.; Pulteney, J.; Monckton, R.; Turner, Sir C.; Baillie, G. (C 66/3473).
1710	4 Oct.	Stamford, Earl of; Meadows, Sir P.; Pulteney, J.; Monckton, R.; Turner, Sir C.; Baillie, G.; Moore, A. (C 66/3474).
1711	12 June	Winchilsea, Earl of; Meadows, Sir P.; Monckton, R.; Turner, Sir C.; Baillie, G.; Moore, A.; Gwyn, F. (C 66/3482).
1712	7 July	Winchilsea, Earl of; Guilford, Lord; Meadows, Sir P.; Monckton, R.; Moore, A.; Gwyn, F.; Foley, T.; Cotton, J. H. (C 66/3488).
1713	15 Sept.	Guilford, Lord; Meadows, Sir P.; Monckton, R.; Moore, A.; Cotton, Sir J. H.; Sharp, J.; Pytts, S.; Vernon, T. (C 66/3493).
1714	13 Dec.	Berkeley of Stratton, Lord; Astley, Sir J.; Molesworth, R.; Cockburn, J.; Hutcheson, A.; Chetwynd, J.; Cooke, C.; Docminique, P. (C 66/3503).
1715	12 May	Suffolk, Earl of; Astley, Sir J.; Molesworth, R.; Cockburn, J.; Hutcheson, A.; Chetwynd, J.; Cooke, C.; Docminique, P. (C 66/3504).
1716	5 Jan.	Suffolk, Earl of; Astley, Sir J.; Cockburn, J.; Chetwynd, J.; Cooke, C.; Docminique, P.; Addison, J.; Molesworth, J. (C 66/3511).
1717	13 July	Suffolk, Earl of; Chetwynd, J.; Cooke, Sir C.; Docminique, P.; Molesworth, J.; Pelham, T.; Pulteney, D.; Bladen, M. (C 66/3520).

1718 31 Jan.   Holdernesse, Earl of; Chetwynd, J.; Cooke, Sir C.; Docminique, P.; Molesworth, J.; Pelham, T.; Pulteney, D.; Bladen, M. (C 66/3521).

1719 11 May   Westmorland, Earl of; Chetwynd, J.; Cooke, Sir C.; Docminique, P.; Molesworth, J.; Pelham, T.; Pulteney, D.; Bladen, M. (C 66/3532).

1720 24 June   Westmorland, Earl of; Chetwynd, J.; Cooke, Sir C.; Docminique, P.; Pelham, T.; Pulteney, D.; Bladen, M.; Ashe, E. (C 66/3538).

1721 4 Sept.   Westmorland, Earl of; Chetwynd, J.; Docminique, P.; Pelham, T.; Pulteney, D.; Bladen, M.; Ashe, E.; Plumer, R. (C 66/3545).

1721 14 Oct.   Westmorland, Earl of; Chetwynd, J.; Docminique, P.; Pelham, T.; Bladen, M.; Ashe, E.; Plumer, R.; Hobart, Sir J. (C 66/3546).

1727 8 Aug.   Westmorland, Earl of; Chetwynd, J.; Docminique, P.; Pelham, T.; Bladen, M.; Ashe, E.; Bridgeman, Sir O.; Carey, W. (C 66/3566).

1728 1 June   Westmorland, Earl of; Docminique, P.; Pelham, T.; Bladen, M.; Ashe, E.; Bridgeman, Sir O.; Carey, W.; Frankland, Sir T. (C 66/3569).

1730 14 May   Westmorland, Earl of; Docminique, P.; Pelham, T.; Bladen, M.; Ashe, E.; Bridgeman, Sir O.; Brudenell, Hon. J.; Croft, Sir A. (C 66/3580).

1735 22 May   Fitzwalter, Earl; Pelham, T.; Bladen, M.; Ashe, E.; Bridgeman, Sir O.; Brudenell, Hon. J.; Croft, Sir A.; Plumer, R. (C 66/3593).

1737 27 June   Monson, Lord; Pelham, T.; Bladen, M.; Ashe, E.; Brudenell, Hon. J.; Croft, Sir A.; Plumer, R.; Herbert, Hon. R. S. (C 66/3597).

1741 5 May   Monson, Lord; Bladen, M.; Ashe, E.; Brudenell, Hon. J.; Plumer, R.; Herbert, Hon. R. S.; Keene, B.; Pelham, T. (C 66/3604).

1743 31 Dec.   Monson, Lord; Bladen, M.; Ashe, E.; Brudenell, Hon. J.; Plumer, R.; Herbert, Hon. R. S.; Keene, B.; Gilmour, Sir C. (C 66/3613).

1745 5 Jan.   Monson, Lord; Bladen, M.; Ashe, E.; Brudenell, Hon. J.; Plumer, R.; Herbert, Hon. R. S.; Phillips, Sir J.; Pitt, J. (C 66/3616).

1745 24 May   Monson, Lord; Bladen, M.; Ashe, E.; Brudenell, Hon. J.; Plumer, R.; Herbert, Hon. R. S.; Pitt, J.; Leveson Gower, Hon. B. (C 66/3616).

1746 26 Feb.   Monson, Lord; Ashe, E.; Brudenell, Hon. J.; Plumer, R.; Herbert, Hon. R. S.; Pitt, J.; Leveson Gower, Hon. B.; Grenville, J. (C 66/3618).

1746 20 Nov.   Monson, Lord; Plumer, R.; Herbert, Hon. R. S.; Pitt, J.; Leveson Gower, Hon. B.; Grenville, J.; Dupplin, Viscount; Fane, F. (C 66/3620).

1748   5 Nov.   Halifax, Earl of; Plumer, R.; Herbert, Hon. R. S.; Pitt, J.; Leveson Gower, Hon. B.; Grenville, J.; Dupplin, Viscount; Fane, F. (C 66/3625).

1748   30 Dec.   Halifax, Earl of; Herbert, Hon. R. S.; Pitt, J.; Leveson Gower, Hon. B.; Grenville, J.; Dupplin, Viscount; Fane, F.; Robinson, Sir T. (C 66/3625).

1749   23 June   Halifax, Earl of; Herbert, Hon. R. S.; Pitt, J.; Grenville, J.; Dupplin, Viscount; Fane, F.; Robinson, Sir T.; Townshend, Hon. C. (C 66/3627).

1749   21 Dec.   Halifax, Earl of; Herbert, Hon. R. S.; Pitt, J.; Grenville, Hon. J.; Dupplin, Viscount; Fane, F.; Townshend, Hon. C.; Stone, A. (C 66/3628).

1752   6 Jan.   Halifax, Earl of; Pitt, J.; Grenville, Hon. J.; Dupplin, Viscount; Fane, F.; Townshend, Hon. C.; Stone, A.; Oswald, J. (C 66/3635).

1754   6 April   Halifax, Earl of; Pitt, J.; Grenville, Hon. J.; Fane, F.; Stone, A.; Oswald, J.; Edgcumbe, Hon. R.; Pelham, T. (C 66/3643).

1755   29 Dec.   Halifax, Earl of; Fane, F.; Stone, A.; Oswald, J.; Pelham, T.; Talbot, Hon. J.; Jenyns, S.; Rigby, R. (C 66/3650).

1756   13 April   Halifax, Earl of; Stone, A.; Oswald, J.; Pelham, T.; Talbot, Hon. J.; Jenyns, S.; Rigby, R.; Hamilton, W. G. (C 66/3652).

1756   13 Dec.   Halifax, Earl of; Stone, A.; Oswald, J.; Pelham, T.; Jenyns, S.; Rigby, R.; Hamilton, W. G.; Sloper, W. (C 66/3655).

1760   14 Jan.   Halifax, Earl of; Stone, A.; Pelham, T.; Jenyns, S.; Hamilton, W. G.; Sloper, W.; Eliot, E.; Bacon, E. (C 66/3666).

1761   21 March   Sandys, Lord; Stone, A.; Jenyns, S.; Eliot, E.; Bacon, E.; Yorke, Hon. J.; Thomas, Sir E.; Rice, G. (C 66/3675).

1761   4 Dec.   Sandys, Lord; Jenyns, S.; Eliot, E.; Bacon, E.; Yorke, Hon. J.; Thomas, Sir E.; Rice, G.; Roberts, J. (C 66/3682).

1763   5 Jan.   Sandys, Lord; Jenyns, S.; Eliot, E.; Bacon, E.; Yorke, Hon. J.; Thomas, Sir E.; Rice, G.; Orwell, Lord (C 66/3686).

1763   1 March   Townshend, Hon. C.; Jenyns, S.; Eliot, E.; Bacon, E.; Yorke, Hon. J.; Thomas, Sir E.; Rice, G.; Orwell, Lord (C 66/3687).

1763   23 April   Shelburne, Earl of; Jenyns, S.; Eliot, E.; Bacon, E.; Yorke, Hon. J.; Rice, G.; Orwell, Lord; Gascoyne, B. (C 66/3690).

1763   17 Sept.   Hillsborough, Earl of; Jenyns, S.; Eliot, E.; Bacon, E.; Yorke, Hon. J.; Rice, G.; Orwell, Lord; Gascoyne, B. (C 66/3692).

1764   2 May   Hillsborough, Earl of; Jenyns, S.; Eliot, E.; Bacon, E.; Rice, G.; Orwell, Lord; Gascoyne, B.; Dyson, J. (C 66/3695).

1765   12 Aug.   Dartmouth, Lord; Jenyns, S.; Eliot, E.; Yorke, Hon. J.; Rice, G.; Roberts, J.; Dyson, J.; Fitzherbert, W. (C 66/3702).

1766   3 Jan.   Dartmouth, Lord; Jenyns, S.; Eliot, E.; Rice, G.; Roberts, J.; Dyson, J.; Fitzherbert, W.; Palmerston, Viscount (C 66/3704).

1766   18 Aug.   Hillsborough, Earl of; Jenyns, S.; Eliot, E.; Rice, G.; Roberts, J.; Dyson, J.; Fitzherbert, W.; Palmerston, Viscount (C66/3707).

1766   22 Oct.   Hillsborough, Earl of; Jenyns, S.; Eliot, E.; Rice, G.; Roberts, J.; Dyson, J.; Fitzherbert, W.; Robinson, Hon. T. (C 66/3709).

1766	18 Dec.	Nugent, R.; Jenyns, S.; Eliot, E.; Rice, G.; Roberts, J.; Dyson, J.; Fitzherbert, W.; Robinson, Hon. T. (C 66/3711).
1768	12 July[1]	Jenyns, S.; Eliot, E.; Rice, G.; Roberts, J.; Dyson, J.; Fitzherbert, W.; Robinson, Hon. T. (C 66/3718).
1768	30 Dec.	Jenyns, S.; Eliot, E.; Rice, G.; Roberts, J.; Fitzherbert, W.; Robinson, Hon. T.; Lisburne, Viscount (C 66/3720).
1770	25 April	Jenyns, S.; Eliot, E.; Roberts, J.; Fitzherbert, W.; Spencer, Lord R.; Greville, Lord; Northey, W. (C 66/3725).
1771	2 Feb.	Jenyns, S.; Eliot, E.; Roberts, J.; Fitzherbert, W.; Spencer, Lord R.; Greville, Lord; Whately, T. (C 66/3730).
1772	10 Feb.	Jenyns, S.; Eliot, E.; Roberts, J.; Gascoyne, B.; Spencer, Lord R.; Greville, Lord; Jolliffe, W. (C 66/3735).
1772	27 Aug.	Jenyns, S.; Eliot, E.; Gascoyne, B.; Spencer, Lord R.; Greville, Lord; Jolliffe, W.; Garlies, Lord (C 66/3737).
1774	26 Jan.	Jenyns, S.; Eliot, E.; Gascoyne, B.; Spencer, Lord R.; Jolliffe, W.; Keene, W.; Greville, Hon. C. F. (C 66/3744).
1776	15 March	Jenyns, S.; Gascoyne, B.; Spencer, Lord R.; Jolliffe, W.; Keene, W.; Greville, Hon. C. F.; Eden, W. (C 66/3758).
1777	17 June	Jenyns, S.; Gascoyne, B.; Spencer, Lord R.; Jolliffe, W.; Greville, Hon. C. F.; Eden, W.; de Grey, T. (C 66/3765).
1779	14 July	Jenyns, S.; Spencer, Lord R.; Greville, Hon. C. F.; Eden, W.; de Grey, T.; Stuart, A.; Gibbon, E. (C 66/3775).
1779	15 Nov.	Carlisle, Earl of; Jenyns, S.; Spencer, Lord R.; Greville, Hon. C. F.; Eden, W.; de Grey, T.; Stuart, A.; Gibbon, E. (C 66/3777).
1780	16 Sept.	Carlisle, Earl of; Spencer, Lord R.; Eden, W.; de Grey, T.; Stuart, A.; Gibbon, E.; Sloane, H.; Langlois, B. (C 66/3781).
1780	12 Dec.	Grantham, Lord; Spencer, Lord R.; Eden, W.; de Grey, Hon. T.; Stuart, A.; Gibbon, E.; Sloane, H.; Langlois, B. (C 66/3783).
1782	2 Jan.	Grantham, Lord; Eden, W.; Stuart, A.; Gibbon, E.; Sloane, H.; Fergusson, Sir A.; Storer, A. M.; Talbot, J. C. (C 66/3790).

Secretary 1696–1782

Although the appointment of the Secretary in 1696 was recorded as an act of the Board, it seems clear that the individual in question had already been nominated by the crown.[2] From 1707 the position of the crown was overtly recognised and the Secretary was admitted to office by the Board on the receipt of a letter from a Secretary of State signifying the royal nomination.[3] In 1722 the Board made an unsuccessful attempt to secure the right of appointment.[4] The office was held singly

---

[1] The enrolled letters patent are dated 8 July in error (T 53/51 p. 125; *JCTP 1768–75*, 38).
[2] CO 391/9 p. 7; BM Add. MS 9729 ff. 140–1.
[3] *JCTP 1704–9*, 356.
[4] *CSPC (America & West Indies) 1722–3*, 42–3.

throughout the period except for the years 1753–8 when it was filled by two Secretaries acting jointly.[1] The salary, originally £500, was increased to £700 in 1764.[2]

LIST OF APPOINTMENTS

1696	25 June	Popple, W.	1753	6 June	{	Hill, T.
1707	19 May	Popple, W.			{	Pownall, J.
1722	17 May	Popple, A.	1758	25 Oct.		Pownall, J.
1737	19 Oct.	Hill, T.	1776	23 Jan.		Cumberland, R.

Deputy Secretary 1696–1782

The office of Deputy Secretary, or Chief Clerk, was created in 1696 with a salary of £100.[3] In 1712 the Deputy Secretary was granted an additional allowance of £100 from the contingency account of the office.[4] In 1764 the salary was fixed at £300.[5]

LIST OF APPOINTMENTS

1696		Popple, W.	1758	12 April	Rogers, R.
1707		Drift, A.	1764	4 July	Bradbury, S.
1714	20 Dec.	Wheelock, B.	1781	4 Dec.	Roberts, W.
1735	9 April	Gellibrand, S.			

Solicitor and Clerk of Reports 1730–82

This office was created in 1730.[6] It was granted to joint holders in 1779.[7] The salary, which formed part of the contingent expenses of the Board, was fixed at £200 in 1730.[8] J. Pownall received an additional allowance of £100 from 1752 to 1753 as did Sedgwick and Bradbury from 1758 to 1764.[9] In 1764 the salary was fixed at £150.[10]

LIST OF APPOINTMENTS

1730	18 Aug.	Burrish, O.	1764	4 July		Silvester, E.
1737	3 June	Popple, W.	1765	31 May		Cumberland, R.
1745	1 May	Pownall, J.	1776	23 Jan.		Serle, A.[11]
1753	6 June	Sedgwick, E.	1779	15 June	{	Goddard, J.
1763	28 Sept.	Bradbury, S.			{	Elliott, G.

[1] During Cumberland's absences from the office, the duties of Secretary were undertaken by Elliott, the Solicitor and Clerk of Reports (*JCTP 1776–82*, 343, 432–4).
[2] CO 389/36 pp. 35–8; *JCTP 1764–7*, 90.   [3] CO 389/36 pp. 35–8.
[4] *JCTP 1709–15*, 340. Earlier attempts to secure an increase in salary had been unsuccessful (*CTB*, xv, 409; CO 389/36 pp. 82–3, 393).
[5] *JCTP 1764–7*, 90.   [6] *CSPC (America & West Indies) 1730*, 231–2; *JCTP 1729–34*, 139.
[7] *JCTP 1776–82*, 257.   [8] *JCTP 1729–34*, 139.
[9] CO 388/83.   [10] *JCTP 1764–7*, 90–1.
[11] During Serle's absence the duties of the office were carried out at follows: by the Clerks, Palmer and Goddard 21 May 1776–26 Dec. 1777 and by Goddard and Elliott 26 Dec. 1777–15 June 1779 (*JCTP 1776–82*, 28, 257).

Clerks 1696–1782

In 1696 provision was made for four Clerks, three with salaries of £80 and one with a salary of £60.[1] The total number of Clerks was raised to five in 1700 and to six in 1701, slight alterations being made in their salaries from time to time.[2] In 1708 the establishment was fixed at seven Clerks, one at £80, one at £70, one at £60, two at £50 and two at £40.[3] This arrangement remained unaltered until 1764 when a new establishment was authorised consisting of nine Clerks with salaries of £100, £90, £80, £70, £60, £55, £50, £45 and £40.[4] At the time of the suppression of the Board in 1782 the number of Clerks had fallen to seven due to the fact that the vacancies which had occurred in 1777 and 1781 had not been filled.[5]

LIST OF APPOINTMENTS

1696		Barker, W.	1735	5 June	Matthias, G.
1696		Skynner, C.	1736	30 March	Hill, T.
1696		Whitworth, C.	1738	14 June	Tutté, J.
1697	25 March	Carroll, M.	1738	14 June	Sedgwick, E.
1700	6 Aug.	Drift, A.	1741	24 June	Pownall, J.
1700	6 Aug.	Wheelock, B.	1745	27 June	Bradbury, S.
1701	11 March	Bruges, W.	1748	19 Jan.	Blucke, R.
1701	4 Nov.	Loggan, J.	1749	23 May	Cranwell, R.
1703	13 May	Estwick, N.	1752	5 Dec.	Peacock, J.
By 1708		{ Gellibrand, S.	1753	22 Nov.	Dancer, F.
		{ Bertin, M.	1756	14 Jan.	Heron, H.
By 1710		Hudson, I.	1758	16 Feb.	Palmer, J. S.
By 1714		{ Sanderson, A.	1758	18 April	Green, R.
		{ Gray, W.	1760	28 March	Cuckow, D.
1714	20 Dec.	Hoskins, W.	1761	14 March	Berkeley, W.
By 1715		Holford, T.	1764	4 July	Lewis, J.
1717	22 March	Popple, A.	1764	29 Nov.	Nelme, L. D.
1721	7 Nov.	Spencer, J.	1765	22 April	Roberts, W.
1722	17 May	Gedney, T.	1765	22 April	Owens, E.
1727	18 April	Popple, H.	1765	22 April	Davis, C.
1727	18 April	Lanham, R.	1765	22 April	Samber, J. S.
1727	10 May	Rogers, R.	1766	31 July	Wilks, S.
1727	12 Aug.	Bradley, G.	1770	24 Jan.	Pownall, J. L.
1735	15 April	Campion, W.	1770	24 Jan.	Powell, J. J.

[1] CO 389/36 pp. 35–8.
[2] ibid. pp. 106–7, 136–8; CO 391/14 pp. 194–5, 208; CO 391/15 pp. 103–4; CO 391/16 pp. 354.
[3] JCTP 1704–9, 451.
[4] JCTP 1764–7, 90–1. Provision was made for these amounts to be increased as the pensions granted to retired officials on this occasion fell in (ibid.; T 1/579 Schedule 3).
[5] JCTP 1776–82, 125, 442. Although Palmer retired in 1777 he was allowed to remain on the establishment at full salary until 1782 (T 1/579 Schedule 3).

1770	24 Jan.	Lloyd, W.	1775	6 July	Clark, F. R.
1772	21 Dec.	Pownall, G.	1779	7 Oct.	Hughes, W.
1775	11 April	Goddard, J.			

Office Keepers 1696–1782

In 1696 provision was made for two Office or Chamber Keepers, sometimes known as Doorkeepers, each with a salary of £40.[1] On the abolition of the office of second Messenger in 1701 the salary of Child, one of the Office Keepers, was raised to £45 and he was given the additional title of Assistant Messenger.[2] On the death of Clarke in 1728 his office was abolished and all the duties were entrusted to Tregonning who had succeeded Child as Office Keeper and Assistant Messenger in 1721.[3] Thereafter the Board was served by one Office Keeper with a salary of £45.

LIST OF APPOINTMENTS

1696	3 July	Child, D.	1740	7 Oct.	Simpson, S.
1696	3 July	Clarke, S.	1742	8 July	Armitage, G.
1721	7 March	Tregonning, R.	1745	8 May	Willis, R.
1733	27 Feb.	Campion, W.	1758	19 Dec.	Terrie, T.
1735	15 April	Hutchinson, J.	1767	27 Feb.	Bonnick, W.

Messengers 1696–1782

In 1696 provision was made for two Messengers, each with a salary of £40.[4] On the death of How in 1701 one of the offices was abolished and all the duties were entrusted to the remaining Messenger, Gray, who was given the additional title of Assistant Chamber Keeper and an increased salary of £45.[5] In 1756 the then Messenger was appointed Porter and held the two offices concurrently until the suppression of the Board.[6]

LIST OF APPOINTMENTS

1696	3 July	Gray, J.	1723	10 Jan.	Wilson, J.
1696	3 July	How, R.	1749	19 Dec.	Serle, E.

Necessary Woman 1696–1782

In 1696 provision was made for a Necessary Woman with a salary of £30.[7]

---

[1] CO 389/36 pp. 35–8. [2] ibid. pp. 136–8; CO 391/14 pp. 194–5. [3] *JCTP 1723–8*, 425.
[4] CO 389/36 pp. 35–8. [5] ibid. pp. 136–8; CO 391/14 pp. 194–5. [6] *JCTP 1754–8*, 258.
[7] CO 389/36 pp. 35–8.

LIST OF APPOINTMENTS

1696	6 July	Wood, M.	By 1741		Griffin, B.
1701	25 March	Wright, M.	1760	5 Nov.	Wright, A.
By 1716		Fry, M.	1777	29 April	Serle, M.

Porter 1724–82

This office was created in 1724. The salary of £40, which originally formed part of the contingent expenses of the office, was made a charge on the establishment in 1728.[1] In 1756 the then Messenger was appointed Porter and held the two offices concurrently until the suppression of the Board.[2]

LIST OF APPOINTMENTS

1724	15 July	Griffin, G.
1756	7 Oct.	Serle, E.

Counsel 1718–82

The 1696 commission empowered the Board to call upon the Attorney or Solicitor General or any of the King's Counsel for advice on legal matters.[3] From 1704 the Attorney and Solicitor General each received a standing allowance of 100 guineas in respect of their services in this connection.[4] In 1718 the Board was accorded the services of a permanent Counsel whose function was to report on all matters of law which were not considered to be of sufficient importance to require the opinion of the Attorney or Solicitor General.[5] West, the first holder of the office, was selected from amongst the King's Counsel. In 1725 his successor, Fane, was appointed Counsel specifically for the affairs of the Board of Trade.[6] In 1727, however, he was appointed a King's Counsel at large, a course that was followed in the cases of Lamb and Jackson. Having received their appointments from the crown by letters patent under the great seal, the Counsel were assigned to the service of the Board by means of a letter from one of the Secretaries of State.[7] In 1782 the function of reporting on colonial acts, which had previously been carried out by the Board's Counsel, was entrusted to a Counsel attached to the office of the Secretary of State who had charge of colonial business.[8]

[1] JCTP 1723–8, 106, 425. [2] JCTP 1754–8, 258.
[3] Commission of 15 May 1696 (C 66/3386); CTB, xviii, 84, 442.
[4] CTB, xix, 244. Their Clerks received allowances of 10 guineas (ibid. xxii, 34).
[5] CSPC (America & West Indies) 1717–18, 198; JCTP 1715–18, 369.
[6] Letters patent of 19 Aug. 1725 (C 66/3561).
[7] JCTP 1723–8, 195; JCTP 1742–9, 214–15; JCTP 1768–75, 185.
[8] This office was held by William Selwyn 1782–3, 1783–96, James Mansfield 1783 and William Baldwin 1796–1813. James Stephen was appointed in 1813 and, between 1825 and 1836, also held the office of Law Clerk to the Board of Trade (D. M. Young, The Colonial Office in the Early 19th Century (London 1961), 58 n. 2; D. B. Swinfen, Imperial Control of Colonial Legislation 1813–1865

In 1718 a salary of £300, payable at the Exchequer, was attached to the office.[1] In 1721 this salary was discontinued and a new arrangement was made whereby the Counsel was paid by the Treasury Solicitor. Thereafter his remuneration consisted of a fixed allowance calculated on the basis of twice weekly attendances at the Board at three guineas a time and a further fee of three guineas for each report on cases or colonial acts submitted to him by the Board.[2]

In the following list the dates are, except in the case of West, those of the letters patent.

LIST OF APPOINTMENTS

1718	23 April	West, R.	1746	12 Nov.	Lamb, M.
1725	19 Aug.	Fane, F.	1770	14 April	Jackson, R.

(Oxford 1970), 21–32; PRO 30/8/184 f. 54). I am grateful to Mr. Michael Collinge for the last reference.

[1] *CTB*, xxxii, 441.

[2] T 29/24, pt. ii p. 38; T 52/31 pp. 159–60; T 1/238 f. 271; AO 1/2321/48; CO 389/37 pp. 247–9.

COMMITTEE OF THE PRIVY COUNCIL
FOR TRADE AND PLANTATIONS 1784—6

Members 1784–6

Between 1784 and 1786 the Board of Trade took the form of a Committee of the Privy Council. The number of Members was not fixed and they received no salary.[1]

LIST OF APPOINTMENTS

1784	5 March	Aylesford, Earl of	1784	5 March	Jenkinson, C.
1784	5 March	Effingham, Earl of	1784	5 March	Dundas, H.
1784	5 March	Clarendon, Earl of	1784	5 March	Grenville, J.
1784	5 March	Campbell, Lord F.	1784	5 March	Grenville, W. W.
1784	5 March	London, Bishop of	1784	8 March	Howe, Viscount
1784	5 March	de Ferrers, Lord	1784	8 March	Goodricke, Sir J.
1784	5 March	Grantham, Lord	1784	11 June	Mulgrave, Lord
1784	5 March	Walsingham, Lord	1785	10 Dec.	Eden, W.
1784	5 March	Grantley, Lord	1786	13 Jan.	Carmarthen,
1784	5 March	Sydney, Lord			Marquess of
1784	5 March	Harley, Hon. T.	1786	13 Jan.	Pitt, Hon. W.
1784	5 March	Yorke, Hon. Sir J.			

[1] PC 2/129 p. 60.

COMMITTEE OF THE PRIVY COUNCIL
FOR TRADE AND PLANTATIONS 1786–1870
General Department
President 1786–1870

This office was created in 1786. Appointments were made by the crown by order in council.[1] The President was, as such, unpaid until 1826 when a salary of £2000 was provided.[2] However, before this date it was the usual practice for him to hold concurrently some other office to which remuneration was attached. This practice was continued until 1845, payment of the salary from the Board being suspended while the President held such an office.[3]

LIST OF APPOINTMENTS

1786	23 Aug.	Hawkesbury, Lord	1841	3 Sept.	Ripon, Earl of
1804	6 June	Montrose, Duke of	1843	10 June	Gladstone, W. E.
1806	5 Feb.	Auckland, Lord	1845	5 Feb.	Dalhousie, Earl of
1807	26 March	Bathurst, Earl	1846	6 July	Clarendon, Earl of
1812	29 Sept.	Clancarty, Earl of	1847	22 July	Labouchere, H.
1818	24 Jan.	Robinson, Hon. F. J.	1852	27 Feb.	Henley, J. W.
1823	21 Feb.	Huskisson, W.	1852	28 Dec.	Cardwell, E.
1827	3 Sept.	Grant, C.	1855	31 March	Stanley of Alderley,
1828	11 June	Vesey Fitzgerald, W.			Lord
1830	2 Feb.	Herries, J. C.	1858	26 Feb.	Henley, J. W.
1830	22 Nov.	Auckland, Lord	1859	3 March	Donoughmore, Earl of
1834	5 June	Poulett Thomson, C.	1859	6 July	Milner Gibson, T.
1834	15 Dec.	Baring, A.	1866	6 July	Northcote, Sir S. H.
1835	18 April	Poulett Thomson, C.	1867	8 March	Richmond, Duke of
1839	29 Aug.	Labouchere, H.	1868	9 Dec.	Bright, J.

Vice President 1786–1868

This office was created in 1786. Appointments were made by the crown by order in council.[4] The Vice President was, as such, unpaid until 1817 when a salary of £2000

---

[1] PC 2/131 pp. 403–4.

[2] The salary was established by 7 Geo. IV, c 32 which superseded a temporary arrangement, made in 1825, whereby £2000 had been added to Huskisson's salary as Treasurer of the Navy in view of his additional responsibilities as President (T 52/103 pp. 186–8, 421; BT 5/35 p. 77).

[3] The position of President was held concurrently with the offices of Chancellor of the Duchy of Lancaster 1786–1803, Joint Postmaster General 1804–6, 1814–16, Master of the Mint 1807–14, 1830–4, 1835, 1839–41, 1843–5 and Treasurer of the Navy 1818–30, 1834.

[4] PC 2/131 pp. 403–4.

was provided.[1] However, both before and after this date it was usual for him to hold concurrently some other office to which remuneration was attached.[2] Payment of the salary from the Board was suspended in these circumstances. The office was abolished in 1868.[3]

LIST OF APPOINTMENTS

1786	23 Aug.	Grenville, W. W.	1845	5 Feb.	Clerk, Sir G.
1789	8 Aug.	Graham, Marquess of	1846	8 July	Milner Gibson, T.
1790	20 Oct.	Ryder, Hon. D.	1848	8 May	Granville, Earl
1801	18 Nov.	Glenbervie, Lord	1852	11 Feb.	Stanley of Alderley, Lord
1804	8 Feb.	Bond, N.			
1804	6 June	Rose, G.	1852	27 Feb.	Colchester, Lord
1806	5 Feb.	Temple, Earl	1853	4 Jan.	Stanley of Alderley, Lord
1807	30 March	Rose, G.			
1812	29 Sept.	Robinson, Hon. F. J.	1855	31 March	Pleydell Bouverie, Hon. E.
1818	24 Jan.	Wallace, T.			
1823	3 April	Grant, C.	1855	13 Aug.	Lowe, R.
1828	5 Feb.	Lewis, T. F.	1858	6 April	Donoughmore, Earl of
1828	30 May	Courtenay, T. P.	1859	3 March	Lovaine, Lord
1830	22 Nov.	Poulett Thomson, C.	1859	18 June	Wilson, J.
1834	20 Dec.	Lowther, Viscount	1859	12 Aug.	Cowper, Hon. W. F.
1835	6 May	Labouchere, H.	1860	22 Feb.	Hutt, W.
1839	29 Aug.	Sheil, R. L.	1865	29 Nov.	Goschen, G. J.
1841	28 June	Maule, Hon. F.	1866	12 March	Monsell, W.
1841	3 Sept.	Gladstone, W. E.	1866	10 July	Cave, S.
1843	10 June	Dalhousie, Earl of			

Members 1786–1870

As constituted in 1786 the Board of Trade took the form of a Committee of the Privy Council composed partly of the holders of certain offices *ex officio* and partly of specifically nominated Members. The *ex officio* Members fell into three groups. The first consisted of the holders of the offices of Archbishop of Canterbury, First Lord of the Treasury, First Lord of the Admiralty, Secretary of State, Chancellor of the Exchequer and Speaker of the House of Commons. The second consisted of the holders of the offices of Chancellor of the Duchy of Lancaster, Paymaster General, Treasurer of the Navy and Master of the Mint, provided that they were members of the Privy Council. The third consisted of such members of the Privy Council of the United Kingdom as held offices in Ireland.[4] The nominated Members were headed

---

[1] 57 Geo. III, c 66; BT 5/26 p. 226.

[2] The position of Vice President was held concurrently with the offices of Joint Paymaster General 1786–1800, 1801–3, 1804–7, 1813–17, Treasurer of the Navy 1800–1, 1807–12, 1830–4, 1834–5, Surveyor of Woods 1803–4, Lord of the Treasury 1812–13, Master of the Mint 1835–9, 1841–3, 1845–6 and Paymaster General 1848–68.

[3] By 30 & 31 Vict., c 72 provision was made for the office of Vice President to be replaced by that of Parliamentary Secretary on the next vacancy. Accordingly the former office ceased to exist on the resignation of Cave in Dec. 1868.

[4] PC 2/131 pp. 403–4.

by the President and Vice President. The rest, who were appointed by the crown by successive orders in council, received no salary and varied in number. Appointments continued to be made with some degree of regularity until 1823 after which there were none until the years 1846–8 when three Members were appointed. Ryan, the last surviving nominated Member, died in 1875.

In the following list *ex officio* Members are omitted.

LIST OF APPOINTMENTS

1786	23 Aug.	Campbell, Lord F.	1802	17 Feb.	Long, C.
1786	23 Aug.	London, Bishop of	1802	3 March	Grant, Sir W.
1786	23 Aug.	Grantley, Lord	1803	22 June	Bragge, C.
1786	23 Aug.	Kenyon, Sir L.	1805	1 May	Thynne, Lord G.
1786	23 Aug.	Harley, Hon. T.	1805	1 May	Thynne, Lord J.
1786	23 Aug.	Yorke, Hon. Sir J.	1805	1 May	Smyth, J.
1786	23 Aug.	Goodricke, Sir J.	1805	1 May	Bond, N.
1786	23 Aug.	Eden, W.	1805	1 May	Pole Carew, R.
1786	23 Aug.	Grenville, J.	1805	1 May	Sullivan, J.
1786	23 Aug.	Orde, T.	1806	12 Feb.	Henley, Lord
1788	25 Jan.	London, Bishop of	1806	14 May	Donoughmore, Earl of
1789	8 Aug.	Sydney, Viscount	1806	18 June	Carysfort, Earl of
1790	24 Feb.	Villiers, Hon. J. C.	1807	28 Jan.	Corry, I.
1790	3 March	Arden, Sir R. P.	1807	15 April	Whitworth, Lord
1790	3 March	Ryder, Hon. D.	1807	13 May	Clancarty, Earl of
1790	3 March	Wynne, Sir W.	1808	30 March	Redesdale, Lord
1793	21 June	Bayham, Viscount	1809	6 Feb.	Nicholl, Sir J.
1796	17 March	Douglas, S.	1809	11 Oct.	London, Bishop of
1797	29 March	Banks, Sir J.	1809	20 Dec.	Sheffield, Lord
1798	31 Oct.	Scott, Sir W.	1812	13 Aug.	Robinson, Hon. F. J.
1799	13 March	Hawkesbury, Lord	1813	30 Nov.	London, Bishop of
1799	17 July	Scott, Sir J.	1814	16 Dec.	Huskisson, W.
1802	17 Feb.	Beresford, J.	1823	3 April	Arbuthnot, C.
1802	17 Feb.	Foster, J.	1846	21 Jan.	Nicholl, J.
1802	17 Feb.	Wickham, W.	1848	15 April	Ryan, Sir E.
1802	17 Feb.	Rose, G.	1848	15 April	Stephen, J.

Secretaries 1786–1867

In 1786 provision was made for the two active Clerks of the Privy Council, Cotterell and Fawkener, to serve as Secretaries to the Board for which they were accorded allowances of £500 each in addition to their other remuneration. At the same time Elliott, the former Solicitor and Clerk of Reports of the earlier Board, was appointed a Clerk of the Privy Council, with a salary of £500, for the particular purpose of acting as one of the Secretaries.[1] Elliott died in the following year and was not replaced. At the time of the reorganisation of the Privy Council Office in 1808 the

[1] BT 5/4 pp. 4, 11–14. The two other Clerks of the Privy Council at this date, Hon. Robert Walpole and Sir George Chetwynd, took no part in the business of the Board or Council.

separate allowances paid to Cotterell and Fawkener in respect of their work for the Board ceased.[1] Cotterell appears to have undertaken the bulk of the duties and after his resignation in 1810 the Clerks of the Privy Council took less and less part in the business of the Board and their position soon became purely nominal.[2] However, as late as 1830 the then Clerks were ordered to attend its service and their names and those of their successors continued to be included in lists of the establishment until 1845.[3] Apart from Cotterell and Fawkener they have not been included in these lists.

Immediately following Cotterell's resignation in 1810 an Assistant Secretary was appointed and it seems clear that, from this date, the holder of this office was effectively the senior permanent official of the Board. Thomas Lack, the first Assistant Secretary, was selected from amongst the Clerks on the establishment. Until 1822 he held concurrently the position and salary of a Clerk, receiving an additional £200 in view of his increased responsibility.[4] In the latter year the assistant secretaryship was made a distinct office with a salary of £1250.[5] In 1825 the salary was raised to £1500 which was, with one exception, the amount received by all subsequent holders of the office.[6] In 1829 a second office of Assistant Secretary was created and conferred upon Hume who had acted as part-time assistant to the Board for the previous four years.[7] From 1829 to 1867 it was the practice for the Board to have the services of two Joint Assistant Secretaries or, as they came increasingly to be called, Joint Secretaries.[8]

In 1836 provision was made for one of the joint secretaryships to be filled by a person with legal qualifications. This official, sometimes known as the Legal Secretary, assumed, in addition to the general responsibilities which he shared with his colleague, the functions of the Law Clerk whose office was abolished in that year.[9]

In 1853 it was recommended that the Joint Secretaries should be replaced by a single Chief Secretary when a vacancy occurred.[10] However, the implementation of this recommendation was delayed on account of the special position of Farrer. Although only an Assistant Secretary, he in fact carried the whole responsibility for the Marine Department. In recognition of this he was in 1863 given the special position of Marine Secretary with a salary of £1200 rising by annual increments of £100 to £1500 on the understanding that he would succeed to the office of Joint

---

[1] BT 5/18 p. 212.

[2] An examination of the out letters of the Board (BT 3) after 1810 indicates a rapid decline in the number of occasions on which Clerks of the Council signed letters on behalf of the Board.

[3] BT 5/39 pp. 339–41; *Royal Kal.* (1845), 162; ibid. (1846), 162. As late as 1848 Shaw Lefevre was still describing the office which he had held as that of 'Assistant Secretary' (HC 543, pt. i, p. 227 (1847–8) xviii, pt. i, 291).

[4] BT 5/20 pp. 95–6, 328. Lack's salary as a Clerk, which had been £450 in 1810, was raised to £700 in 1812 (BT 5/15 pp. 315–22; BT 5/21 pp. 349–51). He also received an allowance of £150 which had been granted in 1795 in consideration of his services to the President (BT 5/9 p. 416) and a further allowance of £200 from the Council Office, granted in 1808 (BT 5/18 pp. 244–6).

[5] BT 5/29 pp. 438–44; BT 5/30 pp. 182–4, 406.

[6] BT 5/34 pp. 67–70, 242. In 1851 Booth was granted an additional £500 a year in respect of his special responsibility for the Railway Department (BT 3/41 pp. 368–9).

[7] BT 5/38 pp. 260–2, 269. In 1827 Hume had been granted an allowance of £500 a year for his services to the Board (BT 5/36 pp. 229–31).

[8] In order to avoid confusion with the distinct grade of Assistant Secretary, introduced in 1853, the holders of these offices are described as 'Secretaries' throughout these lists.

[9] BT 5/43 pp. 248–9; BT 3/43 p. 259. The holders of this office were: Le Marchant 1836–41, Shaw Lefevre 1841–8, Le Marchant 1848–50, Booth 1850–65 and Farrer 1865–7.

[10] [Cd. 1713] pp. 132–3, 134–5 HC (1854) xxvii, 164–5, 166–7.

Secretary on the next vacancy.[1] The vacancy occurred in 1865 when Farrer was duly appointed.[2]

In 1867 one of the joint secretaryships was abolished and the occupant of the remaining office was thereafter known as the Permanent Secretary.[3]

LIST OF APPOINTMENTS

1786	25 Aug.	Cotterell, S.	1847	6 Aug.	Porter, G. R. (v. MacGregor)
1786	25 Aug.	Fawkener, W.			
1786	25 Aug.	Elliott, G.	1848	15 May	Le Marchant, Sir D. (v. Shaw Lefevre)
1810	25 Aug.	Lack, T.	1850	10 Oct.	Booth, J. (v. Le Marchant)
1829	17 July	Hume, J. D.			
1836	8 Feb.	Le Marchant, D. (v. Lack)	1852	6 Oct.	Emerson Tennent, Sir J. (v. Porter)
1840	24 Jan.	MacGregor, J. (v. Hume)	1865	30 Sept.	Farrer, T. H. (v. Booth)
1841	19 June	Shaw Lefevre, J. G. (v. Le Marchant)			

Permanent Secretary 1867–70

On the abolition of the second joint secretaryship in 1867 the title Permanent Secretary was given to the remaining Secretary. The salary attached to the office was £1500.[4]

APPOINTMENT

1867   2 Jan.   Farrer, T. H.

Parliamentary Secretary 1868–70

This office came into existence in 1868 on the resignation of the last Vice President of the Board in accordance with an act of the previous year. The salary attached to it was £1500.[5]

APPOINTMENT

1868   14 Dec.   Shaw Lefevre, G. J.

---

[1] T 1/6433B/13012; BT 3/64 no. 379.
[2] BT 5/73, 30 Sept. 1865.
[3] HC 47 pp. 8, 12, 16–17 (1867) xxxix, 220, 224, 228–9; BT 5/75, 2 Jan. 1867.
[4] HC 47 pp. 8, 12, 14, 16–17 (1867) xxxix, 220, 224, 226, 228–9; BT 5/75, 2 Jan. 1867.
[5] 30 & 31 Vict., c 72; BT 5/76, 14 Dec. 1868.

Assistant Secretaries 1853–70

The term Assistant Secretary was first introduced into the Board of Trade in 1810 to denote those officials who were, in the absence of the Clerks of the Privy Council, effectively the senior permanent officials of the department. In order to avoid confusion these officials have been described as 'Secretaries' throughout these lists.[1] In 1853 the term was again adopted to denote a distinct grade in the department. It was recommended in that year that each of the three divisions of the office should be placed in the immediate charge of an Assistant Secretary with a salary of £700 rising by annual increments of £50 to £1000.[2] In the event no Assistant Secretary was appointed for the General Department but the other two offices were filled by the former Secretaries of the distinct Railway and Marine Departments. The office of Assistant Secretary for the Railway Department was left vacant in 1860 and combined with that of Legal Assistant in 1865.[3] In 1863 Farrer, the Assistant Secretary for the Marine Department was given the special position of Marine Secretary.[4]

In 1867 provision was made for four Assistant Secretaries. Two of these were drawn from the office and placed in immediate charge of the Commercial and Marine Departments, the former being given a salary of £1000 with a personal allowance of £100 and the latter a salary of £800 rising by annual increments of £50 to £1000. The other two, who were given responsibility for the Harbour and Railway Departments, were required to have legal qualifications and were appointed from outside the office. Their salaries were fixed at £800 rising by annual increments of £50 to £1200.[5]

LIST OF APPOINTMENTS

1853	April	Simmons, J. L. A. (Railways)	1867	2 Jan.	Trevor, C. C. (Harbours)
1853	April	Farrer, T. H. (Marine)	1867	2 Jan.	Herbert, R. G. W. (Railways)
1854	29 June	Galton, D. (Railways)	1867	2 Jan.	Gray, T. (Marine)
1865	5 July	Fane, W. D. (Railways)	1870	1 Feb.	Malcolm, W. R. (Railways)
1867	2 Jan.	Mallet, L. (Commercial)			

Chief Clerk 1786–1825

This office was created in 1786 and abolished in 1825.[6] The salary attached to it was originally £500. An additional allowance of £200 from the contingent fund was made

[1] See p. 42 n. 8.
[2] [Cd. 1713] pp. 134–5, 143 HC (1854) xxvii, 166–7, 175.
[3] BT 3/57 no. 35; BT 5/73, 5 July 1865.
[4] See p. 42.
[5] HC 47 pp. 8–9, 17 (1867) xxxix, 220–1, 229; BT 5/75, 2 Jan. 1867.
[6] BT 5/4 pp. 11–15; BT 5/21 pp. 349–51; BT 5/34 pp. 67–70.

available in 1797. In 1805 the salary was raised to £800 thus making the total remuneration £1000.[1]

APPOINTMENT

1786 25 Aug. Chalmers, G.

Clerks 1786–1822

The establishment of 1786 made provision for six Clerks in addition to the Chief Clerk, one at £200, one at £150, one at £120 and three at £100.[2] In 1792 the salaries were altered so that one Clerk received £190, two £140 and three £100.[3] In 1797 additional allowances of £110, £110, £60 and £50 were made available from the contingent fund for the four most senior Clerks.[4] In 1805 the number of Clerks was increased to seven and a general salary increase took place. The progressive principle was introduced to provide maxima of £650, £450, £350, £275, £200, £150 and £120 after ten years' service.[5] In 1812 an eighth Clerk was appointed and the maxima of the salaries were fixed at £850, £700, £470, £375, £280, £210, £160 and £120.[6] In 1822 the Clerks were divided into the three grades of First Class, Second Class (or Senior) and Third Class (or Junior).[7]

LIST OF APPOINTMENTS

1786	25 Aug.	Chetwynd, Hon. R.	1798	4 Jan.	Dowley, G.
1786	25 Aug.	Porter, J.	1801	15 July	Penny, R.
1786	25 Aug.	Budge, W.	1805	16 Oct.	Sowerby, J.
1786	25 Aug.	Lack, T.	1806	23 Aug.	Eden, A.
1786	25 Aug.	Sowerby, J.	1806	24 Sept.	Suft, R. F.
1786	22 Sept.	Wood, G.	1811	24 Sept.	Noyes, C.
1792	24 Jan.	Barton, J.	1812	16 July	Webb, S.
1794	10 Dec.	Stacey, W.	1816	4 April	Lack, E. J.
1795	10 Oct.	Govett, C.			

Supernumerary Clerks 1786–1812; 1843–5

The clerical establishment of 1786 was from the first found to be inadequate with the result that Elliott, one of the Secretaries, brought Gordon into the office where he was employed as an Extra Clerk. Gordon continued in the service of the Board after Elliott's death in 1787 and in 1789 was given supernumerary status with a regular

[1] BT 5/4 pp. 11–15; BT 5/10 pp. 390–1; BT 5/15 pp. 315–22, 346.
[2] BT 5/4 pp. 11–15. [3] BT 5/7 p. 364.
[4] BT 5/10 pp. 390–1. [5] BT 5/15 pp. 315–22.
[6] BT 5/21 pp. 349–51. In 1808 two Clerks, Porter and T. Lack were appointed Under Clerks of the Privy Council with additional allowances of £300 (£200 in peace time) in order to facilitate the progress of business (BT 5/18 pp. 241–6, 251–2). In 1810 Lack was granted a further additional allowance of £200 as Assistant Secretary (BT 5/20 pp. 95–6, 328).
[7] BT 5/30 pp. 182–4, 406.

salary of £50 from the contingent account and the prospect of succeeding to a place on the establishment at the next vacancy.[1] From this time it was the practice for there to be one Supernumerary Clerk in the office who usually succeeded to a place on the establishment when a vacancy occurred.[2] In 1802 a second such Clerk was appointed.[3] In 1805 the number was reduced to one when one of the Supernumeraries was appointed to a clerkship on the enlarged establishment.[4] The other office was discontinued in 1812 when the remaining Clerk was appointed a Clerk on the establishment.[5] Until 1805 the usual salary was £50. In 1805 it was fixed at £100 rising after ten years by two increments of £5 to £110.[6] Apart from Granville (1843–5) no Supernumeraries were appointed after 1812.

LIST OF APPOINTMENTS

1786		Gordon, A.	1801	15 July	Sowerby, J.
1792	20 Feb.	Stacey, W.	1802	26 July	Milne, A.
1795	29 March	Govett, C.	1809	14 March	Noyes, C.
1795	10 Oct.	Dowley, G.	1811	24 Sept.	Webb, S.
1798	22 Feb.	Watts, H.			
1800	6 Aug.	Penny, R.	1843	27 April	Granville, A. A. B.

First Class Clerk 1822–9

On the revision of the clerical establishment in 1822 provision was made for one First Class Clerk with a salary of £700 rising by annual increments of £10 to £800.[7] The office was abolished in 1829.[8]

APPOINTMENT

1822   25 March   Porter, J.

Senior (Second Class) Clerks 1822–53

On the revision of the clerical establishment in 1822 provision was made for a grade of 'Second Class Clerks'. After the abolition of the first class clerkship in 1829 these Clerks were usually known as Senior Clerks and have been so described in these lists. The salary scale attached to the grade was £300 rising by annual increments of £10 to £500.[9] The number of Senior Clerks varied considerably. Beginning at three

[1] BT 5/5 p. 190.
[2] However, Milne was not appointed to either of the places which fell vacant during his period of office (1802–9).
[3] BT 5/13 pp. 146–7.   [4] BT 5/15 pp. 315–22.   [5] BT 5/21 pp. 349–51.
[6] BT 5/9 p. 90; BT 5/10 p. 115; BT 5/12 pp. 49, 320–1; BT 5/13 pp. 146–7; BT 5/15 pp. 315–22. Stacey was granted an additional allowance of £50 in 1793 (BT 5/9 p. 90).
[7] BT 5/29 pp. 438–44; BT 5/30 pp. 182–4, 406.
[8] BT 5/38 pp. 143–4, 260–2.
[9] BT 5/29 pp. 438–44; BT 5/30 pp. 182–4, 406.

in 1822 it was raised to four in 1823 and to five in 1834.[1] It was reduced to four in 1842 and to three in 1846, being raised again to four in 1849.[2] In 1851 three Clerks from the Statistical Department were incorporated in the grade bringing the total to seven.[3] In 1853 a new grade of Senior Clerk was created. The former Senior Clerks retained their offices and were generally known as Old Senior Clerks thereafter.[4]

LIST OF APPOINTMENTS

1822	25 March	Sowerby, J.	1842	5 Jan.	Lack, R. W.
1822	25 March	Penny, R.	1849	4 July	Nailer, R.
1822	25 March	Suft, R. F.	1849	4 July	Larkins, W. F.
1823	3 July	Noyes, C.	1851	Jan.	Irving, T.
1827	22 Nov.	Webb, S.	1851	Jan.	Sivrac, C. A. G.
1834	3 June	Lack, E. J.	1851	Jan.	Ward, T. P.
1842	5 Jan.	Lack, F.			

Junior (Third Class) Clerks 1822–57

On the revision of the clerical establishment in 1822 provision was made for a grade of 'Third Class Clerks'. After the abolition of the first class clerkship in 1829 these Clerks were usually known as Junior Clerks and have been so described in these lists. The salary scale attached to the grade was £100 rising, after three years, by annual increments of £10 to £300. In 1842 the starting level was fixed at £90.[5] The number of Junior Clerks varied considerably. Beginning at three in 1822 it was reduced to two in 1834, being raised to four in 1842, to five in 1847 and to six in 1848.[6] It was reduced to five in 1849 but raised again to six in 1850.[7]

At the reorganisation of 1853 the number of Junior Clerks was fixed in principle at eight.[8] In the event this objective proved impossible to achieve. The consolidation of the General, Railway, Corn and Marine Departments produced a total of eleven Junior Clerks. Pressure of business necessitated increases to twelve in 1854 and to thirteen in January 1855.[9] The number fell to twelve in November 1855 but was again increased to thirteen in 1856.[10] The salary scale attached to the grade in 1853 was £100 rising by annual increments of £15 to £300.[11] The grade was abolished in 1857.[12]

---

[1] BT 5/29 pp. 438–44; BT 5/30 pp. 182–4, 406; BT 5/31 pp. 337–8; BT 5/42 p. 108. Although the appointments of R. F. Suft (1822) and C. Noyes (1823) were described as supernumerary they resulted in permanent additions being made to the grade.

[2] BT 5/50, 5 Jan. 1842; BT 5/55, 29 Aug. 1846; BT 5/58, 4 July 1849.

[3] BT 3/41 pp. 89–93.

[4] [Cd. 1713] p. 142 (1854) xxvii, 174. Of the former Senior Clerks only Larkins was appointed to the new grade.

[5] BT 5/29 pp. 438–44; BT 5/30 pp. 182–4, 406; BT 5/50, 5 Jan. 1842.

[6] BT 5/29 pp. 438–44; BT 5/30 pp. 182–4, 406; BT 5/42 p. 108; BT 5/50, 5 Jan., 16 March and 13 July 1842; BT 5/56, 11 Jan. 1847; BT 5/57, 24 Feb. 1848.

[7] BT 5/58, 4 July 1849; HC 211 p. 12 (1851) xxxi, 326.

[8] [Cd. 1713] pp. 142–3 HC (1854) xxvii, 174–5.

[9] Royal Kal. (1854), 160; BT 3/47 pp. 144–7; BT 5/63, 29 Jan. 1855.

[10] BT 5/63, 10 Nov. 1855; BT 5/64, 30 July 1856.

[11] [Cd. 1713] pp. 142–3 HC (1854) xxvii, 174–5.   [12] BT 3/51 no. 19; BT 5/65, 30 April 1857.

LIST OF APPOINTMENTS

1822	25 March	Noyes, C.		1849	4 July	Pocklington, R.
1822	25 March	Webb, S.		1850		Blair, W. E.
1822	25 March	Lack, E. J.		1853	April	Joyce, G.
1823	3 July	Leeves, E.		1853	April	Suft, H. M.
1827	22 Nov.	Lack, R. W.		1853	April	Owen, H.
1830	13 Nov.	Nailer, R.		1853	April	Boys, W.
1842	5 Jan.	Larkins, W. F.		1853	April	Bucknall, W. M.
1842	5 Jan.	Adderley, G. A.		1853	April	Fanshawe, J. G.
1842	16 March	Hobart, V. H.		1853	April	Swanston, G. J.
1842	13 July	Hobart, F. J.		1853	April	Calcraft, H. G.
1845	1 Aug.	Courtenay, F. F.		1854	22 April	Mayo, J. J.
1845	11 Dec.	Granville, A. A. B.		1855	29 Jan.	Lack, H. R.
1847	11 Jan.	Hornby, P. H.		1856	30 July	Doyle, J. V. T.
1848	24 Feb.	Mallet, L.		1856	30 July	Gray, T.
1849	15 Jan.	Baring, H.				

Senior Clerks 1853–7

This grade was created in 1853. The number of Senior Clerks was then fixed at six.[1] It was increased to seven in 1856.[2] The salary scale was £300 rising by annual increments of £20 to £600.[3] The grade was abolished in 1857.[4]

LIST OF APPOINTMENTS

1853	April	Noyes, C.		1853	April	MacGregor, D.
1853	April	Larkins, W. F.		1853	April	Mallet, L.
1853	April	Valpy, R.		1856	30 July	Suft, H. M.
1853	April	Hobart, Lord				

Old Senior Clerks 1853–63

This grade was so described to distinguish it from the new class of Senior Clerks created in 1853. It was composed of six of the seven former Senior Clerks in the General Department and the two former Senior Clerks in the Railway Department and later included one of the former Assistants in the Statistical Department.[5] The

---

[1] [Cd. 1713] pp. 142, 143, 145–6, 157 HC (1854) xxvii, 174, 175, 177–8, 189. The grade was initially recruited from the holders of the following offices: Registrar (Noyes), Registrar in Railway Department (MacGregor), Senior Clerk (Larkins), Junior Clerk (Hobart and Mallet) and Assistant in Statistical Department (Valpy).

[2] BT 5/64, 30 July 1856.   [3] [Cd. 1713] p. 143 HC (1854) xxvii, 175.

[4] BT 3/51 no. 19; BT 5/65, 30 April 1857.

[5] [Cd. 1713] pp. 142, 157, 158 HC (1854) xxvii, 174, 189, 190; BT 5/65, 30 April 1857. The former Clerks in the Railway Department, McKenzie and Lambert, were appointed Second Class Clerks in 1857 but were allowed to retain the salaries of Old Senior Clerks.

salary scale attached to the grade in 1853 was £300 rising by annual increments of £15 to £500. The amount of the annual increments was raised to £20 in 1857.[1] The grade ceased to exist in 1863 when its remaining members were appointed to the new class of Senior Clerks.[2]

LIST OF APPOINTMENTS

1853	April	Lack, F.		1853	April	Ward, T. P.
1853	April	Lack, R. W.		1853	April	McKenzie, F.
1853	April	Nailer, R.		1853	April	Lambert, C.
1853	April	Irving, T.		1855		Oswald, W. D.
1853	April	Sivrac, C. A. G.				

Copyists 1853–4

In 1853 provision was made for the appointment of a class of Copyists, whose number was to depend upon the amount of work to be done in the department. The salary scale was fixed at £80 rising by annual increments of £5 to £180. In certain special cases Copyists were to be transferred to a higher grade with a salary scale beginning at the amount that they were receiving at the time of their promotion and rising by annual increments of £10 to £250.[3] During the course of 1853 eight Copyists were appointed and in the following year the class was divided into two grades designated Senior and Junior Supplementary Clerks.[4]

LIST OF APPOINTMENTS

1853	Baker, S.	1853	Doyle, J. V. T.
1853	Lack, H. R.	1853	Fonblanque, B. A.
1853	Parsley, J. W.	1853	Gray, T.
1853	Simkins, A. L.	1853	Pattrickson, W.

Senior Supplementary Clerks 1854–70

In 1854 the Copyists or Supplementary Clerks were divided into senior and junior grades.[5] The number of Senior Supplementary Clerks was at first fixed at four. It was increased to six in 1855, to twelve in 1857 and to thirteen in 1859, being reduced to nine in 1863.[6] After the abolition of the grade of Junior Supplementary Clerk in 1864 these Clerks were known simply as Supplementary Clerks.[7] The salary scale

---

[1] [Cd. 1713] p. 146 HC (1854) xxvii, 178; BT 5/65, 30 April 1857.

[2] *Royal Kal.* (1864), 164. The Clerks in question were R. W. Lack, Irving and Ward.

[3] [Cd. 1713] pp. 140, 143, 158–9 HC (1854) xxvii, 172, 175, 190–1.

[4] BT 3/43 pp. 210–12; BT 3/47 pp. 270–2; BT 5/63, 29 Jan. 1855; *Royal Kal.* (1854), 160; ibid. (1855), 159.

[5] BT 3/47 pp. 270–2; BT 5/63, 29 Jan. 1855; *Royal Kal.* (1854), 160; ibid. (1855), 159.

[6] BT 5/63, 29 Jan. 1855; BT 3/51 no. 19; BT 5/65, 30 April 1857; BT 5/67, 23 March 1859; *Royal Kal.* (1864), 164.

[7] BT 5/72, 27 Aug. 1864; *Royal Kal.* (1865), 164.

originally attached to the grade was £80 rising by annual increments of £10 to £250.[1] In 1857 it was increased to £100 rising by annual increments of £10 to £300.[2] In 1863 the starting level was raised to £150 and in 1865 a scale beginning at £180 and rising by annual increments of £10 to £280 was substituted.[3]

LIST OF APPOINTMENTS

1854		Baker, S.	1857	30 April	Lee, N.
1854		Lack, H. R.	1857	30 April	Leaker, W. W.
1854		Simkins, A. L.	1857	30 April	Walsh, J.
1854	June	Michelsen, E. H.	1857	30 April	Jones, D.
1855	29 Jan.	Parsley, J. W.	1859	23 March	Laws, R.
1855	29 Jan.	Gray, T.	1861	Jan.	Rowe, J. L.
1855	29 Jan.	Pattrickson, W.	1861	2 Dec.	Brooksby, C. W.
1856	30 July	Berry, T.	1864	27 Aug.	Scott, C.
1856	30 July	Stoneham, A.	1864	27 Aug.	Cart, R.
1857	30 April	Hillman, F. G.	1868		Cox, F. R.[4]
1857	30 April	Pettet, C.	1868		Simmonds, G. H.[5]

Junior Supplementary Clerks 1854–64

In 1854 the Copyists or Supplementary Clerks were divided into senior and junior grades.[6] The number of Junior Supplementary Clerks was at first fixed at ten. Successive increases brought it to twenty-one in 1857. In that year it was fixed in principle at twenty.[7] In 1863 when the number had fallen to sixteen provision was made for the grade to be abolished and its members appointed to junior clerkships or senior supplementary clerkships.[8] This process was brought to an end in the following year when the grade ceased to exist.[9] The salary scale attached to the grade was originally £80 rising by annual increments of £5 to £180. In 1857 a scale beginning at £100 and rising by annual increments of £5 to £150 was substituted.[10]

LIST OF APPOINTMENTS

1854	Parsley, J. W.	1854	Laws, R.
1854	Doyle, J. V. T.	1854	Hillman, F. G.
1854	Gray, T.	1854	Rowe, J. L.
1854	Pattrickson, W.	1854	Pettet, C.
1854	Berry, T.	1854	Brooksby, C. W.

[1] BT 5/63, 29 Jan. 1855.   [2] BT 5/65, 30 April 1857.
[3] BT 3/64 no. 379; BT 5/73, 26 May 1865.
[4] Transferred to Board from Ramsgate Harbour Commissioners as Extra Clerk 17 Feb. 1863 (BT 20/2 no. 750). Listed as Supplementary Clerk from 1868 (*Staff Lists*, 18; *Royal Kal.* (1869), 166).
[5] Appointed Extra Clerk in Meteorological Department 30 April 1864 (BT 5/72). Listed as Supplementary Clerk from 1868 (*Staff Lists*, 18; *Royal Kal.* (1869), 166).
[6] BT 3/47 pp. 270–2; BT 5/63, 29 Jan. 1855; *Royal Kal.* (1854), 160; ibid. (1855), 159.
[7] BT 3/51 no. 19.   [8] BT 3/64 no. 379.
[9] BT 5/72, 27 Aug. 1864.   [10] BT 5/63, 29 Jan. 1855; BT 5/65, 30 April 1857.

1855	29 Jan.	Lee, N.	1857	30 April	Jamieson, R.
1855	29 Jan.	Leaker, W. W.	1857	30 April	Scott, C.
1855	29 Jan.	Walsh, J.	1857	30 April	Bolton, T. R.
1855	29 Jan.	Babington, T. H.	1857	30 April	Gray, J.
1855	29 Jan.	Jones, D.	1857	30 April	Cart, R.
1855	29 Jan.	Townsend, R.	1857	May	Ough, G. N.
1855	29 Jan.	Bell, C. L.	1857	June	Moorhead, W. H.
1855	29 Jan.	Spence, H. D. M.	1857	July	Hare, T. J.
1855	29 Jan.	Stoneham, A.	1857	Oct.	Monkhouse, W. C.
1855	12 March	Emerson Tennent, W. W.	1857	Nov.	Browne, J.
			1858	Jan.	Gibson, G.
1855	Nov.	Jennings, F. T.	1859	Feb.	Fairfield, A. R.
1855	Nov.	Spence, L. M. D.	1859	April	Reed, J. M.
1855	Dec.	Bicknell, F.	1859	April	Roscoe, E.
1856		Paskin, C. S.	1860	Dec.	Bradstreet, W. C.
1856	Aug.	Jackson, R.	1861	Jan.	Lyons, W. D. W.
1856	Oct.	Dobson, H. A.	1861	Jan.	Bicknell, E. J.

First Class Clerks 1857–63

This grade was created in 1857. The number of First Class Clerks was then fixed at seven with one supernumerary.[1] It was reduced to five in 1859.[2] The grade was abolished in 1863.[3] The salary scale was £450 rising by annual increments of £25 to £600.[4]

LIST OF APPOINTMENTS

1857	30 April	Noyes, C.	1857	30 April	Mallet, L.
1857	30 April	Larkins, W. F.	1857	30 April	Mayo, J. J.
1857	30 April	Valpy, R.	1857	30 April	Suft, H. M.[5]
1857	30 April	Hobart, Lord	1862	14 Nov.	McKenzie, F.
1857	30 April	MacGregor, D.			

Second Class Clerks 1857–63

This grade was created in 1857. The number of Second Class Clerks was then fixed at seven.[6] It was increased to eight in 1860.[7] The grade was abolished in 1863.[8] The salary scale was £300 rising by annual increments of £20 to £450.[9]

[1] BT 5/65, 30 April 1857.
[2] BT 5/67, 10 Feb. and 23 March 1859.
[3] BT 3/64 no. 379.
[4] BT 5/65, 30 April 1857.
[5] Supernumerary.
[6] BT 5/65, 30 April 1857.
[7] BT 5/68, 29 Aug. 1860.
[8] BT 3/64 no. 379.
[9] BT 5/65, 30 April 1857.

LIST OF APPOINTMENTS

1857	30 April	McKenzie, F.		1857	30 April	Swanston, G. J.
1857	30 April	Lambert, C.		1857	30 April	Lack, H. R.
1857	30 April	Blair, W. E.		1860	29 Aug.	Gray, T.
1857	30 April	Owen, H.		1862	14 Nov.	Hornby, P. H.
1857	30 April	Bucknall, W. M.				

Third Class Clerks 1857–63

This grade was created in 1857 when the number of Third Class Clerks was fixed at thirteen.[1] It was increased to fourteen in 1862.[2] The grade was abolished in 1863.[3] The salary scale was £100 rising by annual increments of £15 to £300.[4]

LIST OF APPOINTMENTS

1857	30 April	Joyce, G.		1857	30 April	Spence, H. D. M.
1857	30 April	Hornby, P. H.		1857	30 April	Emerson Tennent,
1857	30 April	Boys, W.				W. W.
1857	30 April	Fanshawe, J. G.		1857	30 April	Jennings, F. T.
1857	30 April	Pocklington, R.		1857	30 April	Blackwood, II. S.
1857	30 April	Calcraft, H. G.		1860	28 Jan.	Spence, L. M. D.
1857	30 April	Doyle, J. V. T.		1860	29 Aug.	Bell, C. L.
1857	30 April	Gray, T.		1862	14 Nov.	Paskin, C. S.
1857	30 April	Babington, T. H.		1862	14 Nov.	Hare, T. J.

Assistants 1863–70

This grade was created in 1863 when the number of Assistants was fixed at four.[5] In 1866 it was provided that the grade should be abolished as vacancies occurred.[6] The number of Assistants fell to three in 1867 and to two in 1870.[7] The salary scale was £600 rising by annual increments of £25 to £800.[8]

LIST OF APPOINTMENTS

1863	July	Larkins, W. F.		1863	July	Valpy, R.
1863	July	MacGregor, D.		1863	July	Mallet, L.

[1] BT 5/65, 30 April 1857.　　[2] BT 5/70, 14 Nov. 1862.
[3] BT 3/64 no. 379.　　[4] BT 5/65, 30 April 1857.
[5] BT 3/64 no. 379.　　[6] HC 47 p. 8 (1867) xxxix, 220.
[7] BT 5/75, 2 Jan. 1867; BT 20/2 no. 750.　　[8] BT 3/64 no. 379.

Senior Clerks 1863–70

This grade was created in 1863. The number of Senior Clerks was then fixed at sixteen with a salary scale of £320 rising by annual increments of £20 to £500.[1] It was increased to seventeen in 1865 and reduced again to sixteen in 1866.[2] In 1867 the grade was given new responsibilities and the top of the salary scale was raised to £600. The number was then fixed at fifteen although two former Senior Clerks, Bunter and Hornby, were also allowed to remain on the establishment on the old salary scale.[3] In 1868 the appointment of four additional Senior Clerks was authorised thus bringing the total to twenty-one. At the same time it was provided that, when either of the Senior Clerks on the old scale vacated his office, the number should be reduced to twenty.[4]

LIST OF APPOINTMENTS

1863	July	Lack, R. W.	1865	20 May	Bunter, F.
1863	July	Irving, T.	1865	28 June	Emerson Tennent,
1863	July	Ward, T. P.			W. W.
1863	July	Blair, W. E.	1865	11 Oct.	Jennings, F. T.
1863	July	Swanston, G. J.	1867	2 Jan.	Stoneham, A.
1863	July	Lack, H. R.	1867	2 Jan.	Bell, C. L.
1863	July	Gray, T.	1867	2 Jan.	Pattrickson, W.
1863	July	Hornby, P. H.	1867	2 Jan.	Dobson, H. A.
1863	July	Eveniss, G. H.[5]	1867	2 Jan.	Bolton, T. R.
1863	July	Boys, W.	1868	7 May	Lee, N.
1863	July	Fanshawe, J. G.	1868	7 May	Gray, J.
1863	July	Pocklington, R.	1868	7 May	Monkhouse, W. C.
1863	July	Calcraft, H. G.	1868	7 May	Browne, J.
1863	July	Doyle, J. V. T.	1869	8 Dec.	Owen, H.
1863	July	Babington, T. H.	1870	9 Aug.	Fairfield, A. R.
1863	July	Lowrie, W.[5]			

Junior Clerks 1863–70

This grade was created in 1863. Twenty-four Junior Clerks were then appointed.[6] Provision was made for thirty-five such Clerks in 1867 but by 1870 the number had reached only thirty.[7] The salary scale was £100 rising by annual increments of £15 to £300.[8]

---

[1] BT 3/64 no. 379.

[2] BT 5/73, 20 May 1865 (Supernumerary appointment); Ind. 20470 no. 358; HC 47 p. 15 (1867) xxxix, 227.

[3] HC 47 p. 14 (1867) xxxix, 226; BT 5/75, 2 Jan. 1867.   [4] BT 5/76, 7 May 1868.

[5] Transferred from the Harbour Department of the Admiralty (BT 3/64 nos. 358, 379).

[6] BT 3/64 no. 379; *Royal Kal.* (1864), 164.

[7] HC 47 pp. 12, 14 (1867) xxxix, 224, 226; BT 5/75, 2 Jan. 1867; *Royal Kal.* (1870), 166.

[8] BT 3/64 no. 379; BT 5/75, 2 Jan. 1867.

LIST OF APPOINTMENTS

1863	July	Joyce, G.	1864	29 Feb.	Leaker, W. W.
1863	July	Emerson Tennent, W. W.	1865	Jan.	Pearson, E. J.
			1865	12 May	Pearson, A. E.
1863	July	Jennings, F. T.	1865	12 May	Bingham, R. P. P.
1863	July	Spence, L. M. D.	1865	27 June	Bateman, A. E.
1863	July	Bell, C. L.	1865	15 Nov.	Brophey, E.
1863	July	Paskin, C. S.	1867	6 Feb.	Walker, I. B.
1863	July	Hare, T. J.	1867	6 Feb.	Price, T. E.
1863	July	Drage, B. J.[1]	1867	6 Feb.	Martyn, J. W.
1863	July	Pattrickson, W.	1867	2 March	Fitzgerald, D.
1863	July	Lee, N.	1867	2 March	Bence Jones, H. R.
1863	July	Jones, D.	1867	2 March	Newport, H. R.
1863	July	Jackson, R.	1867	2 March	Emberson, A. H.
1863	Nov.	Dobson, H. A.	1867	2 March	Heron Maxwell, R. C.
1863	Nov.	Bolton, T. R.	1867	22 Aug.	Graves, H. C. P.
1863	Nov.	Gray, J.	1868	17 Feb.	Napier, W. E.
1863	Nov.	Ough, G. N.	1868	17 Feb.	Waddington, S.
1863	Nov.	Moorhead, W. H.	1868	17 Feb.	Clark, J. H.
1863	Nov.	Moorhouse, W. C.	1868	Feb.	Seton, B. W.
1863	Nov.	Browne, J.	1868	March	Taylor, J.
1863	Nov.	Fairfield, A. R.	1868	11 May	Blomefield, T. W. P.
1863	Nov.	Roscoe, E.	1868	2 Sept.	Maude, A. H.
1863	Nov.	Bradstreet, W. C.	1868	25 Nov.	Malan, H. N. de M.
1863	Nov.	Lyons, W. D. W.	1869	12 Jan.	Clarke Travers, B. L. T.
1863	Nov.	Bicknell, E. J.			
1864	29 Feb.	Reed, J. M.	1870	9 Aug.	Acton, E. A. R.
1864	29 Feb.	Pettet, C.			

Corresponding Clerk (Railway Department) 1868–70

This office was created in 1868 with a salary of £400. Originally a temporary appointment, its continuation on a permanent basis was authorised in 1870.[2]

APPOINTMENT

1868   27 Nov.   Peel, C. L.

Law Clerk 1787–1823; 1825–36; 1867–70

This office was created in 1787.[3] The salary, originally £500, was raised to £800 in

---

[1] Transferred from the Harbour Department of the Admiralty (BT 3/64 nos. 358, 379).
[2] BT 5/76, 27 Nov. 1868; Ind. 20470 no. 1252; HC 122 p. 78 (1868–9) xlii, 90.
[3] BT 5/4 pp. 319, 331–2. For the duties of this office, see D. M. Young, *The Colonial Office in the Early 19th Century* (London 1961), 196–200.

1805.[1] The office was abolished in 1823.[2] It was revived in 1825 when provision was made for the Counsel to the Colonial Office to act as Law Clerk to the Board which was made responsible for paying £500 of his total salary of £1500.[3] In 1836 this arrangement was discontinued and provision was made for the duties formerly undertaken by the Law Clerk to be performed by one of the Joint Secretaries.[4] The office of Law Clerk was once again revived in 1867 with a salary beginning at £350 and rising by annual increments of £15 to £500.[5]

LIST OF APPOINTMENTS

1787	10 Aug.	Reeves, J.
1825	30 July	Stephen, J.
1867	2 Jan.	de Hamel, F. H.

Legal Assistant 1845–50; 1853–67

This office was created in 1845 with a salary of £500.[6] It was abolished in 1850.[7] It was revived in 1853 when the former Legal Assistant to the Railway Department was appointed Legal Assistant to the Board generally. The salary scale was then fixed at £500 rising by annual increments of £25 to £700.[8] In 1857 it was increased to £600 rising by annual increments of £40 to £800 and in 1863 the Legal Assistant was granted an additional personal allowance of £200.[9] In 1865 he was also appointed Assistant Secretary for the Railway Department.[10] The office was abolished in 1867.[11]

LIST OF APPOINTMENTS

1845	22 March	Northcote, S. H.
1853	April	Barron, A.
1856	7 July	Fane, W. D.

Registrar 1842–63; 1867–70

The office of Registrar and Keeper of Official Papers was created in 1842 with a salary of £500 rising by annual increments of £10 to £550.[12] In 1853 it was united with that of Librarian and accorded a salary of £600 rising by annual increments of

---

[1] BT 5/4 pp. 319, 331–2; BT 5/15 pp. 315–22.
[2] BT 5/31 pp. 227–9.
[3] BT 5/34 pp. 67–70. For the office of Counsel to the Colonial Office, see p. 36 n. 8.
[4] BT 5/42 pp. 248–9.
[5] HC 47 pp. 18–19 (1867) xxxix, 230–1; BT 5/75, 2 Jan. 1867.
[6] BT 5/53, 22 March 1845   [7] BT 3/41 pp. 89–93; BT 3/43 p. 258.
[8] [Cd. 1713] pp. 136–7, 143, 157 HC (1854) xxvii, 168–9, 175, 189.
[9] BT 3/51 no. 19; BT 3/64 no. 369.   [10] BT 5/73, 5 July 1865.
[11] HC 47 pp. 8–9 (1867) xxxix, 220–1; BT 5/75, 2 Jan. 1867; BT 20/1 no. 525.
[12] BT 5/50, 5 Jan. 1842.

£25 to £800.[1] In 1857 the salary was fixed at £800.[2] The office was abolished in 1863.[3] It was revived in 1867 with a salary of £300 rising by annual increments of £10 to £400.[4]

LIST OF APPOINTMENTS

1842	5 Jan.	Noyes, C.
1853	April	Bowring, E. A.
1867	2 Jan.	Parsley, J. W.

Librarian 1842–70

The office of Librarian, known until 1845 as that of Assistant Registrar and Librarian, was created in 1842 with a salary of £300.[5] In 1849 it was combined with the post of Précis Writer.[6] In 1853 the offices of Librarian and Registrar were united and accorded a salary of £600 rising by annual increments of £25 to £800.[7] In 1857 the salary was fixed at £800.[8] On the abolition of the office of Registrar in 1863 that of Librarian was continued as a distinct post with a salary of £450 rising by annual increments of £25 to £600.[9]

LIST OF APPOINTMENTS

1842	5 Jan.	Adderley, E. H.	1847	8 Nov.	Bowring, E. A.
1845	17 June	Campbell, P. L.	1863	Dec.	Bucknall, W. M.
1845	11 Dec.	Courtenay, F. F.			

Précis Writer 1846–9

This office was created in 1846 with a salary of £300.[10] In 1849 it was combined with that of Librarian with which it remained united thereafter.[11]

APPOINTMENT

1846   29 Aug.   de Lousada, F.

---

[1] [Cd. 1713] pp. 138–40, 143, 145, 157 (1854) xxvii, 170–2, 175, 177, 189.
[2] BT 3/51 no. 19.   [3] BT 3/64 nos. 379, 652.   [4] BT 5/75, 2 Jan. 1867.
[5] BT 5/50, 5 Jan. 1842.   [6] BT 3/38 pp. 155–6.
[7] [Cd. 1713] pp. 143, 145, 157 HC (1854) xxvii, 175, 177, 189.
[8] BT 3/51 no. 19.
[9] BT 3/64 no. 3. In 1866 it was recommended that, when a suitable opportunity occurred, the salary should be reduced to £300 rising by annual increments of £15 to £500 (HC 47 pp. 9, 14 (1867) xxxix, 221, 226).
[10] BT 5/55, 29 Aug. 1846; HC 543 pt. i, pp. 228–9 (1847–8) xviii, pt. i, 292–3.
[11] BT 3/38 pp. 155–6; BT 3/64 no. 379.

Accountant 1851–70

This office was created in 1851. Originally it was attached exclusively to the Marine Department but in 1853 it was transferred to the Board generally.[1] The salary was originally £800. In 1853 provision was made for it to rise by annual increments of £25 to £1000. In 1857 a scale beginning at £700 and rising by annual increments of £50 to £1000 was established.[2] In 1867 a new scale was introduced beginning at £800 and rising by annual increments of £50 to £1000.[3]

LIST OF APPOINTMENTS

| 1851 | 8 Aug. | Williams, H. R. |
| 1869 | 19 June | Hamilton, R. G. C. |

Deputy Accountant 1855–7; 1863–70

The office of Deputy or Assistant Accountant was created in 1855 with a salary of £300 rising by annual increments of £20 to £500.[4] It was discontinued in 1857 when provision was made for its functions to be undertaken by one of the First Class Clerks.[5] It was revived as a separate office in 1863 with a salary of £500 rising by annual increments of £20 to £600.[6]

LIST OF APPOINTMENTS

1855	10 Nov.	Mayo, J. J.
1863	July	Owen, H.
1869	12 Oct.	Stoneham, A.

Bookkeeper 1863–70

This office was created in 1863 with a salary of £300 rising by annual increments of £15 to £450.[7]

LIST OF APPOINTMENTS

| 1863 | July | Stoneham, A. |
| 1867 | 2 Jan. | Jackson, R. |

[1] BT 13/4 pt. i, 19 April 1869; [Cd. 1713] pp. 137, 149–54, 157 HC (1854) xxvii, 169, 181–6, 189.
[2] BT 3/44 pp. 313–15; BT 3/51 no. 19.
[3] HC 47 p. 14 (1867) xxxix, 226; BT 5/77, 19 June 1869.
[4] BT 5/63, 10 Nov. 1855. Oswald was described as 'Assistant Accountant' in 1855 (*Royal Kal.* (1855), 159); his tenure of the office cannot be verified from the records of the Board.
[5] BT 3/51 no. 19; BT 5/65, 30 April 1857; BT 5/70, 14 Nov. 1862.
[6] BT 3/64 no. 379.
[7] BT 3/64 no. 379.

Chief of Meteorological Department 1854–65

This office was created in 1854.[1] It was not filled after the death of its holder in 1865, the duties being transferred to the Royal Society in the following year.[2] Originally the total remuneration was £600 which was made up of two salaries of £300, one paid by the Board and the other by the Admiralty. In 1863 a single salary of £800, paid by the Board, was substituted.[3]

APPOINTMENT

1854 29 July   Fitzroy, R.

Surveyor General of Steam Ships 1854–70

This office was created in 1854.[4] The salary scale was originally £350 rising by annual increments of £25 to £500. In 1857 it was raised to £450 rising by annual increments of £25 to £600.[5]

APPOINTMENT

1854 17 Aug.   Robertson, R.

Nautical Assessors 1857–70

The employment of Nautical Assessors by the Board was authorised by the Merchant Shipping Act 1854.[6] One Nautical Assessor was appointed in 1857 and a second in 1862. The remuneration consisted of a salary of £200 and an allowance of £2 a day for the duration of each enquiry undertaken.[7]

LIST OF APPOINTMENTS

1857 28 July   Harris, H.
1862 30 Oct.   Baker, R. B.

[1] BT 3/50 no. 778. For the organisation of the duties of the department, see BT 3/47 pp. 474–87; BT 5/67, 14 Jan. and 10 Feb. 1859. In 1864 G. H. Simmonds was attached to the department as an Extra Clerk (BT 5/72, 30 April 1864).
[2] HC 47 pp. 7, 15 (1867) xxxix, 219, 227. In June 1866 a former Senior Clerk, Babington, was appointed on a temporary basis to carry out the duties of the office. In December of the same year they were entrusted to the Extra Clerk, G. H. Simmonds (BT 5/74, 9 June and 7 Dec. 1866).
[3] BT 3/64 no. 379.
[4] 17 & 18 Vict., c 104, s 305; BT 5/63, 29 Jan. and 1 May 1855; BT 3/47 pp. 474–87.
[5] BT 3/47 pp. 474–87; BT 3/51 no. 19; HC 38 p. 11 (1857 (2)) xxvi, 345.
[6] 17 & 18 Vict., c 104, s 434.
[7] BT 5/65, 28 July 1857; BT 5/70, 30 Oct. 1862.

Draftsman 1863–70

The functions of Draftsman were undertaken by McKenzie who was originally appointed a Clerk in the Railway Department in 1842.[1] Until 1863 he was ranked in the ordinary clerical grades of the office. In 1859 he was, although only a Second Class Clerk, given the salary of a First Class Clerk in view of his special services.[2] In 1863 the position of Draftsman was made a distinct office with a salary of £450 rising by annual increments of £25 to £600.[3]

APPOINTMENT

1863   July   McKenzie, F.

Translator 1868–70

This office was created in 1868 with a salary of £300.[4]

APPOINTMENT

1868   9 Jan.   Schebenmeyer, C. F. A.

Private Secretary to President 1823–70

During Liverpool's period of office as President (1786–1804) the duties of Private Secretary appear to have been undertaken by T. Lack, one of the Clerks, who was granted an additional allowance of £150 a year in 1795 'for faithful services particularly in attendance on the President'.[5] It was not until 1823 that a distinct office of Private Secretary was created. A salary of £300 was provided at the same time.[6] Presidents usually appointed their Private Secretaries from outside the office. When Clerks on the establishment served in this capacity they received the salary of the Private Secretary in addition to their other remuneration.

LIST OF APPOINTMENTS

Huskisson	1823–7	1823	3 July	Leeves, E.
Grant	1827–8	1827	4 Sept.	Grant, W.
Vesey Fitzgerald	1828–30	1828	12 June	Fitzgerald, E. M.
Herries	1830	*No appointment traced*		
Auckland	1830–4	1830	Nov.	Lack, E. J.
Poulett Thomson	1834	*No appointment traced*		

[1] BT 5/50, 5 Jan. 1842.   [2] BT 3/55 no. 179.   [3] BT 3/64 no. 379.
[4] BT 20/1 no. 470; BT 5/76, 9 Jan. 1868.
[5] BT 5/9 p. 416. Lack had received payment of £100 in 1786 for similar services to Liverpool (then Jenkinson) in his capacity as a member of the Board of 1784–6 (PC 2/131 pp. 266–8).
[6] BT 5/31 pp. 337–8.

Baring	1834–5	1834 Dec.	Rawson, R. W.
Poulett Thomson	1835–9	1835 2 May	Symonds, A.
Labouchere	1839–41	1839 8 Oct.	Laing, S.
Ripon	1841–3	1841 4 Sept.	Gordon, A.
Gladstone	1843–5	1843 June	Northcote, S. H.
Dalhousie	1845–6	1845 Feb.	Courtenay, F. F.
Clarendon	1846–7	1846 July	Bowring, E. A.
Labouchere	1847–52	1847 6 Aug.	McCullagh, W. T.
		1848 20 March	Mallet, L.
		1848 10 May	Baring, T. G.
		1851	Mallet, L.
Henley	1852	1852 Feb.	Henley, J. J.
Cardwell	1852–5	1853 6 Jan.	Cardwell, C.
Stanley of Alderley	1855–8	1855 March	Mallet, L.
Henley	1858–9	1858 26 Feb.	Henley, J. J.
Donoughmore	1859	*No appointment traced*	
Milner Gibson	1859–66	1859 4 July	Calcraft, H. G.
Northcote	1866–7	1866 7 July	Herbert, Hon. A. E. W. M.
		1867 23 Jan.	Abbot, Hon. R. C. E.
Richmond	1867–8	1867 13 March	Peel, C. L.
Bright	1868	1868 10 Dec.	Calcraft, H. G.

Private Secretary to Vice President 1830–68

This office was apparently created in 1830 when an allowance was first made available for a Private Secretary to the Vice President. It was usually held by Clerks on the establishment. The allowance, which was originally £50, was increased to £100 in 1841 and to £150 in 1843.[1]

LIST OF APPOINTMENTS

Poulett Thomson	1830–4	1830 Nov.	Rawson, R. W.
Lowther	1834–5	*No appointment traced*	
Labouchere	1835–9	1835 6 May	Lack, E. J.
Sheil	1839–41	1839 Aug.	Lack, E. J.
Maule	1841	1841 June	Lack, E. J.
Gladstone	1841–3	1841 4 Sept.	Rawson, R. W.
		1842	Northcote, S. H.
Dalhousie	1843–5	1843 June	Courtenay, F. F.
Clerk	1845–6	1845 Feb.	Clerk, J.
Milner Gibson	1846–8	1846 Sept.	Ward, T. P.
Granville	1848–52	1848 June	Bowring, E. A.
Colchester	1852–3	1852 Feb.	Larkins, W. F.
Stanley of Alderley	1853–5	1853 Feb.	Bowring, E. A.
		1853 April	Hobart, Lord

[1] BT 5/40 pp. 131, 430; BT 3/32 pp. 35–6; BT 5/49, 4 Sept. 1841; BT 5/51, 24 June 1843.

Pleydell Bouverie	1855	*No appointment traced*		
Lowe	1855–8	1855	Aug.	Swanston, G. J.
		1857		Gray, T.
Donoughmore	1858–9	1858	April	Straton, J. W.
Lovaine	1859	1859	March	Emerson Tennent, W. W.
Wilson	1859	*No appointment traced*		
Cowper	1859–60	1859	Aug.	Kingscote, A.
Hutt	1860–5	1860	Feb.	Emerson Tennent, W. W.
Goschen	1865–6	1865	Nov.	Emerson Tennent, W. W.
Monsell	1866	1866	March	Emerson Tennent, W. W.
Cave	1866–8	1866	July	Emerson Tennent, W. W.

Private Secretaries to Secretaries 1842–70

Under an arrangement which originated in 1842 each of the two Joint Secretaries was accorded the services of a Clerk on the establishment who acted as his 'Assistant' or Private Secretary, in consideration of which the Clerks in question received additional allowances.[1] At first these allowances were fixed at £150 for one of the Clerks and £50 for the other. In 1863 the allowance of each was fixed at £100.[2]

Both the Permanent Secretary (1867) and the Parliamentary Secretary (1868) had the services of Clerks as Private Secretaries each of whom received additional allowances of £150.[3]

LISTS OF APPOINTMENTS

PRIVATE SECRETARIES TO JOINT SECRETARIES

MacGregor	1840–7	1842	16 March	Lack, F.
Shaw Lefevre	1841–8	1842	16 March	Hobart, V. H.
Porter	1847–52	1847	Aug.	Lack, F.
Le Marchant	1848–50	1848	May	Hobart, V. H.
Booth	1850–65	1850	Oct.	Hobart, Lord
		By 1859		Hornby, P. H.
		1863		Spence, L. M. D.
Emerson Tennent	1852–67	By 1859		Fanshawe, J. G.
Farrer	1865–7	1865	Sept.	Browne, J.

PRIVATE SECRETARY TO PERMANENT SECRETARY

Farrer	1867	1867	Jan.	Browne, J.

PRIVATE SECRETARY TO PARLIAMENTARY SECRETARY

Shaw Lefevre	1868	1868	Dec.	Pearson, A. E.

[1] BT 5/50, 16 March 1842.
[2] ibid.; BT 3/43 pp. 257–60; BT 3/64 no. 379.
[3] HC 47 pp. 12, 14 (1867) xxxix, 224, 226; BT 5/75, 2 Jan. 1867.

Office Keeper 1786–1870

Provision was made for an Office Keeper in the establishment of 1786. The salary was originally £50.[1] The Office Keeper was granted board wages of one shilling a day in 1789 and an additional annual allowance of £25 in 1798.[2] In 1805 the salary was fixed at £130. It was increased to £180 in 1843 and to £200 in 1844.[3] In 1863 an additional allowance of £50 was made available in consideration of the Office Keeper's wife undertaking the duties of Housekeeper.[4] In 1866 a scale of £200 rising by annual increments of £10 to £250 was provided.[5]

LIST OF APPOINTMENTS

1786	10 Nov.	Cooper, T.	1826	24 July	Howe, E.
1789	8 Oct.	Hyde, T.	1843	2 Aug.	Mitchell, G.
1795	3 Dec.	Stokes, J.	1858		Mallett, W.
1807	17 Oct.	Noyes, W.	1867	18 Feb.	Burgess, H. T.

Assistant Office Keeper 1843–70

In 1843 provision was made for one of the Messengers to act as Assistant Office Keeper with a salary of £110 rising after five years to £120.[6] In 1867 the salary was fixed at £150.[7]

LIST OF APPOINTMENTS

1843	2 Aug.	Joy, W.
1865		Burgess, H. T.
1867		Macdonald, K.

Housekeeper (Necessary Woman) 1786–1863

Provision was made for a Housekeeper or Necessary Woman in the establishment of 1786. The salary was originally £50.[8] It was increased to £90 in 1805 and to £100 in 1815. In 1849 it was reduced to £70.[9] In 1863 the office was abolished and its duties were transferred to the Office Keeper's wife.[10]

[1] BT 5/4 pp. 11–14.
[2] BT 5/5 p. 375; BT 5/11 p. 136.
[3] BT 5/15 pp. 315–22; BT 5/51, 2 Aug. 1843; BT 5/52, 14 June 1844.
[4] [Cd. 1713] p. 147 HC (1854) xxvii, 179; BT 3/64 no. 410.
[5] HC 47 pp. 12–14 (1867) xxxix, 224, 226.
[6] BT 5/51, 2 Aug. 1843.   [7] BT 20/1 no. 333.
[8] BT 5/4 pp. 11–14.
[9] BT 5/15 pp. 315–22; BT 5/24 p. 79; BT 3/35 pp. 645–6; BT 3/38 pp. 264–5; BT 3/63 no. 22.
[10] [Cd. 1713] p. 147 HC (1854) xxvii, 179; BT 3/63 nos. 22, 88; BT 3/64 no. 410.

LIST OF APPOINTMENTS

1786	25 Aug.	Stacey, E.
1838	5 Jan.	Vodoz, C.

Messengers and Extra Messengers 1786–1870

The establishment of 1786 provided for three Messengers with salaries of £50 each.[1] In 1787 board wages of one shilling a day were granted to them. In 1805 the salaries were fixed at £100 and in 1808 it was arranged that they should rise to £130 after ten years.[2] In 1840 a Junior Messenger was appointed who was to succeed to one of the ordinary posts when a vacancy occurred. The salary attached to this office was originally £75. It was increased to £95 in 1843 and in 1844 an arrangement was made whereby the Junior Messenger received £90 at first and, after three years of probation, was placed on a scale beginning at £100 and rising by annual increments of £5 to £120.[3] By 1852 the number of Messengers had reached five.[4] In the following year it was increased to ten when the Office Keeper, Porter and three Messengers of the former Railway Department were fully absorbed into the establishment of the Board. At the same time the Messengers were divided into three classes. Three were placed in the first class with salaries of £120 and attached to the President, the Vice President and the senior Joint Secretary, three were placed in the second class with salaries of £100 and four were placed in the third class with salaries of £85.[5] In 1864 the total number of Messengers was increased to eleven.[6]

From 1841 to 1843 a 'permanent supernumerary' or Extra Messenger was attached to the Board at £1 5s a week and from 1858 there were usually two or three Extra Messengers in its service at the same rate of pay.[7]

LISTS OF APPOINTMENTS

MESSENGERS

1786	25 Aug.	Mills, J.	1810	7 March	Cloud, C.
1786	25 Aug.	King, T.	1814	1 Dec.	Howe, E.
1786	5 Dec.	Hyde, T.	1816	5 Jan.	Hurt, J.
1789	8 Oct.	Fabbri, C.	1816	29 March	Underdown, J.
1792	29 Nov.	Pillett, E. J. B.	1816	9 Dec.	Mitchell, T.
1794	6 Jan.	Stokes, J.	1821	22 May	Grant, W.
1795	3 Dec.	Noyes, W.	1826	3 Oct.	Hill, J.
1803	15 June	Mackett, T.	1827	11 Jan.	Mitchell, G.
1807	17 Oct.	Shergold, J.	1831	2 Dec.	Bidgood, R.

[1] BT 5/4 pp. 11–14.
[2] ibid. pp. 320–1; BT 5/15 pp. 315–22; BT 5/18 pp. 301–2.
[3] BT 5/48, 14 July 1840; BT 5/51, 2 Aug. 1843; BT 5/52, 11 May 1844.
[4] *Royal Kal.* (1852), 160.
[5] [Cd. 1713] p. 147 HC (1854) xxvii, 179; *Royal Kal.* (1854), 160.
[6] *Royal Kal.* (1865), 164.
[7] BT 5/49, 23 Feb. 1841; BT 5/51, 2 Aug. 1843; *Royal Kal.* (1859), 165; ibid. (1870), 166; HC 90 p. 11 (1865) xxxvi, 283.

1838	4 Dec.	Maguire, J.	1854		Quelch, F.
1840	14 July	Joy, W.	1857		Barrow, C.
1843	2 Aug.	Manning, E.	1858		Scarrott, G.
1844	11 May	Barber, D.	1858	May	Macdonald, K.
1845	22 March	Scott, W.	1858		Dickinson, F.
1845	22 July	Westley, J.	1861	Jan.	Holiday, G. F.
1845	21 Nov.	Hardie, T.	1862	Oct.	Simmons, T.
1849		Ridler, T.	1864		Parsons, W. J.
1850	2 July	Mallett, W.	1865	May	Eltenton, G.
1851		Burgess, H. T.	1865	May	Turner, H.
1853	April	Hardie, T.	1865	May	Selby, W. C.
1853	April	Mitchell, T.	1865	July	Pace, S.
1853	April	Sanders, J.	1867		Pallett, G. W.
1853	April	Brown, B. T.	1869	May	Fish, R.
1853	April	Scoons, W. B.			

EXTRA MESSENGERS

1841	23 Feb.	Manning, E.	1865	May	Howells, J.
1858	July	Johnson, W.	1866	Jan.	Fish, R.
1858	22 Oct.	Holiday, G. F.	1866	April	Pallett, G. W.
1859		Simmons, T.	1866	June	Lloyd, F.
1861		Parsons, W. J.	1868	May	Watton, C.
1862	9 Dec.	Eltenton, G.	1869	Sept.	Rossiter, W. H.

Porter 1787–1870

The office of Porter or Doorkeeper was created in 1787. The remuneration was originally 15s a week.[1] In 1805 a salary of £75 was provided. This was raised to £100 in 1808 and to £120 in 1827.[2] In 1844 the Porter was appointed at £1 1s a week and in 1850 the salary was fixed at £90 a year.[3]

LIST OF APPOINTMENTS

1787	10 March	Adams, J.	1845		Bidgood, R.
1809	14 March	Cloud, C.	1850	22 June	Quelch, F.
1810	7 March	Hurt, J.	1854		Davison, W.
1816	5 Jan.	Scott, W.	1859	May	Johnson, W.
1844	11 June	Youde, T.	1865	April	Hill, F.

[1] BT 5/4 p. 211.
[2] BT 5/15 pp. 315–22; BT 5/18 p. 302; BT 5/36 p. 447.
[3] BT 5/52, 11 June 1844; BT 5/59, 22 June 1850.

Firelighter 1864–70

The office of Firelighter and Lamp Trimmer, which had previously been filled on a part-time basis, was given an established position in 1864.[1] The salary was £1 10s a week (£78 a year).[2]

APPOINTMENT

1864   Jan.   Burgess, W.

Corn Department

Receiver and Comptroller of Corn Returns 1821–65

In 1770 the Treasury was given statutory authority to appoint a Receiver of Corn Returns.[3] In 1821 the responsibility for these returns was transferred to the Board of Trade together with the right to appoint the Receiver.[4] In 1827 the title of the office was changed to Comptroller of Corn Returns and the right of appointment vested nominally in the crown.[5] In 1865 the Corn Department was abolished and the office of Comptroller combined with that of Superintendent of the Statistical Department.[6]

In 1821 Dowding, who had held office under the Treasury, was reappointed with a salary of £800.[7] In 1822 the salary scale was assimilated to that of a First Class Clerk in the General Department: £700 rising by annual increments of £10 to £800.[8] The salary was fixed at £600 in 1842 and reduced to £500 in 1851.[9]

LIST OF APPOINTMENTS

| 1821 | 24 July | Dowding, W. | 1842 | 5 Jan. | Joyce, G. |
| 1822 | 17 July | Jacob, W. | 1851 | | Jadis, H. F. |

Deputy Receiver and Comptroller of Corn Returns 1821–65

This office, originally known as that of Principal Clerk of Corn Returns, was created in 1821 with a salary of £300.[10] In 1822 the salary scale was assimilated to that of a Senior (Second Class) Clerk in the General Department: £300 rising by annual increments of £10 to £500.[11] It was fixed at £500 rising by annual increments of £10

---

[1] BT 12/1 no. 11.   [2] HC 90 p. 11 (1865) xxxvi, 283.

[3] 10 Geo. III, c 39, s 6. The earlier holders of the office were William Cooke 1770–8, John Barnes 1778–9, John James Catherwood 1779–1813 and William Dowding 1813–21. For the organisation of the office during this period, see TM 25 May 1813 (T 29/123 pp. 359–61).

[4] 1 & 2 Geo. IV, c 87, s 4; BT 5/29 pp. 381–4.   [5] 7 & 8 Geo. IV, c 58, s 3.

[6] 27 & 28 Vict., c 87; BT 13/1, Board of Trade to Treasury, 23 Nov. 1864; Ind. 20470 no. 4.

[7] BT 5/29 pp. 381–4.   [8] BT 5/30 pp. 325–6, 406.

[9] BT 5/50, 5 Jan. 1842; HC 238 p. 12 (1852) xxix, 326.

[10] BT 5/29 pp. 381–4.   [11] BT 5/30 pp. 325–6.

to £550 in 1842, at £450 rising by annual increments of £10 to £500 in 1843 and at £400 in 1851.[1] The office was abolished in 1865.[2]

LIST OF APPOINTMENTS

1821	24 July	Joyce, G.	1843	11 May	Jadis, H. F.
1842	5 Jan.	Lack, E. J.	1851		Bunter, F.

Clerks 1821–53

In 1821 provision was made for one Clerk in the Corn Department apart from the Deputy Receiver or Principal Clerk. The salary was then fixed at £90.[3] In the following year it was assimilated to that of a Junior (Third Class) Clerk in the General Department: £100 rising after three years by annual increments of £10 to £300.[4] About the same time a second Clerk was appointed.[5] The number was increased to three in 1842 but reduced to two in 1848 and to one in 1850.[6] In 1853 the remaining Clerk was incorporated into the ordinary establishment of the Board as a Junior Clerk.[7]

LIST OF APPOINTMENTS

1821	24 July	Jadis, H. F.	1834	31 Jan.	Joyce, G.
1822		Nedham, W. T.	1842	5 Jan.	Jadis, H. F.
1825	26 Jan.	Lack, F.	1842	13 July	Blair, W. E.
1827	12 July	Carey, J.	1843	10 Aug.	Lack, E. J.
1829	26 Jan.	Rawson, R. W.			

Statistical Department

Superintendent 1834–70

In April 1832 G. R. Porter was engaged by the Board on a temporary basis to arrange and make abstracts from parliamentary returns.[8] In 1834 he was given an established position as Superintendent of the Statistical Department with a salary of £525 rising by annual increments of £25 to £600.[9] In 1838 the salary was raised to £800.[10] In

[1] BT 5/50, 5 Jan. 1842; BT 5/51, 11 May 1843; HC 238 p. 12 (1852) xxix, 326.
[2] BT 13/1, Board of Trade to Treasury, 23 Nov. 1864; BT 5/73, 20 May 1865.
[3] BT 5/29 pp. 381–4.   [4] BT 5/30 pp. 182–4, 406.
[5] The appointment of a second Clerk was authorised in the establishment of 1822 (ibid.). The appointment was probably made in that year although it is not until 1824 that such a Clerk occurs in office (Royal Kal. (1824), 135).
[6] BT 5/50, 13 July 1842; BT 5/57, 24 Feb. 1848; HC 268 p. 13 (1849) xxxi, 327; HC 211 p. 12 (1851) xxxii, 326; BT 3/41 pp. 89–93.
[7] Royal Kal. (1854), 160.
[8] BT 5/40 pp. 506–7.
[9] BT 5/41 pp. 543–5. After 1844 the holder of this office was often described as 'Chief' of the Statistical Department (Royal Kal. (1844), 163; ibid. (1845), 162).
[10] BT 5/45 pp. 283–5, 412–13.

1840 Porter was appointed Superintendent of the Railway Department with an additional salary of £200 which he retained after his connection with that department ceased in 1845.[1] Fonblanque was appointed at £800 in 1847 but his salary was raised to £1000 in 1865 when the office of Superintendent was united with that of Comptroller of Corn Returns.[2]

LIST OF APPOINTMENTS

1834	31 Jan.	Porter, G. R.
1847	22 Oct.	Fonblanque, W. A.

Junior Clerks 1834–51

In 1834 the clerical establishment of the Statistical Department was fixed at three Junior Clerks.[3] A fourth such Clerk was appointed in 1838.[4] In 1842 the number was reduced to three.[5] In 1851 these were incorporated into the ordinary establishment of the Board.[6] The salary scale was £90 rising after three years by annual increments of £10 to £300.[7]

LIST OF APPOINTMENTS

1834	31 Jan.	Rawson, R. W.	1841	6 July	Ward, T. P.
1834	11 Nov.	Irving, T.	1841	14 Aug.	Bowring, E. A.
1834	11 Nov.	Oswald, W. D.	1847	8 Nov.	Mallet, L.
1838	3 July	Hankey, F.	1848	24 Feb.	Baring, H.
1838	4 Dec.	Sivrac, C. A. G.	1849	15 Jan.	Fanshawe, J. G.
1840		Deedes, H. C.			

Senior Clerk 1838–51

There was one Senior Clerk in the Statistical Department from 1838 until 1851 when the clerical staff of the department was absorbed into the ordinary establishment of the Board. The salary scale attached to the office was £300 rising by annual increments of £10 to £500.[8]

LIST OF APPOINTMENTS

1838	3 July	Rawson, R. W.
1842	5 Jan.	Irving, T.

[1] BT 3/29 pp. 535–8; BT 5/55, 19 Nov. 1846; HC 543, pt. i, p. 230 (1847–8) xviii, pt. i, 294.
[2] BT 12/1 no. 366; BT 13/1, Treasury to Board of Trade, 4 Jan. 1865.
[3] BT 5/41 pp. 543–5; BT 5/42 p. 267. Of the Clerks appointed in 1834 Irving and Oswald had already been temporarily engaged on statistical work for the Board for about two years; Rawson was transferred from the Corn Department.
[4] BT 5/45 pp. 283–5, 412–13.   [5] BT 5/50, 5 Jan. 1842.
[6] BT 3/41 pp. 89–93; *Royal Kal.* (1852), 160.   [7] BT 5/45 pp. 283–5, 412–13.
[8] BT 5/45 pp. 412–13; BT 3/41 pp. 89–93; *Royal Kal.* (1852), 160.

Assistants 1842–63

The designation Assistant was introduced into the Statistical Department in 1842. Two Assistants were then appointed. Rawson was given the function of assisting the Superintendent in the general business of the department while Valpy was placed in immediate charge of the new agricultural branch. Rawson was given a salary of £450 rising by annual increments of £10 to £550 while his successor, Oswald, received £350 rising by annual increments of £10 to £500. Valpy's salary was fixed at £250 rising by annual increments of £10 to £400.[1] Valpy was appointed a Senior Clerk on the ordinary establishment in 1853 and Oswald's office was discontinued in the following year.[2] However, Valpy was generally known as Assistant in the Statistical Department from 1856 and this title was officially restored to him in 1859.[3] In 1863 he was appointed to the newly created grade of Assistant.[4]

LIST OF APPOINTMENTS

1842	5 Jan.	Rawson, R. W.
1842	5 Jan.	Valpy, R.
1842	13 July	Oswald, W. D.

Railway Department

Members of the Railway Board 1844–5

In 1844 the functions of the Board of Trade in relation to railways were transferred to a distinct Board composed of the President or Vice President of the Board of Trade, the Inspector General or Assistant Inspector General of Railways, the Superintendent or Senior Member of the Board and the two Joint Secretaries of the department who all served *ex officio*.[5] The Board was abolished in 1845 when its functions were again undertaken by the Board of Trade itself.[6]

Commissioners of Railways 1846–51

In 1846 the powers formerly exercised by the Board of Trade in relation to railways were transferred to a statutory body known as the Commissioners of Railways. Provision was made for five such Commissioners of whom the President and two others were to receive salaries of £2000 and £1500 respectively while the other two offices were to be unpaid. The President and the two unpaid Commissioners were enabled to sit in the House of Commons.[7] In the event only one of the unpaid offices

---

[1] BT 5/50, 5 and 12 Jan. and 13 July 1842.
[2] [Cd. 1713] p. 157 HC (1854) xxvii, 189; HC 172 p. 12 (1854) xl, 364; HC 140 p. 11 (1854–5) xxxi, 417; *Royal Kal.* (1854), 160; ibid. (1855), 159.
[3] *Royal Kal.* (1856), 160; BT 5/67, 10 Feb. 1859.   [4] BT 3/64 no. 379.
[5] BT 5/52, 6 Aug. 1844.   [6] BT 5/54, 10 July 1845.
[7] 9 & 10 Vict., c 105; MT 13/7 pp. 561–3.

was ever filled and the second salaried commissionership was left vacant after the resignation of Alderson in 1848. Thereafter there were only three Commissioners, of whom the President and the unpaid Commissioner were President and Vice President of the Board of Trade respectively. The Commissioners of Railways were abolished in 1851.[1]

In the following list the names of salaried Commissioners are preceded by an asterisk.

LISTS OF APPOINTMENTS

PRESIDENT

| 1846 | 29 Aug. | *Strutt, E. |
| 1848 | 10 April | Labouchere, H. |

OTHER COMMISSIONERS

| 1846 | 4 Nov. | Granville, Earl | 1846 | 4 Nov. | *Brandreth, H. H. |
| 1846 | 4 Nov. | *Ryan, E. | 1848 | 11 March | *Alderson, R. C. |

Superintendent and Senior Member of the Railway Board 1840–5

This office was created in 1840 and conferred upon the Superintendent of the Statistical Department who was granted an additional salary of £200 in respect of his increased responsibility.[2] On the creation of the Railway Board in 1844 the Superintendent was made one of its members and his title was changed to Senior Member of the Board.[3] This office ceased to exist on the abolition of the Board in 1845.[4]

APPOINTMENT

1840   11 Aug.   Porter, G. R.

Law and Corresponding Clerk 1840–4

This office was created in 1840 with a salary of £500.[5] It ceased to exist in 1844 when its holder was appointed one of the Joint Secretaries to the Railway Department.[6]

APPOINTMENT

1840   11 Aug.   Laing, S.

[1] 14 & 15 Vict., c 64.
[2] BT 3/29 pp. 535–8; MT 13/1 pp. 1–2.   [3] BT 5/52, 6 and 13 Aug. 1844.
[4] BT 5/53, 10 July 1845. Porter retained his additional salary until his appointment as Joint Secretary in 1852 (BT 5/55, 19 Nov. 1846; HC 543, pt. i, p. 230 (1847–8) xviii, pt. i, 294).
[5] BT 3/29 pp. 535–8.   [6] BT 5/52, 6 Aug. 1844.

Registrar 1842–53

In 1842 the senior of the Clerks in the Railway Department was given an increased salary and his office was thereafter generally known as that of Registrar.[1] The office ceased to exist in 1853 when the duties of the Registrars of the General and Railway Departments were combined.[2] The salary attached to the office in January 1842 was £300 rising by annual increments of £10 to £500. In July of the same year the starting level was reduced to £250. In 1848 a scale beginning at £350 and rising by annual increments of £15 to £500 was substituted.[3]

LIST OF APPOINTMENTS

1842	5 Jan.	Oswald, W. D.
1842	13 July	MacGregor, D.

Secretaries 1844–53

In 1844 provision was made for two Secretaries to the Railway Board, one to be called the Law Secretary and the other the General Secretary, with salaries of £800 each.[4] Laing, the Law Secretary, resigned shortly after the abolition of the Board in 1845[5] and for the next year all railway business was undertaken by O'Brien, the remaining Secretary, acting alone.

In 1846 the Commissioners of Railways appointed Bruce their Secretary with a salary of £1000.[6] In January 1847 the duties of the office were divided, Bruce becoming Secretary for the General Department, a newly-appointed official, Harness, being made Secretary for the Engineering Department.[7] This arrangement was of short duration. On Bruce's resignation in May 1847, Harness was appointed to undertake all the secretarial functions and the Department was served by a single Secretary thereafter.[8] On the abolition of the Commissioners of Railways in 1851 the Secretary of the Railway Department was placed under the immediate authority of the Legal Joint Secretary of the Board of Trade.[9] The office ceased to exist in 1853 when the Secretary was appointed an Assistant Secretary to the Board.[10]

LIST OF APPOINTMENTS

1844	6 Aug.	Laing, S.	1847	22 Jan.	Harness, H. D.
1844	6 Aug.	O'Brien, D.	1850	3 April	Simmons, J. L. A.
1846	12 Nov.	Bruce, Hon. F. W. A.			

[1] BT 5/50, 5 Jan. and 13 July 1842; BT 5/51, 7 Jan. 1843; *Royal Kal.* (1844), 163.
[2] [Cd. 1713] pp. 138, 157 HC (1854) xxvii, 170, 189.
[3] BT 5/50, 5 Jan. and 13 July 1842; MT 11/12 p. 139.
[4] BT 5/52, 6 Aug. 1844.   [5] BT 5/54, 22 July 1845.
[6] MT 13/6 p. 5; MT 13/7 pp. 403–4, 561–3.
[7] MT 13/7 pp. 81–2.   [8] ibid. p. 267.   [9] BT 3/43 p. 259.
[10] [Cd. 1713] pp. 134–5 HC (1854) xxvii, 166–7.

Assistant Secretary and Assistant 1847–55

This office, originally known as that of Clerk of the Minutes and Correspondence, was created in 1847.[1] The salary, at first £300, was raised in 1848 to £350 rising by annual increments of £10 to £450.[2] In 1850 the office was merged with that of Statistical and Topographical Assistant.[3] In 1853 the Assistant Secretary was absorbed into the ordinary establishment of the Board of Trade and given the new title of Assistant in the Railway Department.[4] This office was abolished in 1855.[5]

LIST OF APPOINTMENTS

1847	9 July	Osborne, Hon. G. G.
1850	2 March	Galton, D.
1852	6 Nov.	Morland, H.

Statistical and Topographical Assistant 1847–50

This office was created in 1847 with a salary of £300.[6] In 1848 provision was made for the salary to rise by annual increments of £10 to £400.[7] In 1850 the office was merged with that of Assistant Secretary to the Railway Department.[8]

APPOINTMENT

1847	3 Feb.	Galton, D.

Clerks 1840–8

On the formation of the Railway Department in 1840 one established Clerk was appointed with a salary of £100 rising after three years by annual increments of £10 to £300.[9] In 1842 this Clerk was granted an increased salary and shortly afterwards acquired the title of Registrar. He was replaced by another Clerk at the original salary.[10] A second Clerk was appointed in 1844.[11] In 1846 both were transferred to the Commissioners of Railways who then appointed a third Clerk.[12] Until 1848 these Clerks were assisted by a number of temporary unestablished Clerks. In that year the clerical establishment was divided into Senior, Junior and Supernumerary grades.[1]

LIST OF APPOINTMENTS

1840	Aug.	Oswald, W. D.	1844	5 Oct.	Lambert, C.
1842	5 Jan.	McKenzie, F.	1846	8 Dec.	Suft, H. M.

[1] MT 13/7 p. 408; MT 13/8 pp. 237–8. [2] MT 11/12 p. 139.
[3] MT 13/12 p. 89. [4] *Royal Kal.* (1854), 160. [5] BT 3/49 no. 475.
[6] MT 13/7 pp. 56, 65–6, 561–3. [7] MT 11/12 p. 139. [8] MT 13/12 p. 89.
[9] BT 3/29 pp. 535–8. [10] BT 5/50, 5 Jan. 1842. [11] BT 5/52, 5 Oct. 1844.
[12] MT 13/6 p. 53. [13] MT 13/9 p. 191.

Senior Clerks 1848–53

On the revision of the clerical establishment of the Railway Department in 1848 provision was made for two Senior Clerks with salaries of £200 rising by annual increments of £10 to £400.[1] In 1851 the salaries were assimilated to those of Clerks of the corresponding rank in the Board of Trade: £300 rising by annual increments of £10 to £500.[2] In 1853 the Clerks were fully incorporated into the establishment of the Board.[3]

LIST OF APPOINTMENTS

1848	18 Feb.	McKenzie, F.
1848	18 Feb.	Lambert, C.

Junior Clerks 1848–53

On the revision of the clerical establishment of the Railway Department in 1848 provision was made for two Junior Clerks. The number was increased to six in 1851 when the grade of Supernumerary Clerk was abolished.[4] The salary scale was originally £100 rising by annual increments of £10 to £200.[5] In 1851 it was assimilated to that of Clerks of the corresponding rank in the Board of Trade: £90 rising after three years by annual increments of £10 to £300.[6] At the time of the reorganisation of 1853 the Clerks were fully incorporated into the establishment of the Board.[7]

LIST OF APPOINTMENTS

1848	18 Feb.	Suft, H. M.	1851	6 Sept.	Bucknall, W. M.
1848	18 Feb.	Owen, H.	1851	6 Sept.	Swanston, G. J.
1851	6 Sept.	Boys, W.	1852	24 Feb.	Calcraft, H. G.
1851	6 Sept.	Vereker, Hon. H. P.			

Supernumerary Clerks 1848–51

On the revision of the clerical establishment of the Railway Department in 1848 provision was made for six Supernumerary Clerks at salaries of £90.[8] In the event only four were appointed.[9] In 1851 all the Supernumeraries were promoted to the rank of Juniors and the grade ceased to exist.[10]

[1] MT 11/12 p. 139; MT 13/9 p. 191.   [2] BT 3/41 pp. 513–18.
[3] [Cd. 1713] p. 157 HC (1854) xxvii, 189; *Royal Kal.* (1854), 160.
[4] MT 13/9 p. 191; MT 13/15 pp. 419–20, 490.
[5] MT 11/12 p. 139.   [6] BT 3/41 pp. 513–18.
[7] [Cd. 1713] p. 157 HC (1854) xxvii, 189; *Royal Kal.* (1854), 160.
[8] MT 11/12 p. 139.
[9] MT 13/9 p. 191; MT 13/10 pp. 304, 336.
[10] MT 13/15 pp. 419–20, 490.

LIST OF APPOINTMENTS

1848	18 Feb.	Boys, W.	1848	28 Sept.	Bucknall, W. M.
1848	18 Feb.	Gordon, H. C.	1849	26 July	Swanston, G. J.
1848	8 Sept.	Vereker, Hon. H. P.			

Private Secretary to President of Railway Commission 1847–8

The President of the Railway Commissioners was provided with the services of a Private Secretary with a salary of £150. Galton, the only holder of this post, received this in addition to his salary as Statistical and Topographical Assistant to the Commissioners.[1] The office was discontinued in 1848 when the presidencies of the Commission and of the Board of Trade were combined.

APPOINTMENT

Strutt	1846–8	1847 21 Feb.	Galton, D.

Legal Assistant 1847–53

This office was created in 1847.[2] The salary, originally £300, was increased in 1848 to £350 rising by annual increments of £15 to £500.[3] The office ceased to exist in 1853 when its holder was appointed Legal Assistant to the Board of Trade generally.[4]

APPOINTMENT

1847 30 Jan.   Barron, A.

Inspector General of Railways 1840–6

This office was created in 1840. Both its holders were officers of the Royal Engineers. The salary was at first fixed at £900 of which the charge to the Board of Trade was £570, the remainder being paid by the Ordnance.[5] On the formation of the Railway Board in 1844 the Inspector General became one of its members and his salary from the Board was raised to £800.[6] The office was discontinued on the appointment of the Commissioners of Railways in 1846.

LIST OF APPOINTMENTS

1840	2 Dec.	Smith, Sir J. M. F.
1842	5 Jan.	Pasley, C. W.

---

[1] MT 13/7 pp. 403–4, 561–3.   [2] MT 13/7 p. 49.   [3] ibid.; MT 11/12 p. 139.
[4] [Cd. 1713] pp. 136–7, 157 HC (1854) xxvii, 168–9, 189; Royal Kal. (1854), 160.
[5] BT 3/29 pp. 666–70; BT 5/48, 2 Dec. 1840.   [6] BT 5/52, 6 Aug. 1844.

Assistant Inspector General of Railways 1844–6

This office was created in 1844.[1] The salary, originally £400, was raised to £500 in 1846.[2] The office was discontinued in the same year when its holder was appointed an Inspector by the Commissioners of Railways.[3]

APPOINTMENT

1844   6 Aug.   Coddington, J.

Inspectors of Railways 1846–70

The Inspectors of Railways, who were selected from amongst officers of the Royal Engineers, came under the authority of the Commissioners of Railways from 1846 to 1851, formed part of the Railway Department of the Board of Trade until 1853 and were placed under the immediate authority of the Board in the latter year. At first the Commissioners were served by a single Inspector, who had previously held the office of Assistant Inspector General of Railways. In 1847 the number of Inspectors was fixed at three.[4] It fell to two in 1850 but was raised again to three in 1853 at which level it remained until 1867.[5] In 1847 the salary of the senior Inspector was fixed at £600 and those of the other two at £400.[6] In 1848 a scale was provided beginning at £600 and rising by annual increments of £50 to £1000.[7] In 1853 this was reduced, for future appointments, to £500 rising by annual increments of £50 to £800.[8] In 1863 it was increased again to £700 rising by annual increments of £50 to £1000.[9]

In 1867 it was provided that there should be four Inspectors, to be divided ultimately into two seniors at £800 rising by annual increments of £50 to £1000 and two juniors at £600 rising by annual increments of £25 to £800, who were to fill the higher posts as vacancies occurred.[10]

LIST OF APPOINTMENTS

1846	Nov.	Coddington, J.	1853	15 April	Tyler, H. W.
1847	28 Jan.	Simmons, J. L. A.	1854	19 July	Yolland, W.
1847	19 Aug.	Wynne, G.	1858	28 April	Ross, G.
1847	24 Aug.	Laffan, R. M.	1861	1 April	Rich, F. H.
1852	6 Nov.	Galton, D.	1867	28 Feb.	Hutchinson, C. S.[11]

---

[1] BT 5/52, 6 Aug. 1844.   [2] ibid.; BT 3/34 p. 182.   [3] MT 13/6 p. 44.
[4] MT 13/6 pp. 44, 76; MT 13/7 pp. 44, 368–9, 406.
[5] MT 13/12 p. 152; [Cd. 1713] p. 157 HC (1854) xxvii, 189.
[6] MT 13/7 pp. 368–9, 406, 561–3.   [7] MT 11/12 p. 139.
[8] [Cd. 1713] p. 155 HC (1854) xxvii, 187.   [9] BT 3/64 no. 379.
[10] HC 47 pp. 12, 14 (1867) xxxix, 222, 224; BT 5/75, 28 Feb. 1867.
[11] Junior Inspector.

Office Keeper 1846–53

This office was created in 1846.[1] The salary, originally £90, was increased in 1848 to £110 rising by annual increments of £5 to £130.[2] The office was abolished in 1853 when the duties were transferred to the Office Keeper of the Board of Trade.[3]

APPOINTMENT

1846   8 Dec.   Hardie, T.

Messengers 1846–53

In 1846 provision was made for three Messengers in the Railway Department.[4] The salaries, originally £70, were increased in 1848 to £80 rising after three years by annual increments of £10 to £100.[5] In 1853 the Messengers were incorporated into the establishment of the Board of Trade.[6]

LIST OF APPOINTMENTS

1846   23 Dec.   Sanders, J.
1846   23 Dec.   Brown, B.T.
1846   23 Dec.   Scoons, W. B.

Porter 1846–53

This office was created in 1846.[7] The salary, originally £70, was increased in 1848 to £80 rising after three years by annual increments of £10 to £100.[8] The office ceased to exist in 1853 when the Porter was appointed one of the Messengers to the Board of Trade.[9]

APPOINTMENT

1846   Mitchell, T.

[1] MT 13/6 pp. 53, 65.   [2] ibid.; MT 11/12 p. 139.
[3] [Cd. 1713] p. 147 HC (1854) xxvii, 179; *Royal Kal.* (1854), 160.
[4] MT 13/6 pp. 53, 65.   [5] ibid.; MT 11/12 p. 139.
[6] [Cd. 1713] p. 147 HC (1854) xxvii, 179; *Royal Kal.* (1854), 160.
[7] MT 13/6 pp. 53, 65.   [8] ibid.; MT 11/12 p. 139.
[9] [Cd. 1713] p. 147 HC (1854) xxvii, 179; *Royal Kal.* (1854), 160.

Marine Department

Secretary 1850–3

This office was created in 1850 with a salary of £800.[1] It ceased to exist in 1853 when the Secretary was appointed an Assistant Secretary to the Board.[2]

APPOINTMENT

1850   15 Aug.   Farrer, T. H.

Clerks 1851–3

Two Clerks were apparently assigned to the Marine Department in 1851, the number being reduced to one in the following year. The remaining Clerk was absorbed into the ordinary establishment of the Board in 1853.[3] No information about their salaries has survived.

LIST OF APPOINTMENTS

1851   Fanshawe, J. G.
1851   Beechey, F. S.

Professional Members 1850–70

Provision was made for two Professional Members, selected from amongst senior officers of the Royal Navy or Merchant Service, on the formation of the Marine Department in 1850. In 1853 they were placed under the immediate direction of the Board of Trade. Their salaries were originally £600.[4] In 1853 a scale was substituted beginning at £500 and rising by annual increments of £50 to £800.[5] In 1857 the starting level was raised to £600 and in 1863 fixed salaries of £800 were provided.[6]

LIST OF APPOINTMENTS

1850	15 Aug.	Beechey, F. W.	1857	26 March	Sulivan, B. J.
1850	15 Aug.	Walker, W. H.	1865	29 May	Bedford, G. A.

---

[1] BT 5/59, 23 Dec. 1850.
[2] [Cd. 1713] pp. 135, 146, 155, 157 HC (1854) xxvii, 167, 178, 187, 189.
[3] *Royal Kal.* (1852), 160; ibid. (1853), 160; ibid. (1854), 160.
[4] BT 5/59, 23 Dec. 1850; BT 3/50 no. 778; [Cd. 1713] pp. 133, 137–8, 156–7 HC (1854) xxvii, 165, 169–70, 188–9.
[5] [Cd. 1713] p. 143 HC (1854) xxvii, 175.   [6] BT 3/51 no. 19; BT 3/64 no. 379.

Accountant 1851–3

See p. 57

Standard Department

Warden of the Standards 1866–70

Following the Standard of Weights, Measures and Coinage Act 1866 the Chief Clerk in the office of the Comptroller of the Exchequer was transferred to the Board of Trade with the title of Warden of the Standards.[1] The salary attached to the office, originally £700, was raised to £900 in 1867.[2]

APPOINTMENT

1866   20 Aug.   Chisholm, H. W.

Clerk 1866–70

This official was transferred from the office of the Comptroller of the Exchequer in 1866 with a salary of £300.[3]

APPOINTMENT

1866   20 Aug.   Chaney, H. J.

Mechanic 1866–70

This official, who also acted as Messenger, was transferred to the Board from the office of the Comptroller of the Exchequer in 1866 with a salary of £85.[4] In 1867 the Mechanic was also appointed Office Keeper to the Standard Department and provision was made for his salary to rise by annual increments of £5 to £100.[5]

APPOINTMENT

1866   20 Aug.   Porter, D.

[1] 29 & 30 Vict., c 82, s 10; BT 5/74, 20 Aug. 1866.
[2] Ind. 20470 no. 664; BT 20/1 no. 435.
[3] BT 5/74, 20 Aug. 1866; HC 47 pp. 8, 13, 17 (1867) xxxix, 220, 225, 229; BT 20/1 nos. 275, 366.
[4] BT 5/74, 20 Aug. 1866; BT 20/1 no. 275; Ind. 20470 no. 554.
[5] BT 20/1 no. 353.

Periodic Lists of Officials

LIST OF OFFICIALS FOLLOWING APPOINTMENT
OF THE COUNCIL 1696

Commissioners
Bridgwater, Earl of
Tankerville, Earl of
Meadows, Sir P.
Blathwayt, W.
Pollexfen, J.
Locke, J.
Hill, A.
Methuen, P.

Secretary
Popple, W.
Deputy Secretary
Popple, W.
Clerks
Barker, W.
Skynner, C.
Whitworth, C.
(1 vacancy)

Office Keepers
Child, D.
Clarke, S.
Messengers
Gray, J.
How, R.
Necessary Woman
Wood, M.

LIST OF OFFICIALS AT ACCESSION OF ANNE
8 MARCH 1702

Commissioners
Stamford, Earl of
Lexington, Lord
Meadows, Sir P.
Blathwayt, W.
Pollexfen, J.
Stepney, G.
Prior, M.
Cecil, Hon. R.

Secretary
Popple, W.
Deputy Secretary
Popple, W.
Clerks
Barker, W.
Carroll, M.
Drift, A.
Wheelock, B.

Bruges, W.
Loggan, J.
Office Keepers
Child, D.
Clarke, S.
Messenger
Gray, J.
Necessary Woman
Wright, M.

LIST OF OFFICIALS AT ACCESSION OF GEORGE I
1 AUGUST 1714

Commissioners
Guilford, Lord
Meadows, Sir P.
Monckton, R.
Moore, A.
Cotton, Sir J. H.
Sharp, J.
Pytts, S.
Vernon, T.

Secretary
Popple, W.
Deputy Secretary
Drift, A.
Clerks
Carroll, M.
Loggan, J.
Gellibrand, S.
Hudson, I.
Sanderson, A.

Gray, W.
(1 vacancy)
Office Keepers
Child, D.
Clarke, S.
Messenger
Gray, J.
Necessary Woman
(?) Wright, M.

LIST OF OFFICIALS AT ACCESSION OF GEORGE II
11 JUNE 1727

Commissioners
Westmorland, Earl of
Chetwynd, J.
Docminique, P.
Pelham, T.
Bladen, M.
Ashe, E.
Plumer, R.
Hobart, Sir J.
Secretary
Popple, A.

Deputy Secretary
Wheelock, B.
Clerks
Gellibrand, S.
Hudson, I.
Sanderson, A.
Gedney, T.
Popple, H.
Lanham, R.
Rogers, R.

Office Keepers
Clarke, S.
Tregonning, R.
Messenger
Wilson, J.
Necessary Woman
Fry, M.
Porter
Griffin, G.
Counsel
Fane, F.

LIST OF OFFICIALS AT ACCESSION OF GEORGE III
25 OCTOBER 1760

Commissioners
Halifax, Earl of
Stone, A.
Pelham, T.
Jenyns, S.
Hamilton, W. G.
Sloper, W.
Eliot, E.
Bacon, E.
Secretary
Pownall, J.

Deputy Secretary
Rogers, R.
Solicitor and
Clerk of Reports
Sedgwick, E.
Clerks
Tutté, J.
Bradbury, S.
Cranwell, R.
Peacock, J.
Palmer, J. S.

Green, R.
Cuckow, D.
Office Keeper
Terrie, T.
Messenger
Serle, E.
Necessary Woman
(vacant)
Porter
Serle, E.
Counsel
Lamb, Sir M.

LIST OF OFFICIALS FOLLOWING APPOINTMENT
OF THE BOARD 1786

President
Hawkesbury, Lord
Vice President
Grenville, W. W.
Secretaries
Cotterell, S.
Fawkener, W.
Elliott, G.

Chief Clerk
Chalmers, G.
Clerks
Chetwynd, Hon. R.
Porter, J.
Budge, W.
Lack, T.
Sowerby, J.
Wood, G.

Office Keeper
(vacant)
Housekeeper
Stacey, E.
Messengers
Mills, J.
King, T.
Hyde, T.

LIST OF OFFICIALS FOLLOWING REORGANISATION
MARCH 1822

President
Robinson, Hon. F. J.
Vice President
Wallace, T.
Secretary
Lack, T.
Chief Clerk
Chalmers, G.
Law Clerk
Reeves, J.
First Class Clerk
Porter, J.
Senior (Second Class)
Clerks
Sowerby, J.
Penny, R.
Suft, R. F.

Junior (Third Class)
Clerks
Noyes, C.
Webb, S.
Lack, E. J.

CORN DEPARTMENT
Receiver of
Corn Returns
Dowding, W.
Deputy Receiver of
Corn Returns
Joyce, G.
Clerks
Jadis, H. F.
Nedham, W. T.

Office Keeper
Noyes, W.
Housekeeper
Stacey, E.
Messengers
Howe, E.
Mitchell, T.
Grant, W.
Porter
Scott, W.

LIST OF OFFICIALS FOLLOWING REORGANISATION
JANUARY 1842

President
Ripon, Earl of
Vice President
Gladstone, W. E.
Secretaries
MacGregor, J.
Shaw Lefevre, J. G.
Registrar
Noyes, C.
Librarian
Adderley, E. H.
Senior Clerks
Suft, R. F.
Webb, S.
Lack, F.
Lack, R. W.
Junior Clerks
Nailer, R.
Larkins, W. F.
Adderley, G. A.
Hobart, V. H.
Private Secretaries
To President
Gordon, A.

To Vice President
Northcote, S. H.
To Secretaries
Lack, F.
(to MacGregor)
Hobart, V. H.
(to Shaw Lefevre)

CORN DEPARTMENT
Comptroller of
Corn Returns
Joyce, G.
Deputy Comptroller of
Corn Returns
Lack, E. J.
Clerks
Jadis, H. F.
Joyce, G.

STATISTICAL DEPARTMENT
Superintendent
Porter, G. R.

Assistants
Rawson, R. W.
Valpy, R.
Senior Clerk
Irving, T.
Junior Clerks
Sivrac, C. A. G.
Ward, T. P.
Bowring, E. A.

RAILWAY DEPARTMENT
Superintendent
Porter, G. R.
Inspector General of
Railways
Pasley, C. W.
Law and
Corresponding Clerk
Laing, S.
Registrar
Oswald, W. D.
Clerk
McKenzie, F.

Office Keeper
Howe, E.
Housekeeper
Vodoz, C.

Messengers
Mitchell, G.
Bidgood, R.

Maguire, J.
Joy, W.
Porter
Scott, W.

LIST OF OFFICIALS FOLLOWING REORGANISATION
APRIL 1853

President
Cardwell, E.
Vice President
Stanley of Alderley,
Lord
Secretaries
Booth, J.
Emerson Tennent,
Sir J.
Assistant Secretaries
Simmons, J. L. A.
(*Railways*)
Farrer, T. H.
(*Marine*)
Registrar and Librarian
Bowring, E. A.
Senior Clerks
Noyes, C.
Larkins, W. F.
Valpy, R.
Hobart, Lord
MacGregor, D.
Mallet, L.
Old Senior Clerks
Lack, F.
Lack, R. W.
Nailer, R.
Irving, T.
Sivrac, C. A. G.
Ward, T. P.
McKenzie, F.
Lambert, C.
Junior Clerks
Joyce, G.
Blair, W. E.
Suft, H. M.

Hornby, P. H.
Owen, H.
Boys, W.
Bucknall, W. M.
Fanshawe, J. G.
Pocklington, R.
Swanston, J. G.
Calcraft, H. G.
Copyists
Baker, S.
Lack, H. R.
Parsley, J. W.
Simkins, A. L.
Doyle, J. V. T.
Fonblanque, B. A.
Gray, T.
Pattrickson, W.
Legal Assistant
Barron, A.
Accountant
Williams, H. R.
Professional Members
(*Marine Department*)
Beechey, F. W.
Walker, W. H.
Inspectors of Railways
Wynne, G.
Galton, D.
Tyler, H. W.
Superintendent of
Statistical Department
Fonblanque, W. A.
Assistant
(*Statistical Department*)
Oswald, W. D.

Assistant
(*Railway Department*)
Morland, H.
Comptroller of
Corn Returns
Jadis, H. F.
Deputy Comptroller o
Corn Returns
Bunter, F.
Private Secretaries
To President
Cardwell, C.
To Vice President
Hobart, Lord
To Secretaries
(Names unknown)
Office Keeper
Mitchell, G.
Assistant Office Keeper
Joy, W.
Housekeeper
Vodoz, C.
Messengers
Maguire, J.
Scott, W.
Hardie, T.
Ridler, T.
Mallett, W.
Mitchell, T.
Sanders, J.
Brown, B. T.
Scoons, W. B.
Burgess, H. T.
Porter
Quelch, F.

LIST OF OFFICIALS FOLLOWING REORGANISATION
APRIL 1857

President
Stanley of Alderley,
Lord
Vice President
Lowe, R.
Secretaries
Booth, J.
Emerson Tennent,
Sir J.
Assistant Secretaries
Farrer, T. H.
(*Marine*)
Galton, D.
(*Railways*)
Registrar and Librarian
Bowring, E. A.
First Class Clerks
Noyes, C.
Larkins, W. F.
Valpy, R.
Hobart, Lord
MacGregor, D.
Mallet, L.
Mayo, J. J.
Suft, H. M.
Old Senior Clerks
Lack, F.
Lack, R. W.
Irving, T.
Oswald, W. D.
Ward, T. P.
Second Class Clerks
McKenzie, F.
Lambert, C.
Blair, W. E.
Owen, H.
Bucknall, W. M.
Swanston, G. J.
Lack, H. R.
Third Class Clerks
Joyce, G.
Hornby, P. H.
Boys, W.
Fanshawe, J. G.
Pocklington, R.

Calcraft, H. G.
Doyle, J. V. T.
Gray, T.
Babington, T. H.
Spence, H. D. M.
Emerson Tennent,
W. W.
Jennings, F. T.
Blackwood, H. S.
*Senior Supplementary
Clerks*
Baker, S.
Michelsen, E. H.
Parsley, J. W.
Pattrickson, W.
Berry, T.
Stoneham, A.
Hillman, F. G.
Pettet, C.
Lee, N.
Leaker, W. W.
Walsh, J.
Jones, D.
*Junior Supplementary
Clerks*
Laws, R.
Rowe, J. L.
Brooksby, C. W.
Townsend, R.
Bell, C. L.
Spence, L. M. D.
Bicknell, F.
Paskin, C. S.
Jackson, R.
Dobson, H. A.
Jamieson, R.
Scott, C.
Bolton, T. R.
Gray, J.
Cart, R.
(5 vacancies)
Legal Assistant
Fane, W. D.
Accountant
Williams, H. R.

Professional Members
(*Marine Department*)
Walker, W. H.
Sulivan, B. J.
Inspectors of Railways
Wynne, G.
Tyler, H. W.
Yolland, W.
*Superintendent of
Statistical Department*
Fonblanque, A. W.
*Comptroller of
Corn Returns*
Jadis, H. F.
*Deputy Comptroller of
Corn Returns*
Bunter, F.
*Chief of Meteorological
Department*
Fitzroy, R.
*Surveyor General
of Steam Ships*
Robertson, R.
Nautical Assessor
Harris, H.
*Private Secretaries
To President*
Mallet, L.
To Vice President
Gray, T.
To Secretaries
(Names unknown)
Office Keeper
Mitchell, G.
Assistant Office Keeper
Joy, W.
Housekeeper
Vodoz, C.
Messengers
Scott, W.
Hardie, T.
Sanders, J.
Brown, B. T.
Scoons, W. B.
Quelch, F.

Mallett, W.
Burgess, H. T.

Mitchell, T.
Barrow, C.

Porter
Davison, W.

LIST OF OFFICIALS FOLLOWING REORGANISATION
JULY 1863

President
 Milner Gibson, T.
Vice President
 Hutt, W.
Secretaries
 Booth, J.
 Emerson Tennent,
  Sir J.
Marine Secretary
 Farrer, T. H.
Superintendent of
Statistical Department
 Fonblanque, A. W.
Legal Assistant
 Fane, W. D.
Assistants
 Larkins, W. F.
 MacGregor, D.
 Valpy, R.
 Mallet, L.
Senior Clerks
 Lack, R. W.
 Irving, T.
 Ward, T. P.
 Blair, W. E.
 Swanston, G. J.
 Lack, H. R.
 Gray, T.
 Hornby, P. H.
 Eveniss, G. H.
 Boys, W.
 Fanshawe, J. G.
 Pocklington, R.
 Calcraft, H. G.
 Doyle, J. V. T.
 Babington, T. H.
 Lowrie, W.
Junior Clerks
 Joyce, G.
 Emerson Tennent,
  W. W.

Jennings, F. T.
Spence, L. M. D.
Bell, C. L.
Paskin, C. S.
Hare, T. J.
Drage, B. J.
Pattrickson, W.
Lee, N.
Jones, D.
Jackson, R.
Dobson, H. A.
Bolton, T. R.
Gray, J.
Ough, G. N.
Moorhead, W. H.
Monkhouse, W. C.
Browne, J.
Fairfield, A. R.
Roscoe, E.
Bradstreet, W. C.
Lyons, W. D. W.
Bicknell, E. J.
Senior Supplementary
Clerks
 Michelsen, E. H.
 Parsley, J. W.
 Berry, T.
 Hillman, F. G.
 Pettet, C.
 Leaker, W. W.
 Laws, R.
 Rowe, J. L.
 Brooksby, C. W.
Junior Supplementary
Clerks
 Scott, C.
 Cart, R.
 Reed, J. M.

Comptroller of
Corn Returns
 Jadis, H. F.
Deputy Comptroller of
Corn Returns
 Bunter, F.
Professional Members
(Marine Department)
 Walker, W. H.
 Sulivan, B. J.
Surveyor General
of Steam Ships
 Robertson, R.
Nautical Assessors
 Harris, H.
 Baker, R. B.
Chief of Meteorological
Department
 Fitzroy, R.
Inspectors of Railways
 Tyler, H. W.
 Yolland, W.
 Rich, F. H.
Accountant
 Williams, H. R.
Deputy Accountant
 Owen, H.
Bookkeeper
 Stoneham, A.
Draftsman
 McKenzie, F.
Librarian
 Bucknall, W. H.
Private Secretaries
To President
 Calcraft, H. G.
To Vice President
 Emerson Tennent,
  W. W.

To Secretaries
 Spence, L. M. D.
  (to Booth)
 Fanshawe, J. G. (to
  Emerson Tennent)
Office Keeper
 Mallet, W.
Assistant Office Keeper
 Joy, W.

Messengers
 Scott, W.
 Hardie, T.
 Sanders, J.
 Mitchell, T.
 Burgess, H. T.
 Quelch, F.

 Scarrott, G.
 Macdonald, K.
 Holiday, G. F.
 Simmons, T.
Extra Messenger
 Parsons, W. J.
Porter
 Johnson, W.

LIST OF OFFICIALS FOLLOWING REORGANISATION
JANUARY 1867

President
 Richmond, Duke of
Vice President
 Cave, S.
Permanent Secretary
 Farrer, T. H.
Assistant Secretaries
 Mallet, L.
  (*Commercial*)
 Trevor, C. C.
  (*Harbour*)
 Herbert, R. G. W.
  (*Railway*)
 Gray, T. (*Marine*)
*Superintendent of
Statistical Department
and Comptroller of
Corn Returns*
 Fonblanque, A. W.
Accountant
 Williams, H. R.
Assistants
 Larkins, W. F.
 MacGregor, D.
 Valpy, R.
Senior Clerks
 Swanston, G. J.
 Lack, H. R.
 Hornby, P. H.
 Eveniss, G. H.
 Boys, W.
 Fanshawe, J. G.
 Pocklington, R.
 Calcraft, H. G.

 Doyle, J. V. T.
 Bunter, F.
 Emerson Tennent,
  W. W.
 Jennings, F. T.
 Stoneham, A.
 Bell, C. L.
 Pattrickson, W.
 Dobson, H. A.
 Bolton, T. R.
Junior Clerks
 Drage, B. J.
 Lee, N.
 Gray, J.
 Ough, G. N.
 Monkhouse, W. C.
 Browne, J.
 Fairfield, A. R.
 Roscoe, E.
 Bradstreet, W. C.
 Lyons, W. D. W.
 Reed, J. M.
 Pettet, C.
 Leaker, W. W.
 Pearson, E. J.
 Pearson, A. E.
 Bingham, R. P. P.
 Bateman, A. E.
 Walker, I. B.
 Price, T. E.
 Martyn, J. W.
 Fitzgerald, D.
 Bence Jones, H. R.

 Newport, H. R.
 Emberson, A. H.
 Heron Maxwell,
  R. C.
Supplementary Clerks
 Michelsen, E. H.
 Berry, T.
 Hillman, F. G.
 Laws, R.
 Rowe, J. L.
 Brooksby, C. W.
 Scott, C.
 Cart, R.
Professional Members
(Marine Department)
 Walker, W. H.
 Bedford, G. A.
*Surveyor General
of Steam Ships*
 Robertson, R.
Nautical Assessors
 Harris, H.
 Baker, R. B.
Inspectors of Railways
 Tyler, H. W.
 Yolland, W.
 Rich, F. H.
 (1 vacancy)
Draftsman
 McKenzie, F.
Librarian
 Bucknall, W. H.
Deputy Accountant
 Owen, H.

84

Bookkeeper
  Jackson, R.
Law Clerk
  de Hamel, F. H.
Registrar
  Parsley, J. W.
Private Secretaries
 To President
  Peel, C. L.
 To Vice President
  Emerson Tennent,
   W. W.
 To Permanent Secretary
  Browne, J.
Office Keeper
  Burgess, H. T.

Assistant Office Keeper
  Macdonald, K.
Messengers
  Mitchell, T.
  Quelch, F.
  Scarrott, G.
  Holiday, G. F.
  Simmons, T.
  Parsons, W. J.
  Eltenton, C.
  Turner, H.
  Selby, W. C.
  Pace, S.
  Pallett, G.

Extra Messengers
  Fish, R.
  Lloyd, F.
Porter
  Hill, F.
Firelighter
  Burgess, W.

STANDARD
DEPARTMENT
Warden of the Standards
  Chisholm, H. W.
Clerk
  Chaney, H. J.
Mechanic
  Porter, D.

Alphabetical List of Officials

Abbot, Hon. Reginald Charles Edward *Private Secretary to President* (Northcote) 23 Jan.–March 1867 (BT 5/75).

Abdy, Sir Robert, 1st Bart. *Commissioner* (*Trade*) 7 Nov. 1660.

Acton, Eugene A. Roger *Junior Clerk* 9 Aug. 1870 (BT 5/78).

Adams, James *Porter* 10 March 1787–c. 14 March 1809 (BT 5/4 p. 211). D. by 14 March 1809 (BT 5/18 p. 471).

Adderley, Edward Hale *Librarian* 5 Jan. 1842–21 Jan. 1845 (BT 5/50). Res. 21 Jan. 1845 (BT 5/53).

Adderley, George Augustus *Junior Clerk* 5 Jan. 1842–c. 1843 (BT 5/50). Last occ. 1843 (*Royal Kal.* (1843), 163).

Addison, Joseph *Commissioner* 5 Jan. 1716–13 July 1717.

Ailesbury, Robert (Bruce) 1st Earl of *Member* 13 Dec. 1678 (PC 2/64 p. 395), 23 Feb. 1681 (PC 2/69 p. 222).

Albemarle, Christopher (Monck) 2nd Duke of *Member* 22 April 1679 (PC 2/68 p. 6).

Albemarle, George (Monck) 1st Duke of *Commissioner* (*Trade*) 7 Nov. 1660, 20 Oct. 1668, 16 April 1669.

Albin, Benjamin *Commissioner* (*Trade*) 20 Oct. 1668, 16 April 1669.

Alderson, Ralph Carr *Commissioner of Railways* 11 March–29 Dec. 1848 (*London Gazette* no. 20836). Left office 29 Dec. 1848 on app. as Secretary, Chelsea Hospital (ibid. no. 20931).

Alington, William (Alington) 3rd Lord *Commissioner* (*Plantations*) 30 July 1670–27 Sept. 1672. *Commissioner* 27 Sept. 1672–21 Dec. 1674.

Allen, William *Commissioner* (*Trade*) 7 Nov. 1660.

Anglesey, Earl of *see* **Annesley,** Arthur

Annesley, Arthur (cr. Earl of **Anglesey** 20 April 1661) *Commissioner* (*Trade*) 7 Nov. 1660, 20 Oct. 1668, 16 April 1669.
 Commissioner (*Plantations*) 1 Dec. 1660.
 Member 12 March 1675 (PC 2/64 p. 395), 22 April 1679 (PC 2/68 p. 6).

Arbuthnot, Charles *Member* 3 April 1823 (PC 2/205 p. 43).

Arden, Sir Richard Pepper, kt. *Member* 3 March 1790 (PC 2/134 p. 534).

Arlington, Henry (Bennet) 1st Lord (cr. Earl of **Arlington** 22 April 1672) *Commissioner* (*Trade*) 20 Oct. 1668, 16 April 1669.
 Member 12 March 1675 (PC 2/64 p. 395), 22 April 1679 (PC 2/68 p. 6).

Armitage, George *Office Keeper* 8 July 1742–8 May 1745 (*JCTP 1742–9*, 27). Dis. 8 May 1745 (ibid. 164).

Ashe, Edward *Commissioner* 24 June 1720–20 Nov. 1746.

Ashe, Sir Joseph, kt. *Commissioner* (*Trade*) 7 Nov. 1660.

Ashley, Lord *see* **Cooper,** Sir Anthony Ashley

Astley, Sir Jacob, 1st Bart. *Commissioner* 13 Dec. 1714–13 July 1717.

Auckland, 1st Lord *see* **Eden,** William

Auckland, George (Eden) 2nd Lord *President* 22 Nov. 1830–5 June 1834 (PC 2/211A p. 413).

Aylesford, Heneage (Finch) 4th Earl of *Member* 5 March 1784 (PC 2/129 p. 56).

Babington, Thomas Henry *Junior Supplementary Clerk* 29 Jan. 1855–30 April 1857 (BT 5/63). *Third Class Clerk* 30 April 1857–July 1863 (BT 5/65). *Senior Clerk* July 1863–2 June 1866 (BT 3/64 no. 379; *Royal Kal.* (1864), 164). Res. 2 June 1866 (Ind. 20470 no. 358).

Bacon, Edward *Commissioner* 14 Jan. 1760–12 Aug. 1765.

Baillie, George *Commissioner* 12 May 1710–7 July 1712.

Baker, Robert Benjamin *Nautical Assessor* 30 Oct. 1862 (BT 5/70).

Baker, Samuel *Copyist* 1853–4 (BT 5/67, 10 Feb. 1859; *Royal Kal.* (1854), 160). *Senior Supplementary Clerk* 1854–12 Dec. 1860 (BT 3/47 pp. 270–2; *Royal Kal.* (1855), 159). Res. 12 Dec. 1860 (BT 3/58 no. 867).

Banks, Sir Joseph, 1st Bart. *Member* 29 March 1797 (PC 2/148 p. 117).

Barber, Dean *Messenger* 11 May 1844–c. 2 July 1850 (BT 5/52). D. by 2 July 1850 (BT 5/59).

Barber, Richard *Clerk (Plantations)* app. 6 March 1671 (Journal (Plantations) 1670–2, 41); no further occ.

Baring, Alexander *President* 15 Dec. 1834–18 April 1835 (PC 2/215 p. 884).

Baring, Henry *Junior Clerk (Statistical Department)* 24 Feb. 1848–15 Jan. 1849 (BT 5/57). *Junior Clerk* 15 Jan. 1849–8 March 1853 (BT 5/58). Res. 8 March 1853 (Ind. 20456 no. 500).

Baring, Thomas George *Private Secretary to President* (Labouchere) 10 May 1848–1851 (BT 5/57; *Royal Kal.* (1851), 160). Probably left office 1851 on app. as Private Secretary to Sir George Grey as Home Secretary (*Royal Kal.* (1852), 158).

Barker, William *Clerk* 1696–c. 1710 (CO 389/36 pp. 136–8). Last occ. 1710 (Chamberlayne, *Present State* (1710), 660). Probably d. by 26 Jan. 1712 (Prob 6/88).

Barron, Arthur *Legal Assistant (Railway Department)* 30 Jan. 1847–April 1853 (MT 13/7 p. 49). *Legal Assistant* April 1853–13 June 1856 (HC (1854), xxvii, 189; *Royal Kal.* (1854), 160). D. 13 June 1856 (*Gent. Mag.* (1856), cxxxix, 126).

Barrow, Charles *Messenger* probably app. 1857; occ. 1858 (*Royal Kal.* (1858), 161). No further occ.

Barton, John *Clerk* 24 Jan. 1792–4 April 1816 (BT 5/7 p. 364). Res. 4 April 1816 (BT 5/24 p. 428).

Bateman, Alfred Edmund *Junior Clerk* 27 June 1865 (BT 5/73).

Bath, John (Granville) 1st Earl of *Member* 16 Feb. 1689 (PC 2/73 p. 8).

Bathurst, Henry (Bathurst) 3rd Earl *President* 26 March 1807–29 Sept. 1812 (PC 2/172 p. 393).

Bayham, John Jeffreys (Pratt) *styled* Viscount *Member* 21 June 1793 (PC 2/138 p. 353).

Bedford, George Augustus *Professional Member (Marine Department)* 29 May 1865 (BT 5/73).

Beechey, Frederick Stapleton *Clerk (Marine Department)* probably app. 1851; occ. 1852 (*Royal Kal.* (1852), 160). No further occ.

Beechey, Frederick William *Professional Member (Marine Department)* 15 Aug. 1850–29 Nov. 1856 (BT 3/50 no. 778). D. 29 Nov. 1856 (*Gent. Mag.* (1857), cxl, 108).

Bell, Charles Loraine *Junior Supplementary Clerk* 29 Jan. 1855–29 Aug. 1860 (BT 5/63). *Third Class Clerk* 29 Aug. 1860–July 1863 (BT 5/68). *Junior Clerk* July 1863–2 Jan. 1867 (BT 3/64 no. 379; *Royal Kal.* (1864), 164). *Senior Clerk* 2 Jan. 1867 (BT 5/75).

Bence Jones, Henry Robert *Junior Clerk* 2 March 1867 (BT 5/75).

Beresford, John *Member* 17 Feb. 1802 (PC 2/160 p. 220).

Berkeley, George (Berkeley) 9th Lord (cr. Earl of **Berkeley** 11 Sept. 1679) *Commissioner* (*Trade*) 16 April 1669.
    Member 26 July 1678 (PC 2/66 pp. 371, 378), 30 Oct. 1685 (PC 2/71 p. 148).

Berkeley, Sir William, kt. *Commissioner* (*Plantations*) 1 Dec. 1660.

Berkeley, Wilson *Clerk* 14 March 1761–2 May 1782 (*JCTP 1759–63*, 180). Office abolished 2 May 1782 (*JCTP 1776–82*, 472; T 1/579 Schedule 3).

Berkeley of Stratton, John (Berkeley) 1st Lord *Commissioner* (*Trade*) 7 Nov. 1660, 20 Oct. 1668, 16 April 1669.
    Commissioner (*Plantations*) 1 Dec. 1660.
    Member 12 March 1675 (PC 2/64 p. 395).

Berkeley of Stratton, William (Berkeley) 4th Lord *First Lord* 13 Dec. 1714– 12 May 1715.

Berry, Thomas *Junior Supplementary Clerk* 1854–30 July 1856 (BT 5/67, 10 Feb. 1859). *Senior Supplementary Clerk* 30 July 1856–1 Dec. 1868 (BT 5/64). Ret. 1 Dec. 1868 (BT 20/1 no. 604).

Bertin, Matthew *Clerk* occ. from 22 Jan. 1708 to 1710 (*JCTP 1704–9*, 451; Chamberlayne, *Present State* (1710), 660).

Bicknell, Edward James *Junior Supplementary Clerk* Jan. 1861–Nov. 1863 (BT 3/59 no. 49). *Junior Clerk* Nov. 1863–5 Aug. 1865 (BT 3/64 no. 624). D. 5 Aug. 1865 (BT 20/1 no. 271).

Bicknell, Frank *Junior Supplementary Clerk* Dec. 1855–16 March 1859 (BT 3/49 no. 804; Ind. 20458 no. 2250). Res. 16 March 1859 (BT 3/55 no. 155).

Bidgood, Robert *Messenger* 2 Dec. 1831–1845 (BT 5/40 p. 361; *Royal Kal.* (1845), 162). *Porter* probably app. 1845; occ. from 1846 to 1850 (*Royal Kal.* (1846), 162; ibid. (1850), 161).

Bingham, Reginald Potenger Peregrine *Junior Clerk* 12 May 1865 (BT 5/73).

Birch, John *Commissioner* (*Trade*) 20 Oct. 1668, 16 April 1669.

Blackwood, Hans Stevenson *Third Class Clerk* 30 April 1857–1862 (BT 5/65). Res. 1862 (*Royal Kal.* (1862), 164; BT 20/1 no. 43).

Bladen, Martin *Commissioner* 13 July 1717–15 Feb. 1746. D. 15 Feb. 1746 (T 53/42 p. 383).

Blair, William Edward *Clerk* (*Corn Department*) 13 July 1842–1850 (BT 5/50; *Royal Kal.* (1851), 160). *Junior Clerk* 1850–30 April 1857 (HC 211 p. 12 (1851) xxxii, 326; BT 3/41 pp. 89–93; *Royal Kal.* (1852), 160). *Second Class Clerk* 30 April 1857–July 1863 (BT 5/65). *Senior Clerk* July 1863–2 Jan. 1867 (BT 3/64 no. 379; *Royal Kal.* (1864), 164). Ret. 2 Jan. 1867 (HC 47 p. 16 (1867) xxxix, 228; BT 5/75).

Blathwayt, William *Secretary* pd. as 'Assistant' (Secretary) from 29 Sept. 1675 to 24 June 1696 (BM Add. MS 9767 p. 16; ibid. 9768 p. 76). Remained in office until abolition of Committee.
    Commissioner 15 May 1696–25 April 1707.

Blomefield, Thomas Wilmot Peregrine *Junior Clerk* 11 May 1868 (BT 5/76).

Blount, Sir Henry, kt.   *Commissioner (Trade)* 20 Oct. 1668, 16 April 1669.

Blucke, Robert   *Clerk* 19 Jan. 1748–20 Sept. 1753 (*JCTP 1742–9*, 268–9). D. 20 Sept. 1753 (*Gent. Mag.* (1753), xxiii, 445).

Bolton, Thomas Richard   *Junior Supplementary Clerk* 30 April 1857–Nov. 1863 (BT 5/65). *Junior Clerk* Nov. 1863–2 Jan. 1867 (BT 3/64 no. 624). *Senior Clerk* 2 Jan. 1867–19 July 1870 (BT 5/75). D. 19 July 1870 (death certificate).

Bond, Nathaniel   *Vice President* 8 Feb.–6 June 1804 (PC 2/164 p. 496). *Member* 1 May 1805 (PC 2/167 p. 360).

Bonnick, William   *Office Keeper* 3 March 1767–2 May 1782 (*JCTP 1764–7*, 371). Office abolished 2 May 1782 (*JCTP 1776–82*, 472; T 1/579 Schedule 3).

Boone, Christopher   *Commissioner (Trade)* 7 Nov. 1660.

Booth, James   *Secretary* 10 Oct. 1850–30 Sept. 1865 (BT 5/59). Res. 30 Sept. 1865 (BT 5/73).

Bouverie *see* **Pleydell Bouverie**

Bowring, Edgar Alfred   *Junior Clerk (Statistical Department)* 14 Aug. 1841–8 Nov. 1847 (BT 5/49). *Librarian* 8 Nov. 1847 April 1853 (BT 5/56). *Registrar and Librarian* April 1853–31 Dec. 1863 ([Cd. 1713] p. 157 HC (1854) xxvii, 189). Ret. 31 Dec. 1863 (BT 3/64 no. 652).

    Private Secretary: to President (Clarendon) probably app. July 1846; occ. 1847 (*Royal Kal.* (1847), 162); *to Vice President* (Granville) June 1848–Feb. 1852 (*Gent. Mag.* (1848), cxxii, 654); (Stanley of Alderley) Feb.–April 1853 (ibid. (1853), cxxxii, 192). Probably left office April 1853 on app. as Registrar and Librarian.

Boys, William   *Supernumerary Clerk (Railway Department)* 18 Feb. 1848–6 Sept. 1851 (MT 13/9 p. 191). *Junior Clerk (Railway Department)* 6 Sept. 1851–April 1853 (MT 13/15 p. 490). *Junior Clerk* April 1853–30 April 1857 ([Cd. 1713] p. 157 HC (1854) xxvii, 189; *Royal Kal.* (1854), 160). *Third Class Clerk* 30 April 1857–July 1863 (BT 5/65). *Senior Clerk* July 1863 (BT 3/64 no. 379; *Royal Kal.* (1864), 164).

Bradbury, Silas   *Clerk* 27 June 1745–14 March 1761 (*JCTP 1742–9*, 170). Res. 14 March 1761 (*JCTP 1759–63*, 180). *Solicitor and Clerk of Reports* 28 Sept. 1763–4 July 1764 (ibid. 381). *Deputy Secretary* 4 July 1764–5 Oct. 1781 (*JCTP 1764–7*, 89, 93, 99). D. 5 Oct. 1781 (*Gent. Mag.* (1781), l, 491).

Bradley, George   *Clerk* 12 Aug. 1727–24 June 1741 (*JCTP 1723–8*, 346). Dis. 24 June 1741 (*JCTP 1735–41*, 390).

Bradstreet, William Carolus   *Junior Supplementary Clerk* Dec. 1860–Nov. 1863 (BT 3/58 no. 800; Ind. 20464 no. 1853). *Junior Clerk* Nov. 1863 (BT 3/64 no. 624).

Bragge, Charles   *Member* 22 June 1803 (PC 2/163 p. 204).

Brandreth, Henry Howland   *Commissioner of Railways* 4 Nov. 1846–20 Feb. 1848 (*London Gazette* no. 20657). D. 20 Feb. 1848 (*Gent. Mag.* (1848), cxxii, 672).

Bridgeman, Sir Orlando, 1st Bart.   *Commissioner (Trade)* 20 Oct. 1668, 16 April 1669.

Bridgeman, Sir Orlando, 2nd Bart.   *Commissioner* 8 Aug. 1727–27 June 1737.

Bridges *see* **Bruges**

Bridgwater, John (Egerton) 2nd Earl of   *Commissioner (Trade)* 20 Oct. 1668, 16 April 1669.

    Member 12 March 1675 (PC 2/64 p. 395), 22 April 1679 (PC 2/68 p. 6).

Bridgwater, John (Egerton) 3rd Earl of   *Member* 14 May 1691 (PC 2/74 p. 172). *First Lord* 15 May 1696–9 June 1699.

Bright, John   *President* 9 Dec. 1868 (PC 2/268 p. 407).

Brooke and Warwick, Earl *see* **Greville**, Lord

Brooksby, Charles W.   *Junior Supplementary Clerk* 1854–2 Dec. 1861 (BT 5/67, 10 Feb. 1859). *Senior Supplementary Clerk* 2 Dec. 1861 (BT 5/69).

Brophey, Edward   *Junior Clerk* 15 Nov. 1865 (BT 5/73). No further occ.

Brouncker, Hon. Henry   *Commissioner (Plantations)* 30 July 1670–27 Sept. 1672. *Commissioner* 27 Sept. 1672–21 Dec. 1674.

Brouncker, William (Brouncker) 2nd Viscount   *Commissioner (Trade)* 7 Nov. 1660.

Brown, Benjamin Thomas   *Messenger (Railway Department)* 23 Dec. 1846–April 1853 (MT 13/6 p. 77). *Messenger* April 1853–27 Dec. 1860 ([Cd. 1713] pp. 147, 157 HC (1854) xxvii, 179, 189; *Royal Kal.* (1854), 160). D. 27 Dec. 1860 (BT 3/60 no. 13).

Browne, Jemmett   *Junior Supplementary Clerk* Nov. 1857–Nov. 1863 (BT 3/52 no. 711; Ind. 20461 no. 1810). *Junior Clerk* Nov. 1863–7 May 1868 (BT 3/64 no. 624). *Senior Clerk* 7 May 1868 (BT 5/76).
Private Secretary to Secretary and Permanent Secretary (Farrer) probably app. Sept. 1865; first occ. 1866 (*Royal Kal.* (1866), 166).

Bruce, Hon. Frederick William Adolphus   *Secretary (Railway Department)* 12 Nov. 1846–18 May 1847 (MT 13/6 p. 5). Res. 18 May 1847 on app. as Consul General, Bolivia (MT 13/7 p. 267; *London Gazette* no. 20756).

Brudenell, Hon. James   *Commissioner* 14 May 1730–9 Aug. 1746. D. 9 Aug. 1746 (T 53/42 p. 383).

Bruges (Bridges), William   *Clerk* 11 March 1701–7 May 1703 (CO 389/36 pp. 107, 136–8). D. 7 May 1703 (CO 391/16 p. 111).

Buckingham, George (Villiers) 2nd Duke of   *Commissioner (Trade)* 20 Oct. 1668, 16 April 1669.
Commissioner (Plantations) 4 April 1671. *Commissioner* 27 Sept. 1672.

Bucknall, William Miles   *Supernumerary Clerk (Railway Department)* 28 Sept. 1848–6 Sept. 1851 (MT 13/10 p. 336). *Junior Clerk (Railway Department)* 6 Sept. 1851–April 1853 (MT 13/15 p. 490). *Junior Clerk* April 1853–30 April 1857 ([Cd. 1713] p. 157 HC (1854) xxvii, 189; *Royal Kal.* (1854), 160). *Second Class Clerk* 30 April 1857–Dec. 1863 (BT 5/65). *Librarian* Dec. 1863 (BT 3/64 no. 652; *Royal Kal.* (1864), 164).

Buckworth, John   *Commissioner (Trade)* 20 Oct. 1668, 16 April 1669.

Budge, William   *Clerk* 25 Aug. 1786–10 Dec. 1794 (BT 5/4 p. 15). Res. 10 Dec. 1794 on app. as Clerk, office of Secretary of State for War (BT 5/9 p. 301).

Bunter, Frederick   *Deputy Comptroller of Corn Returns* probably app. 1851; first occ. 1852 (*Royal Kal.* (1852), 160). Office abolished 1865 (BT 5/73, 20 May 1865). *Senior Clerk* 20 May 1865 (ibid.).

Burgess, Henry T.   *Messenger* probably app. 1851; occ. from 1852 to 1865 (*Royal Kal.* (1852), 160; ibid. (1865), 164). *Assistant Office Keeper* probably app. 1865; occ. from 1866 to 1867 (ibid. (1866), 166; ibid. (1867), 166). *Office Keeper* 18 Feb. 1867 (BT 20/1 no. 333).

Burgess, W.   *Firelighter* Jan. 1864 (BT 12/1 no. 11).

Burrish, Onslow   *Solicitor and Clerk of Reports* 18 Aug. 1730–26 Oct. 1736 (*JCTP 1729–34*, 139). Left office 26 Oct. 1736 (*JCTP 1735–41*, 137).

Calcraft, Henry George   *Junior Clerk (Railway Department)* 24 Feb. 1852–April 1853 (*Staff Lists*, 237; *Royal Kal.* (1853), 160). *Junior Clerk* April 1853–30 April

1857 ([Cd. 1713] p. 157 HC (1854) xxvii, 189; *Royal Kal.* (1854), 160). *Third Class Clerk* 30 April 1857–July 1863 (BT 5/65). *Senior Clerk* July 1863 (BT 3/64 no. 379; *Royal Kal.* (1864), 164).

    Private Secretary to President (Milner Gibson) 4 July 1859–July 1866 (BT 5/67); (Bright) 10 Dec. 1868 (BT 5/76).

Campbell, Lord Frederick *Member* 5 March 1784 (PC 2/129 p. 56), 23 Aug. 1786 (PC 2/131 pp. 403–4).

Campbell, P. L. *Librarian* 17 June–13 Aug. 1845 (BT 5/54). Res. 13 Aug. 1845 (ibid.).

Campion, William *Office Keeper* 27 Feb. 1733–15 April 1735 (*JCTP 1729–34*, 335). *Clerk* 15 April 1735–c. 5 Dec. 1752 (*JCTP 1735–41*, 13–14). D. by 5 Dec. 1752 (*JCTP 1750–3*, 370).

Capel, Hon. Sir Henry, kt. *Member* 16 Feb. 1689 (PC 2/73 p. 8).

Cardwell, Charles *Private Secretary to President* (Cardwell) 6 Jan. 1853–March 1855 (BT 5/61).

Cardwell, Edward *President* 28 Dec. 1852–31 March 1855 (PC 2/236 p. 512).

Carew *see* **Pole Carew**

Carey, James *Clerk (Corn Department)* 12 July 1827–26 Jan. 1829 (BT 5/36 p. 204). Res. 26 Jan. 1829 (BT 5/43 p. 237).

Carey, Walter *Commissioner* 8 Aug. 1727–14 May 1730.

Carlisle, Charles (Howard) 1st Earl of *Commissioner (Trade)* 20 Oct. 1668, 16 April 1669.

    Member 12 March 1675 (PC 2/64 p. 395).

Carlisle, Frederick (Howard) 5th Earl of *First Lord* 15 Nov. 1779–12 Dec. 1780.

Carmarthen, Francis Godolphin (Osborne) *styled* Marquess of *Member* 13 Jan. 1786 (PC 2/131 p. 8).

Carr, Sir Robert, 3rd Bart. *Member* 12 March 1675 (PC 2/64 p. 395), 20 Oct. 1680 (PC 2/69 p. 127).

Carroll, Maurice *Clerk* 25 March 1697–20 Dec. 1714 (CO 389/36 pp. 106, 136–8). Ret. 20 Dec. 1714 (*JCTP 1709–15*, 575).

Cart, Robert *Junior Supplementary Clerk* 30 April 1857–27 Aug. 1864 (BT 5/65). *Senior Supplementary Clerk* 27 Aug. 1864 (BT 5/72).

Carteret, Sir George, 1st Bart. *Commissioner (Trade)* 7 Nov. 1660, 20 Oct. 1668, 16 April 1669.

    Commissioner (Plantations) 1 Dec. 1660, 4 April 1671. *Commissioner* 27 Sept. 1672.

Carysfort, John Joshua (Proby) 1st Earl of *Member* 18 June 1806 (PC 2/170 p. 397).

Cave, Stephen *Vice President* 10 July 1866–Dec. 1868 (PC 2/264 p. 37).

Cavendish, William (Cavendish) *styled* Lord (succ. as 4th Earl of **Devonshire** 23 Nov. 1684) *Member* 22 April 1679 (PC 2/68 p. 6), 16 Feb. 1689 (PC 2/73 p. 8).

Cecil, Hon. Robert *Commissioner* 8 Jan. 1702–25 April 1707.

Chalmers, George *Chief Clerk* 25 Aug. 1786–31 May 1825 (BT 5/4 p. 15). D. 31 May 1825 (*Gent. Mag.* (1825), xcv (2), 564).

Chamberlain, Sir Thomas, kt. *Commissioner (Trade)* 7 Nov. 1660.

Chaney, Henry James *Clerk (Standard Department)* 20 Aug. 1866 (BT 5/74).

Chesterfield, Philip (Stanhope) 2nd Earl of *Member* 23 Feb. 1681 (PC 2/69 p. 222).

Chetwynd, John *Commissioner* 13 Dec. 1714–1 June 1728.

Chetwynd, Hon. Richard (succ. as 5th Viscount **Chetwynd** 12 Nov. 1791) *Clerk* 25 Aug. 1786–24 Jan. 1792 (BT 5/4 p. 15). Res. 24 Jan. 1792 (BT 5/7 p. 364).

Child, Daniel *Office Keeper* 3 July 1696–c. 7 March 1721 (CO 391/9 p. 10). D. by 7 March 1721 (*JCTP 1718–23*, 253).

Child, Josiah *Commissioner (Trade)* 20 Oct. 1668, 16 April 1669.

Chisholm, Henry Williams *Warden of the Standards* 20 Aug. 1866 (BT 5/74).

Chiverton, Richard *Commissioner (Trade)* 7 Nov. 1660.

Clancarty, Richard (le Poer Trench) 2nd Earl of *Member* 13 May 1807 (PC 2/173 p. 47). *President* 29 Sept. 1812–24 Jan. 1818 (PC 2/193 p. 434).

Clare, John (Holles) 2nd Earl of *Commissioner (Plantations)* 1 Dec. 1660.

Clare, Viscount *see* **Nugent,** Robert

Clarendon, George William Frederick (Villiers) 4th Earl of *President* 6 July 1846–22 July 1847 (PC 2/228 p. 571).

Clarendon, Henry (Hyde) 2nd Earl of *Member* 29 June 1680 (PC 2/69 p. 24).

Clarendon, Thomas (Villiers) 1st Earl of *Member* 5 March 1784 (PC 2/129 p. 56).

Clark, Francis Rush *Clerk* 6 July 1775–2 May 1782 (*JCTP 1768–75*, 429). Office abolished 2 May 1782 (*JCTP 1776–82*, 472; T 1/579 Schedule 3).

Clark, John Hall *Junior Clerk* 17 Feb. 1868 (BT 5/76).

Clarke, Samuel *Office Keeper* 3 July 1696–c. 27 Aug. 1728 (CO 391/9 p. 10). D. by 27 Aug. 1728 (*JCTP 1723–8*, 425).

Clarke Travers, Boyle Lorenzo Travers *Junior Clerk* 12 Jan. 1869 (BT 5/77).

Clerk, Sir George, 6th Bart. *Vice President* 5 Feb. 1845–8 July 1846 (PC 2/227 p. 97).

Clerk, James *Private Secretary to Vice President* (Clerk) probably app. Feb. 1845; occ. 1846 (*Royal Kal.* (1846), 162).

Clifford, Sir Thomas, kt. *Commissioner (Trade)* 20 Oct. 1668, 16 April 1669.

Cloud, Charles *Porter* 14 March 1809–7 March 1810 (BT 5/18 p. 471). *Messenger* 7 March 1810–1 Dec. 1814 (BT 5/19 p. 426). Left office 1 Dec. 1814 on app. as Messenger to Secretaries of State (BT 5/23 p. 472).

Cockburn, John *Commissioner* 13 Dec. 1714–13 July 1717.

Coddington, Joshua *Assistant Inspector General of Railways* 6 Aug. 1844–Nov. 1846 (BT 5/52). *Inspector of Railways* Nov. 1846–23 Aug. 1847 (MT 13/6 pp. 1–2, 44). Res. 23 Aug. 1847 (MT 13/7 pp. 464, 481, 506).

Colchester, Charles (Abbot) 2nd Lord *Vice President* 27 Feb. 1852–4 Jan. 1853 (PC 2/235 p. 167).

Colepepper, John (Colepepper) 1st Lord *Commissioner (Trade)* 7 Nov. 1660.

Colepepper, Thomas (Colepepper) 2nd Lord *Commissioner (Plantations)* 4 April 1671. *Vice President* 27 Sept. 1672–21 Dec. 1674.

Colleton, John *Commissioner (Trade)* 7 Nov. 1660.
Commissioner (Plantations) 1 Dec. 1660.

Collins, John *Clerk (Plantations)* app. 12 Aug. 1670 (Journal (Plantations) 1670–2, 3); no further occ.

Cooke, Charles (ktd. 24 Jan. 1717) *Commissioner* 13 Dec. 1714–2 Jan. 1721. D. 2 Jan. 1721 (*Hist. Reg. Chron.* (1721), vi, 3).

Cooper, Sir Anthony Ashley, 2nd Bart. (cr. Lord **Ashley** 20 April 1661; Earl of

Shaftesbury 23 April 1672) *Commissioner (Trade)* 7 Nov. 1660, 20 Oct. 1668, 16 April 1669.
  Commissioner (Plantations) 1 Dec. 1660.
  President 27 Sept. 1672–21 Dec. 1674.
  Member 22 April 1679 (PC 2/68 p. 6).
Cooper, Thomas *Office Keeper* 10 Nov. 1786–8 Oct. 1789 (BT 5/4 p. 72). Left office 8 Oct. 1789 (BT 5/5 p. 375).
Corry, Isaac *Member* 28 Jan. 1807 (PC 2/172 p. 122).
Cotterell, Stephen (ktd. 21 Dec. 1796) *Secretary* 25 Aug. 1786–10 Aug. 1810 (BT 5/4 pp. 11–14). Res. 10 Aug. 1810 (BT 5/20 p. 88).
Cotton, John Hynde (succ. as 3rd Bart. 20 Jan. 1713) *Commissioner* 7 July 1712–13 Dec. 1714.
Courtenay, Francis Foljambe *Private Secretary: to Vice President* (Dalhousie) probably app. June 1843; occ. 1845 (*Royal Kal.* (1845), 162); *to President* (Dalhousie) probably app. Feb. 1845; occ. 1846 (ibid. (1846), 162).
  Junior Clerk 1 Aug.–11 Dec. 1845 (BT 5/54). *Librarian* 11 Dec. 1845–8 Nov. 1847 (ibid.). Res. 8 Nov. 1847 (BT 5/56).
Courtenay, Thomas Peregrine *Vice President* 30 May 1828–22 Nov. 1830 (PC 2/209 pp. 412–13).
Coventry, Hon. Henry *Member* 12 March 1675 (PC 2/64 p. 395), 22 April 1679 (PC 2/68 p. 6).
Coventry, Hon. William (ktd. 26 June 1665) *Commissioner (Trade)* 7 Nov. 1660, 20 Oct. 1668, 16 April 1669.
  Commissioner (Plantations) 1 Dec. 1660.
Cowper, Hon. William Francis *Vice President* 12 Aug. 1859–22 Feb. 1860 (PC 2/250 p. 81).
Cox, Frederick Robert *Extra Clerk* 17 Feb. 1863–1868 (BT 20/2 no. 750). *Supplementary Clerk* 1868–1 April 1870 (*Staff Lists*, 18; *Royal Kal.* (1869), 166). Ret. 1 April 1870 (BT 20/2 no. 750).
Cranwell, Richard *Clerk* 23 May 1749–4 July 1764 (*JCTP 1742–9*, 415). Ret. 4 July 1764 (*JCTP 1764–7*, 89).
Craven, William (Craven) 1st Earl of *Commissioner (Trade)* 20 Oct. 1668, 16 April 1669.
  Member 12 March 1675 (PC 2/64 p. 395), 9 March 1681 (PC 2/68 p. 6).
Crispe, Sir Nicholas, kt. *Commissioner (Trade)* 7 Nov. 1660.
  Commissioner (Plantations) 1 Dec. 1660.
Croft, Sir Archer, 2nd Bart. *Commissioner* 14 May 1730–5 May 1741.
Crow, Sir Sackville, 1st Bart. *Commissioner (Trade)* 7 Nov. 1660.
Cuckow, David *Clerk* 28 March 1760–4 July 1764 (*JCTP 1759–63*, 101). Ret. 4 July 1764 (*JCTP 1764–7*, 89).
Cumberland, Richard *Solicitor and Clerk of Reports* 31 May 1765–23 Jan. 1776 (*JCTP 1764–7*, 175). *Secretary* 23 Jan. 1776–2 May 1782 (*JCTP 1776–82*, 2). Office abolished 2 May 1782 (ibid. 472; T 1/579 Schedule 3).
Dacre, Francis (Lennard) 15th Lord *Commissioner (Plantations)* 1 Dec. 1660.
Dalhousie, James Andrew (Ramsay) 10th Earl of *Vice President* 10 June 1843–5 Feb. 1845 (PC 2/225 p. 242). *President* 5 Feb. 1845–6 July 1846 (PC 2/227 p. 97).
Danby, Earl of *see* **Osborne,** Sir Thomas

Dancer, Francis *Clerk* 22 Nov. 1753–16 Feb. 1758 (*JCTP 1750–3,* 459). Res. 16 Feb. 1758 on app. as Extraordinary Clerk, Admiralty (*JCTP 1754–8,* 376; *Court and City Reg.* (1758), 203).

Dartmouth, William (Legge) 2nd Lord *Commissioner* 19 June 1702–4 Oct. 1710.

Dartmouth, William (Legge) 2nd Earl of *First Lord* 12 Aug. 1765–18 Aug. 1766.

Davis, Chamberlin *Clerk* 22 April 1765–15 June 1779 (*JCTP 1764–7,* 168). Res. 15 June 1779 (*JCTP 1776–82,* 257).

Davison, William *Porter* probably app. 1854; first occ. 1855 (*Royal Kal.* (1855), 160). Res. 28 April 1859 (Ind. 20463 no. 605).

Deedes, Henry Charles *Junior Clerk* (*Statistical Department*) probably app. 1840; first occ. 1841 (*Royal Kal.* (1841), 135). Left office 14 Aug. 1841 on app. as Junior Clerk, Board of Control (BT 5/49; *Royal Kal.* (1842), 164).

de Ferrers, George (Townshend) 11th Lord *Member* 5 March 1784 (PC 2/129 p. 56).

de Grey, Thomas (*styled* Hon. 17 Oct. 1780; succ. as 2nd Lord **Walsingham** 9 May 1781) *Commissioner* 17 June 1777–2 Jan. 1782. *Member* 5 March 1784 (PC 2/129 p. 56).

de Hamel, Felix Hargrave *Law Clerk* 2 Jan. 1867 (BT 5/75).

de Lousada, Francis *Précis Writer* 29 Aug. 1846–March 1849 (BT 5/55). Res. March 1849 (BT 3/38 pp. 155–6).

Denham, John *Commissioner* (*Plantations*) 1 Dec. 1660.

Devonshire, 4th Earl of *see* **Cavendish,** Lord

Devonshire, William (Cavendish) 3rd Earl of *Commissioner* (*Trade*) 16 April 1669.

Dickinson, Frederick *Messenger* probably app. 1858; occ. from 1859 to 1862 (*Royal Kal.* (1859), 165; ibid. (1862), 165).

Digges, Edward *Commissioner* (*Trade*) 7 Nov. 1660.
  Commissioner (*Plantations*) 1 Dec. 1660.

Dobson, Henry Austin *Junior Supplementary Clerk* Oct. 1856–Nov. 1863 (BT 3/50 nos. 716, 730; BT 3/51 no. 42; Ind. 20461 no. 102). *Junior Clerk* Nov. 1863–2 Jan. 1867 (BT 3/64 no. 624). *Senior Clerk* 2 Jan. 1867 (BT 5/75).

Docminique, Paul *Commissioner* 13 Dec. 1714–16 March 1735. D. 16 March 1735 (*CTBP 1735–8,* 122).

Donoughmore, Richard Hely (Hely Hutchinson) 1st Earl of *Member* 14 May 1806 (PC 2/170 p. 157).

Donoughmore, Richard John (Hely Hutchinson) 4th Earl of *Vice President* 6 April 1858–3 March 1859 (PC 2/247 p. 173). *President* 3 March–18 June 1859 (PC 2/249 p. 169).

Douglas, Sylvester (cr. Lord **Glenbervie** 30 Nov. 1800) *Member* 17 March 1796 (PC 2/145 p. 318). *Vice President* 18 Nov. 1801–8 Feb. 1804 (PC 2/159 p. 434).

Dowding, William *Receiver of Corn Returns* 24 July 1821–17 July 1822 (BT 5/29 pp. 381–4). Res. 17 July 1822 (BT 5/30 pp. 348–50).

Dowley, George *Supernumerary Clerk* 10 Oct. 1795–4 Jan. 1798 (BT 5/10 p. 115). *Clerk* 4 Jan. 1798–c. 8 May 1806 (BT 5/11 pp. 48–9). D. by 8 May 1806 (BT 5/16 pp. 301–2).

Downing, Sir George, kt. (cr. Bart. 1 July 1663) *Commissioner* (*Trade*) 7 Nov. 1660, 20 Oct. 1668, 16 April 1669.

Doyle, John Vincent Thomas *Copyist* 1853–4 (BT 5/67, 10 Feb. 1859; *Royal Kal.* (1854), 160). *Junior Supplementary Clerk* 1854–17 Jan. 1855 (BT 3/47 pp. 270–2;

Royal Kal. (1855), 159). Left office 17 Jan. 1855 on app. as Senior Clerk and Financial Officer, Department of Science and Art (BT 5/63). *Junior Clerk* 30 July 1856–30 April 1857 (BT 5/64). *Third Class Clerk* 30 April 1857–July 1863 (BT 5/65). *Senior Clerk* July 1863 (BT 3/64 no. 379; *Royal Kal.* (1864), 164).

Doyle, Robert *Commissioner (Plantations)* 1 Dec. 1660.

Drage, Binyoun John *Junior Clerk* July 1863 (BT 3/62 no. 676; BT 3/64 no. 379; *Royal Kal.* (1864), 164).

Draxe, Sir James, kt. *Commissioner (Trade)* 7 Nov. 1660.
Commissioner (Plantations) 1 Dec. 1660.

Drift, Adrian *Clerk* 6 Aug. 1700–1707 (CO 389/36 pp. 106–7, 136–8). *Deputy Secretary* 1707–20 Dec. 1714 (*JCTP 1704–9*, 356; CO 389/36 pp. 334–6). Left office 20 Dec. 1714 (*JCTP 1709–15*, 575).

Duke, George *Secretary (Trade)* app. following creation of Council 7 Nov. 1660; first occ. 13 Nov. 1660 (*CSPD 1660–1*, 356); received payments as Secretary from 15 May 1661 to 26 July 1664 (*CTB*, i, 244, 615); referred to as 'late' Secretary 14 March 1664 (*CSPD 1663–4*, 515) but apparently still in office 23 Sept. 1667 (*APC (Colonial) 1613–80*, 435); possibly remained in office until app. of new Council 20 Oct. 1668.

du Moulin, Peter *Secretary (Trade)* 22 Oct. 1668–c. July 1672 (*The Rawdon Papers*, ed. J. Bramhall (London 1819), 237–8). Probably left office c. July 1672 on departure from England (*CSPD 1672*, 432; K. H. D. Haley, *William of Orange and the English Opposition 1672–4* (Oxford 1953), 37).

Duncombe, Sir John, kt. *Member* 12 March 1675 (PC 2/64 p. 395).

Dundas, Henry *Member* 5 March 1784 (PC 2/129 p. 56).

Dunkley, William *Commissioner (Trade)* 7 Nov. 1660.

Dupplin, Thomas (Hay) *styled* Viscount *Commissioner* 20 Nov. 1746–6 April 1754.

Dyson, Jeremiah *Commissioner* 2 May 1764–30 Dec. 1768.

Eden, Arthur *Clerk* 23 Aug.–24 Sept. 1806 (BT 5/16 pp. 301–2). Left office 24 Sept. 1806 on app. as Clerk, Office of Auditor of Receipt of Exchequer (ibid. p. 348).

Eden, William (cr. Lord **Auckland** 18 Nov. 1789) *Commissioner* 15 March 1776–2 May 1782. *Member* 10 Dec. 1785 (PC 2/130 p. 436), 23 Aug. 1786 (PC 2/131 pp. 403–4). *President* 5 Feb. 1806–26 March 1807 (PC 2/169 pp. 286, 472).

Edgcumbe, Hon. Richard *Commissioner* 6 April 1754–29 Dec. 1755.

Effingham, Thomas (Howard) 3rd Earl of *Member* 5 March 1784 (PC 2/129 p. 56).

Eliot, Edward *Commissioner* 14 Jan. 1760–15 March 1774.

Elliott, Grey *Acting Solicitor and Clerk of Reports* 26 Dec. 1777–15 June 1779 (*JCTP 1776–82*, 125). *Solicitor and Clerk of Reports* 15 June 1779–2 May 1782 (ibid. 257). Office abolished 2 May 1782 (ibid. 472; T 1/579 Schedule 3). *Secretary* 25 Aug. 1786–June 1787 (BT 5/4 pp. 11–14). D. June 1787 (*Gent. Mag.* (1787), lvii (1), 548).

Eltenton, Charles *Extra Messenger* 9 Dec. 1862–May 1865 (BT 3/62 no. 699). *Messenger* May 1865 (BT 20/1 no. 71).

Emberson, Arthur Henry *Junior Clerk* 2 March 1867 (BT 5/75).

Emerson Tennent, Sir James, kt. *Secretary* 6 Oct. 1852–2 Jan. 1867 (BT 5/60). Res. 2 Jan. 1867 (HC 47 pp. 16–17 (1867) xxxix, 228–9; BT 5/75).

Emerson Tennent, William W. (succ. as 2nd Bart. 6 March 1869) *Junior Supplementary Clerk* 12 March 1855–30 April 1857 (BT 20/2 no. 750). *Third Class Clerk* 30 April 1857–July 1863 (BT 5/65). *Junior Clerk* July 1863–28 June 1865 (BT 3/64 no. 379; *Royal Kal.* (1864), 164). *Senior Clerk* 28 June 1865–1 April 1870 (BT 5/73). Ret. 1 April 1870 (BT 20/2 no. 750).

Private Secretary to Vice President (Lovaine) March–June 1859 (*Foreign Office List* (1869), 173); (Hutt, Goschen, Monsell, Cave) Feb. 1860–Dec. 1868 (ibid.; BT 20/1 no. 223; *Royal Kal.* (1861), 164; ibid. (1868), 166).

Ernle, Sir John, kt. *Member* 22 April 1679 (PC 2/68 p. 6).

Essex, Arthur (Capel) 1st Earl of *Member* 12 March 1675 (PC 2/64 p. 395), 22 April 1679 (PC 2/68 p. 6).

Estwick, Nathaniel *Clerk* 13 May 1703–c. 22 Jan. 1708 (CO 391/16 p. 111). Left office between 22 Jan. 1708 and 21 Feb. 1709 (*JCTP 1704–9*, 451; CO 389/36 pp. 388–9).

Evelyn, John *Commissioner* (*Plantations*) 4 April 1671–27 Sept. 1672. *Commissioner* 27 Sept. 1672–21 Dec. 1674.

Eveniss, George Hathaway *Senior Clerk* July 1863–2 Aug. 1870 (BT 3/62 no. 676; BT 3/64 no. 379; *Royal Kal.* (1864), 164). D. 2 Aug. 1870 (death certificate).

Fabbri, Charles *Messenger* 8 Oct. 1789–29 Nov. 1792 (BT 5/5 p. 375). Left office 29 Nov. 1792 (BT 5/8 p. 326).

Fairfield, Arthur Rowan *Junior Supplementary Clerk* Feb. 1859–Nov. 1863 (BT 3/55 no. 67; Ind. 20463 no. 159). *Junior Clerk* Nov. 1863–9 Aug. 1870 (BT 3/64 no. 624). *Senior Clerk* 9 Aug. 1870 (BT 5/78).

Fane, Francis *Counsel* 19 Aug. 1725–12 Nov. 1746 (C 66/3561, 3570; *JCTP 1723–8*, 195). *Commissioner* 20 Nov. 1746–13 April 1756.

Fane, William Dashwood *Legal Assistant* 7 July 1856–2 Jan. 1867 (BT 5/64). Office abolished 2 Jan. 1867 (BT 5/75; BT 20/1 no. 525).

Assistant Secretary (*Railways*) 5 July 1865–2 Jan. 1867 (BT 5/73). Left office 2 Jan. 1867 (BT 5/75; BT 20/1 nos. 316, 525).

Fanshawe, John Gaspard *Junior Clerk* (*Statistical Department*) 15 Jan. 1849–1851 (BT 5/58; *Royal Kal.* (1851) 160). *Clerk* (*Marine Department*) probably app. 1851; occ. from 1852 to 1853 (*Royal Kal.* (1852), 160; ibid. (1853), 160). *Junior Clerk* April 1853–30 April 1857 ([Cd. 1713] p. 157 HC (1854) xxvii, 189; *Royal Kal.* (1854), 160). *Third Class Clerk* 30 April 1857–July 1863 (BT 5/65). *Senior Clerk* July 1863 (BT 3/64 no. 379; *Royal Kal.* (1864), 164).

Private Secretary to Secretary (Emerson Tennent) first occ. 1859 (BT 6/293 p. 164). Office abolished 2 Jan. 1867 (HC 47 p. 18 (1867) xxxix, 230; BT 5/75).

Farrer, Thomas Henry *Secretary* (*Marine Department*) 15 Aug. 1850–April 1853 (BT 5/59, 23 Dec. 1850). *Assistant Secretary* (*Marine*) April 1853–July 1863 ([Cd. 1713] pp. 135, 156–7 HC (1854) xxvii, 167, 188–9; *Royal Kal.* (1854), 160). *Marine Secretary* July 1863–30 Sept. 1865 (BT 3/64 no. 379; T 1/6433B/13012; *Royal Kal.* (1864), 164). *Secretary* 30 Sept. 1865–2 Jan. 1867 (BT 5/73). *Permanent Secretary* 2 Jan. 1867 (HC 47 pp. 8, 16–17 (1867) xxxix, 220, 228–9; BT 5/75).

Fauconberg, Thomas (Belasyse) 2nd Viscount *Member* 12 March 1675 (PC 2/64 p. 395), 22 April 1679 (PC 2/68 p. 6), 16 Feb. 1689 (PC 2/73 p. 8).

Fawkener, William *Secretary* 25 Aug. 1786–26 July 1811 (BT 5/4 pp. 11–14). D. 26 July 1811 (*Gent. Mag.* (1811), lxxxi (2), 93).

Fergusson, Sir Adam, 3rd Bart. *Commissioner* 2 Jan.–2 May 1782.

Ferrers *see* **de Ferrers**

Finch, Heneage (Finch) 1st Lord *Member* 22 April 1679 (PC 2/68 p. 6).

Finch, Sir John, kt. *Commissioner* (*Plantations*) 30 July 1670–27 Sept. 1672. *Commissioner* 27 Sept.–7 Dec. 1672.

Fish, Robert *Extra Messenger* Jan. 1866–May 1869 (BT 20/1 no. 200). *Messenger* May 1869 (Ind. 20470 no. 1101).

Fisher, William *Commissioner* (*Trade*) 7 Nov. 1660.

Fitzgerald, David *Junior Clerk* 2 March 1867 (BT 5/75).

Fitzgerald, Edward M. *Private Secretary to President* (Vesey Fitzgerald) 12 June 1828–Feb. 1830 (BT 5/37 pp. 16, 251).

Fitzgerald *see also* **Vesey Fitzgerald**

Fitzherbert, William *Commissioner* 12 Aug. 1765–2 Jan. 1772. D. 2 Jan. 1772 (T 53/52 p. 339).

Fitzroy, Robert *Chief of Meteorological Department* 1 Aug. 1854–30 April 1865 (BT 3/50 no. 778). D. 30 April 1865 (*Gent. Mag.* (1865), clvi, 788).

Fitzwalter, Benjamin (Mildmay) 1st Earl *First Lord* 22 May 1735–27 June 1737.

Foley, Thomas *Commissioner* 7 July 1712–15 Sept. 1713.

Fonblanque, Bentham Albany *Copyist* April 1853–7 Jan. 1854 (BT 20/1 no. 158). Res. 7 Jan. 1854 on app. as Clerk, Admiralty (ibid.; Ind. 20457 no. 172).

Fonblanque, William Albany *Superintendent of Statistical Department* 22 Oct. 1847 (BT 5/56).

Ford, Sir Richard, kt. *Commissioner* (*Trade*) 7 Nov. 1660.

Foster, John *Member* 17 Feb. 1802 (PC 2/160 p. 220).

Frankland, Sir Thomas, 3rd Bart. *Commissioner* 1 June 1728–14 May 1730.

Freeman, Sir Ralph, kt. *Commissioner* (*Trade*) 7 Nov. 1660.

Frowde, Corney *Clerk* (*Plantations*) 12 Aug. 1670–27 Sept. 1672 (Journal (Plantations) 1670–2, 3). *Clerk* 24 Oct. 1672–27 Oct. 1673 (Journal (Trade and Plantations) 1672–4, 2). Res. 27 Oct. 1673 (ibid. 51).

Frowde, Philip (ktd. 10 March 1665) *Secretary* (*Plantations*) app. 10 Dec. 1660 (*CSPC* (*America & West Indies*) *1574–1660*, 494); received payments as Secretary from 31 May 1661 to 25 June 1664 (*CTB*, i, 249, 604); apparently still in office 23 Sept. 1667 (*APC* (*Colonial*) *1613–80*, 435); possibly remained in office until app. of new Council 30 July 1670.

Fry, Mary *Necessary Woman* occ. from 1716 to 19 June 1727 (Chamberlayne, *Present State* (1716), 683; CO 389/37 p. 276).

Galloway, Earl of *see* **Garlies, Lord**

Galton, Douglas *Statistical and Topographical Assistant* (*Railway Department*) 3 Feb. 1847–2 March 1850 (MT 13/7 p. 56). *Assistant Secretary* (*Railway Department*) 2 March 1850–6 Nov. 1852 (MT 13/12 p. 98). *Inspector of Railways* 6 Nov. 1852–29 June 1854 (BT 5/60). *Assistant Secretary* (*Railways*) 29 June 1854–18 Jan. 1860 (MT 13/20 no. 147). Res. 18 Jan. 1860 on app. as Assistant Inspector General of Fortification, War Office (BT 3/57 no. 35).

Private Secretary to President of Railway Commission (Strutt) 21 Feb. 1847–April 1848 (MT 13/7 pp. 403–4).

Garlies, John (Stewart) *styled* Lord (succ. as 7th Earl of **Galloway** 24 Sept. 1773) *Commissioner* 27 Aug. 1772–26 Jan. 1774.

Garroway, William *Commissioner* (*Trade*) 20 Oct. 1668, 16 April 1669.

Gascoyne, Bamber *Commissioner* 23 April 1763–12 Aug. 1765; 10 Feb. 1772– 14 July 1779.

Gedney, Thomas *Clerk* 17 May 1722–14 June 1738 (*JCTP 1718–22*, 359). Ret. 14 June 1738 (*JCTP 1735–41*, 243).

Gellibrand, Samuel *Clerk* occ. from 22 Jan. 1708 to 9 April 1735 (*JCTP 1704–9*, 451; *JCTP 1735–41*, 13). *Deputy Secretary* 9 April 1735–14 April 1758 (*JCTP 1735–41*, 13). D. 14 April 1758 (*Gent. Mag.* (1758), xxviii, 197).

Gibbon, Edward *Commissioner* 14 July 1779–2 May 1782.

Gibson, George *Junior Supplementary Clerk* Jan. 1858–Feb. 1862 (BT 3/53 no. 7; Ind. 20462 no. 43). Left office Feb. 1862 on app. as Superintendent, Malta and Alexandria Telegraph (BT 3/61 no. 111).

Gibson *see also* **Milner Gibson**

Gilmour, Sir Charles, 2nd Bart. *Commissioner* 31 Dec. 1743–5 Jan. 1745.

Gladstone, William Ewart *Vice President* 3 Sept. 1841–10 June 1843 (PC 2/223 p. 466). *President* 10 June 1843–5 Feb. 1845 (PC 2/225 p. 242).

Glascock, William *Commissioner* (*Plantations*) 1 Dec. 1660.

Glenbervie, Lord *see* **Douglas**, Sylvester

Goddard, John *Clerk* 11 April 1775–2 May 1782 (*JCTP 1768–75*, 421). Office abolished 2 May 1782 (*JCTP 1776–82*, 472; T 1/579 Schedule 3).
    Acting Solicitor and Clerk of Reports 26 Dec. 1776–15 June 1779 (*JCTP 1776– 82*, 28, 125). *Solicitor and Clerk of Reports* app. 15 June 1779 (ibid. 257). No further occ.

Goderich, Viscount *see* **Robinson**, Hon. Frederick John

Godolphin, George Godolphin, Lord *see* **Osborne**, Hon. George Godolphin

Godolphin, Sidney (Godolphin) 1st Lord *Member* 20 Nov. 1690 (PC 2/74 p. 56).

Goodricke, Sir John, 5th Bart. *Member* 8 March 1784 (PC 2/129 p. 60), 23 Aug. 1786 (PC 2/131 pp. 403–4).

Gordon, Adam *Supernumerary Clerk* probably app. 1786 (BT 5/5 p. 190); occ. as 'Clerk' from 1787 to 1792 (sic) (*Royal Kal.* (1787), 103; ibid. (1792), 103). Probably left office May 1791 on app. as Clerk, Home Office (R. R. Nelson, *The Home Office, 1782–1801* (Durham, N.C. 1969), 166).

Gordon, Alexander *Private Secretary to President* (Ripon) 4 Sept. 1841–June 1843 (BT 5/49).

Gordon, Henry Clarence *Supernumerary Clerk* (*Railway Department*) 18 Feb. 1848–1 June 1849 (MT 13/9 p. 161). Res. 1 June 1849 (MT 13/11 p. 443).

Gorges, Richard (Gorges) 3rd Lord *Commissioner* (*Plantations*) 30 July 1670– 27 Sept. 1672. *Commissioner* 27 Sept. 1672–21 Dec. 1674.

Goschen, George Joachim *Vice President* 29 Nov. 1865–12 March 1866 (PC 2/262 p. 703).

Govett, Clement *Supernumerary Clerk* 29 March–10 Oct. 1795 (BT 5/9 p. 440). *Clerk* 10 Oct. 1795–April 1801 (BT 5/10 p. 115). D. April 1801 (BT 5/12 pp. 320–1; *Gent. Mag.* (1801), lxxi (1), 377).

Gower *see* **Leveson Gower**

Graham, James (Graham) *styled* Marquess of (succ. as 3rd Duke of **Montrose** 23 Sept. 1790) *Vice President* 8 Aug. 1789–20 Oct. 1790 (PC 2/134 p. 182). *President* 6 June 1804–5 Feb. 1806 (PC 2/165 p. 319).

Grant, Charles *Vice President* 3 April 1823–3 Sept. 1827 (PC 2/205 p. 43). *President* 3 Sept. 1827–11 June 1828 (PC 2/208 p. 408).

Grant, Sir William, kt. *Member* 3 March 1802 (PC 2/160 p. 271).

Grant, William *Messenger* 22 May 1821–c. 4 Dec. 1838 (BT 5/29 p. 303). D. by 4 Dec. 1838 (BT 5/46 p. 117).

Grant, William *Private Secretary to President* (Grant) 4 Sept. 1827–June 1828 (BT 5/37 pp. 167, 175).

Grantham, Lord *see* **Robinson**, Hon. Thomas

Grantley, Fletcher (Norton) 1st Lord *Member* 5 March 1784 (PC 2/129 p. 56), 23 Aug. 1786 (PC 2/131 pp. 403–4).

Granville, Arthur Alleyne Bozzi *Supernumerary Clerk* 27 April 1843–11 Dec. 1845 (BT 5/51). *Junior Clerk* 11 Dec. 1845–15 Jan. 1849 (BT 5/54). Res. 15 Jan. 1849 (BT 5/58).

Granville, Granville George (Leveson Gower) 2nd Earl *Commissioner of Railways* 4 Nov. 1846–10 Oct. 1851 (*London Gazette* no. 20657). Office abolished 10 Oct. 1851 (14 & 15 Vict., c 64, s 1).
Vice President 9 May 1848–11 Feb. 1852 (PC 2/231 p. 280).

Graves, Henry Cyril Percy *Junior Clerk* 22 Aug. 1867 (BT 5/75).

Gray, John *Messenger* 3 July 1696–c. 10 Jan. 1723 (CO 391/9 p. 10). D. by 10 Jan. 1723 (*JCTP 1723–8*, 1).

Gray, Joseph *Junior Supplementary Clerk* 30 April 1857–Nov. 1863 (BT 5/65). *Junior Clerk* Nov. 1863–7 May 1868 (BT 3/64 no. 624). *Senior Clerk* 7 May 1868 (BT 5/76).

Gray, Thomas *Copyist* 1853–4 (BT 5/67, 10 Feb. 1859; *Royal Kal.* (1854), 160). *Junior Supplementary Clerk* 1854–29 Jan. 1855 (BT 3/47 pp. 270–2; *Royal Kal.* (1855), 159). *Senior Supplementary Clerk* 29 Jan. 1855–30 July 1856 (BT 5/63). *Junior Clerk* 30 July 1856–30 April 1857 (BT 5/64). *Third Class Clerk* 30 April 1857–29 Aug. 1860 (BT 5/65). *Second Class Clerk* 29 Aug. 1860–July 1863 (BT 5/68). *Senior Clerk* July 1863–2 Jan. 1867 (BT 3/64 no. 379; *Royal Kal.* (1864), 164). *Assistant Secretary* (*Marine*) 2 Jan. 1867 (BT 5/75).
Private Secretary to Vice President (Lowe) probably app. 1857; occ. 1858 (*Royal Kal.* (1858), 161).

Gray, William *Clerk* first occ. 20 Dec. 1714 (*JCTP 1709–15*, 575). D. by 18 April 1727 (*JCTP 1723–8*, 323–4).

Green, Robert *Clerk* 18 April 1758–4 July 1764 (*JCTP 1754–8*, 396). Ret. 4 July 1764 (*JCTP 1764–7*, 89).

Grenville, James (*styled* Hon. 13 Sept. 1749) *Commissioner* 26 Feb. 1746–29 Dec. 1755.

Grenville, James *Member* 5 March 1784 (PC 2/129 p. 56), 23 Aug. 1786 (PC 2/131 pp. 403–4).

Grenville, William Wyndham *Member* 5 March 1784 (PC 2/129 p. 56). *Vice President* 23 Aug. 1786–8 Aug. 1789 (PC 2/131 pp. 403–4).

Greville, Hon. Charles Francis *Commissioner* 26 Jan. 1774–16 Sept. 1780.

Greville, George (Greville) *styled* Lord (succ. as 2nd Earl **Brooke** and Earl of **Warwick** 6 July 1773) *Commissioner* 25 April 1770–26 Jan. 1774.

Grey, Hon. Thomas *Commissioner* (*Trade*) 20 Oct. 1668, 16 April 1669.
Commissioner (*Plantations*) 30 July 1670–1672. D. 1672 (*Complete Peerage*, 2nd ed. VI, 169 n. d).

Grey *see also* **de Grey**

Griffin, Bridget *Necessary Woman* first occ. 1741 (Chamberlayne, *Present State* (1741), pt. ii, 55). D. 25 July 1760 (*Gent. Mag.* (1760), xxx, 347).

Griffin, Gyles *Porter* 15 July 1724–c. 7 Oct. 1756 (*JCTP 1723–8*, 106). D. by 7 Oct. 1756 (*JCTP 1754–8*, 258).

Guilford, Francis (North) 2nd Lord *Commissioner* 7 July 1712–15 Sept. 1713. *First Lord* 15 Sept. 1713–13 Dec. 1714.

Gwyn, Francis *Commissioner* 12 June 1711–15 Sept. 1713.

Halifax, George (Montagu Dunk) 2nd Earl of *First Lord* 5 Nov. 1748–21 March 1761.

Halifax, George (Savile) 1st Viscount (cr. Earl of **Halifax** 16 July 1679; Marquess of Halifax 22 Aug. 1682) *Commissioner (Trade)* 16 April 1669. *Commissioner* 27 Sept. 1672. *Member* 12 March 1675 (PC 2/64 p. 395), 22 April 1679 (PC 2/68 p. 6), 16 Feb. 1689 (PC 2/73 p. 8).

Hamel *see* **de Hamel**

Hamilton, Robert George Crookshank *Accountant* 19 June 1869 (BT 5/77).

Hamilton, William Gerard *Commissioner* 13 April 1756–21 March 1761.

Hankey, Frederick *Junior Clerk (Statistical Department)* 3 July 1838–6 July 1841 (BT 5/45 pp. 412–13). Res. 6 July 1841 (BT 5/49).

Harbord, Sir Charles, kt. *Commissioner (Trade)* 7 Nov. 1660.

Hardie, Thomas *Messenger* 21 Nov. 1845–8 Dec. 1846 (BT 5/54). *Office Keeper (Railway Department)* 8 Dec. 1846–April 1853 (MT 13/6 p. 53). *Messenger* April 1853–12 May 1865 ([Cd. 1713] pp. 147, 157 HC (1854) xxvii, 179, 189; *Royal Kal.* (1854), 160). Ret. 12 May 1865 (BT 20/1 no. 60).

Hare, Theodore J. *Junior Supplementary Clerk* July 1857–14 Nov. 1862 (BT 3/52 nos. 448, 489; Ind. 20461 no. 1208). *Third Class Clerk* 14 Nov. 1862–July 1863 (BT 5/70). *Junior Clerk* July 1863–1865 (BT 3/64 no. 379; *Royal Kal.* (1864), 164). Last occ. 1865 (*Royal Kal.* (1865), 164).

Harley, Hon. Thomas *Member* 5 March 1784 (PC 2/129 p. 56), 23 Aug. 1789 (PC 2/131 pp. 403–4).

Harness, Henry Drury *Secretary (Railway Department)* 22 Jan. 1847–3 April 1850 (MT 13/7 pp. 81–2, 267). Res. 3 April 1850 on app. as Deputy Master of Mint (MT 13/12 p. 152).

Harris, Henry *Nautical Assessor* 28 July 1857 (BT 5/65).

Hawkesbury, Charles, Lord *see* **Jenkinson,** Charles

Hawkesbury, Robert Bankes (Jenkinson) *styled* Lord *Member* 13 March 1799 (PC 2/152 p. 350).

Henley, Joseph John *Private Secretary to President* (Henley) probably app. Feb. 1852; occ. 1853 (sic) (*Royal Kal.* (1853), 160); 26 Feb. 1858–March 1859 (BT 5/66).

Henley, Joseph Warner *President* 27 Feb.–28 Dec. 1852 (PC 2/235 p. 167); 26 Feb. 1858–3 March 1859 (PC 2/247 p. 129).

Henley, Morton Frederick (Eden) 1st Lord *Member* 12 Feb. 1806 (BT 1/26 f. 326).

Herbert, Hon. Auberon Edward William Molyneux *Private Secretary to President* (Northcote) 7 July 1866–c. 23 Jan. 1867 (BT 5/74). Left office by 23 Jan. 1867 (app. of Abbot).

Herbert, Robert George Wyndham *Assistant Secretary (Railways)* 2 Jan. 1867–1 Feb. 1870 (BT 5/75). Res. 1 Feb. 1870 on app. as Assistant Under Secretary, Colonial Office (BT 5/78; *Colonial Office List* (1871), 9).

Herbert, Hon. Robert Sawyer *Commissioner* 27 June 1737–6 Jan. 1752.

Herbert of Chirbury, Henry (Herbert) 1st Lord *Commissioner* 25 April 1707–22 Jan. 1709. D. 22 Jan. 1709.

Heron, Henry *Clerk* 14 Jan. 1756–c. 28 March 1760 (*JCTP 1754–8*, 197). D. by 28 March 1760 (*JCTP 1759–63*, 101).

Heron Maxwell, Robert Charles *Junior Clerk* 2 March 1867 (BT 5/75).

Herries, John Charles *President* 2 Feb.–22 Nov. 1830 (PC 2/211A pp. 4, 305).

Hickman, Sir William, 2nd Bart. *Commissioner* 7 Dec. 1672–21 Dec. 1674.

Hill, Abraham *Commissioner* 15 May 1696–8 Jan. 1702.

Hill, Frederick *Porter* April 1865 (BT 20/1 no. 40).

Hill, Joseph *Messenger* 3 Oct. 1826–c. 2 Dec. 1831 (BT 5/35 p. 276). D. by 2 Dec. 1831 (BT 5/40 p. 361).

Hill, Thomas *Clerk* 30 March 1736–c. 14 June 1738 (*JCTP 1735–41*, 98). D. by 14 June 1738 (ibid. 243).

Hill, Thomas *Secretary* 19 Oct. 1737–20 Sept. 1758 (*JCTP 1735–41*, 215; *JCTP 1750–3*, 430–1). D. 20 Sept. 1758 (*Gent. Mag.* (1758), xxviii, 452).

Hillman, Frederick G. *Junior Supplementary Clerk* 1854–30 April 1857 (BT 5/67, 10 Feb. 1859). *Senior Supplementary Clerk* 30 April 1857 (BT 5/65).

Hillsborough, Wills (Hill) 1st Earl of *First Lord* 17 Sept. 1763–12 Aug. 1765; 18 Aug.–18 Dec. 1766.

Hobart, Frederick John *Junior Clerk* 13 July 1842–1 Aug. 1845 (BT 5/50). Res. 1 Aug. 1845 on app. as Junior Clerk, Board of Control (BT 5/54; *Royal Kal.* (1846), 163).

Hobart, Sir John, 5th Bart. *Commissioner* 14 Oct. 1721–8 Aug. 1727.

Hobart, Vere Henry (*styled* Lord **Hobart** 1 Feb. 1849) *Junior Clerk* 16 March 1842–April 1853 (BT 5/50). *Senior Clerk* April 1853–30 April 1857 ([Cd. 1713] p. 157 HC (1854) xxvii, 189; BT 5/65, 30 April 1857). *First Class Clerk* 30 April 1857–30 July 1863 (BT 5/65). Res. 30 July 1863 (BT 3/64 no. 412).
   Private Secretary : to Secretary (Shaw Lefevre, Le Marchant, Booth) 16 March 1842–April 1853 (BT 5/50; BT 3/43 pp. 257–60); *to Vice President* (Stanley of Alderley) probably app. April 1853; occ. 1854 (*Royal Kal.* (1854), 160). Res. 28 Feb. 1855 (BT 5/63).

Holdernesse, Robert (Darcy) 3rd Earl of *First Lord* 31 Jan. 1718–11 May 1719.

Holford, Thomas *Clerk* app. between 20 Dec. 1714 and 2 Aug. 1715 (*JCTP 1709–15*, 575; *JCTP 1715–18*, 66). D. 4 Nov. 1721 (*JCTP 1718–22*, 327).

Holiday, George Frederick *Extra Messenger* 22 Oct. 1858–Jan. 1861 (BT 3/59 no. 66). *Messenger* Jan. 1861 (ibid.).

Holles, Hon. Denzil (cr. Lord **Holles** 20 April 1661) *Commissioner* (*Trade*) 7 Nov. 1660, 20 Oct. 1668, 16 April 1669.
   Commissioner (*Plantations*) 1 Dec. 1660.
   Member 12 March 1675 (PC 2/64 p. 395), 27 June 1679 (PC 2/68 p. 6).

Hornby, Philip Henry *Junior Clerk* 11 Jan. 1847–30 April 1857 (BT 5/56). *Third Class Clerk* 30 April 1857–14 Nov. 1862 (BT 5/65). *Second Class Clerk* 14 Nov. 1862–July 1863 (BT 5/70). *Senior Clerk* July 1863–1 April 1870 (BT 3/64 no. 379; *Royal Kal.* (1864), 164). Ret. 1 April 1870 (BT 20/2 no. 750).
   Private Secretary to Secretary (Booth) occ. 1859 (BT 6/293 p. 164).

Hoskins, William *Clerk* 20 Dec. 1714–11 April 1727 (*JCTP 1709–15*, 575). Dis. 11 April 1727 (*JCTP 1723–8*, 323).

How, Robert *Messenger* 3 July 1696–c. 4 Nov. 1701 (CO 391/9 p. 10). D. by 4 Nov. 1701 (CO 391/12 p. 194).

Howe, Alexander *Commissioner* (*Plantations*) 1 Dec. 1660.

Howe, Edward *Messenger* 1 Dec. 1814–24 July 1826 (BT 5/23 p. 472). *Office Keeper* 24 July 1826–24 May 1843 (BT 5/35 p. 35). D. 24 May 1843 (BT 3/53 no. 345).

Howe, Richard (Howe) 1st Viscount *Member* 8 March 1784 (PC 2/129 p. 60).

Howells, James *Extra Messenger* May–c. 16 Oct. 1865 (BT 20/1 no. 71). D. by 16 Oct. 1865 (ibid. no. 146).

Hudson, Israel *Clerk* first occ. 1710 (Chamberlayne, *Present State* (1710), 660). D. by 19 Jan. 1748 (*JCTP 1742–9*, 268–9).

Hughes, William *Clerk* 7 Oct. 1779–2 May 1782 (*JCTP 1776–82*, 275–6, 365). Office abolished 2 May 1782 (ibid. 472; T 1/579 Schedule 3).

Hume, James Deacon *Secretary* 17 July 1829–4 Jan. 1840 (BT 5/38 p. 269). Ret. 4 Jan. 1840 (BT 5/48, 28 Feb. 1840).

Hurt, John *Porter* 7 March 1810–5 Jan. 1816 (BT 5/19 p. 426; *Royal Kal.* (1816), 145). *Messenger* probably app. 5 Jan. 1816 when replaced as Porter by Scott (BT 5/52, 21 May 1844). D. by 9 Dec. 1816 (BT 5/25 p. 200).

Huskisson, William *Member* 16 Dec. 1814 (PC 2/196 p. 265).
    President 21 Feb. 1823–3 Sept. 1827 (PC 2/205 p. 34).

Hutcheson, Archibald *Commissioner* 13 Dec. 1714–5 Jan. 1716.

Hutchinson, Charles Scrope *Inspector of Railways* 28 Feb. 1867 (BT 5/75).

Hutchinson, John *Office Keeper* 15 April 1735–c. 7 Oct. 1740 (*JCTP 1735–41*, 13–14). D. by 7 Oct. 1740 (ibid. 347).

Hutt, William *Vice President* 22 Feb. 1860–29 Nov. 1865 (PC 2/251 p. 152).

Hyde, Edward (Hyde) 1st Lord *Commissioner (Trade)* 7 Nov. 1660.
    Commissioner (Plantations) 1 December 1660.

Hyde, Henry *Commissioner (Trade)* 7 Nov. 1660.

Hyde, Hon. Lawrence *Member* 26 Nov. 1679 (PC 2/68 p. 6).

Hyde, Thomas *Messenger* 5 Dec. 1786–8 Oct. 1789 (BT 5/4 p. 105). *Office Keeper* 8 Oct. 1789–c. 3 Dec. 1795 (BT 5/5 p. 375). D. by 3 Dec. 1795 (BT 5/10 p. 144).

Ingram, Arthur *Commissioner (Trade)* 7 Nov. 1660.

Ingram, Sir Thomas, kt. *Commissioner (Trade)* 7 Nov. 1660.

Irving, Thomas *Junior Clerk (Statistical Department)* 11 Nov. 1834–5 Jan. 1842 (BT 5/42 p. 267). *Senior Clerk (Statistical Department)* 5 Jan. 1842–Jan. 1851 (BT 5/50). *Senior Clerk* Jan. 1851–April 1853 (BT 3/41 pp. 89–93). *Old Senior Clerk* April 1853–July 1863 ([Cd. 1713] pp. 142, 157 HC (1854) xxvii, 174, 189; BT 5/65, 30 April 1857). *Senior Clerk* July 1863–24 April 1865 (BT 3/64 no. 379; *Royal Kal.* (1864), 164). Res. 24 April 1865 (BT 20/1 no. 48).

Jackson, Richard *Counsel* 14 April 1770–2 May 1782 (C 66/3725; *JCTP 1768–75*, 185). Office abolished 2 May 1782 (*JCTP 1776–82*, 472).

Jackson, Robert *Junior Supplementary Clerk* Aug. 1856–July 1863 (BT 3/50 no. 633). *Junior Clerk* July 1863–2 Jan. 1867 (BT 3/64 no. 379; *Royal Kal.* (1864), 164). *Bookkeeper* 2 Jan. 1867 (BT 5/75).

Jacob, William *Receiver of Corn Returns* 17 July 1822–July 1827 (BT 5/30 pp. 348–50). *Comptroller of Corn Returns* July 1827–18 Dec. 1841 (7 & 8 Geo. IV, c 58, s 3; *Royal Kal.* (1828), 135). Ret. 18 Dec. 1841 (BT 5/49).

Jadis, Henry Fenton *Clerk (Corn Department)* 24 July 1821–12 July 1827 (BT 5/29 pp. 381–4). Dis. 12 July 1827 (BT 5/36 p. 204); reapp. 5 Jan. 1842 (BT 5/50). *Deputy Comptroller of Corn Returns* 11 May 1843–1851 (BT 5/51; *Royal Kal.*

(1851), 160). *Comptroller of Corn Returns* 1851–Jan. 1865 (*London Gazette* nos. 21187, 21189). Ret. Jan. 1865 (BT 20/1 nos. 2, 25).

Jamieson, Robert   *Junior Supplementary Clerk* 30 April 1857–25 March 1862 (BT 5/65). Res. 25 March 1862 (BT 3/61 no. 220).

Jeffreys, John   *Commissioner* (*Plantations*) 1 Dec. 1660.

Jenkins, Sir Leoline, kt.   *Member* 14 Feb. 1680 (PC 2/68 p. 6).

Jenkinson, Charles (cr. Lord **Hawkesbury** 21 Aug. 1786; Earl of **Liverpool** 1 June 1796)   *Member* 5 March 1784 (PC 2/129 p. 56). *President* 23 Aug. 1786– 6 June 1804 (PC 2/131 pp. 403–4).

Jennings, Frederick Thomas   *Junior Supplementary Clerk* Nov. 1855–30 April 1857 (BT 3/49 no. 644; Ind. 20458 no. 1993). *Third Class Clerk* 30 April 1857– July 1863 (BT 5/65). *Junior Clerk* July 1863–11 Oct. 1865 (BT 3/64 no. 379; *Royal Kal.* (1864), 164). *Senior Clerk* 11 Oct. 1865 (BT 5/73).

Jenyns, Soame   *Commissioner* 29 Dec. 1755–16 Sept. 1780.

Johnson, William   *Extra Messenger* July 1858–May 1859 (BT 3/57 no. 452). *Porter* May 1859–12 April 1865 (ibid.). Left office 12 April 1865 on app. as Office Keeper, Office of Registrar of Designs (BT 20/1 no. 41).

Jolliffe, William   *Commissioner* (*Trade*) 7 Nov. 1660.

Jolliffe, William   *Commissioner* 10 Feb. 1772–14 July 1779.

Jones, Daniel   *Junior Supplementary Clerk* 29 Jan. 1855–30 April 1857 (BT 5/63). *Senior Supplementary Clerk* 30 April 1857–July 1863 (BT 5/65). *Junior Clerk* July 1863–4 May 1865 (BT 3/64 no. 379; *Royal Kal.* (1864), 164). D. 4 May 1865 (death certificate).

Jones *see also* **Bence Jones**

Joy, William   *Messenger* 14 July 1840–2 Aug. 1843 (BT 5/48). *Assistant Office Keeper* 2 Aug. 1843–12 May 1865 (BT 5/51). Ret. 12 May 1865 (BT 20/1 no. 55).

Joyce, George   *Deputy Receiver of Corn Returns* 24 July 1821–July 1827 (BT 5/29 pp. 381–4). *Deputy Comptroller of Corn Returns* July 1827–5 Jan. 1842 (7 & 8 Geo. IV, c 58, s 3; *Royal Kal.* (1828), 135). *Comptroller of Corn Returns* 5 Jan. 1842–1851 (BT 5/50). Left office 1851 (*London Gazette* nos. 21187, 21189).

Joyce, George   *Clerk* (*Corn Department*) 31 Jan. 1834–April 1853 (BT 5/41 pp. 543–5). *Junior Clerk* April 1853–30 April 1857 ([Cd. 1713] pp. 131, 157 HC (1854) xxvii, 163, 189; *Royal Kal.* (1854), 160). *Third Class Clerk* 30 April 1857– July 1863 (BT 5/65). *Junior Clerk* July 1863–Jan. 1865 (BT 3/64 no. 379: *Royal Kal.* (1864), 164). Ret. Jan. 1865 (BT 20/1 nos. 2, 24).

Keene, Benjamin   *Commissioner* 5 May 1741–5 Jan. 1745.

Keene, Whitshed   *Commissioner* 26 Jan. 1774–17 June 1777.

Kendall, Thomas   *Commissioner* (*Trade*) 7 Nov. 1660.
    Commissioner (*Plantations*) 1 Dec. 1660.

Kenyon, Sir Lloyd, 1st Bart.   *Member* 23 Aug. 1786 (PC 2/131 pp. 403–4).

King, Richard   *Commissioner* (*Trade*) 7 Nov. 1660.

King, Thomas   *Messenger* 25 Aug. 1786–c. 6 Jan. 1794 (BT 5/4 p. 15). D. by 6 Jan. 1794 (BT 5/9 p. 131).

Kingscote, A.   *Private Secretary to Vice President* (Cowper) probably app. Aug. 1859; occ. 1860 (*Royal Kal.* (1860), 165).

Labouchere, Henry   *Vice President* 6 May 1835–29 Aug. 1839 (PC 2/216 p. 379). *President* 29 Aug. 1839–3 Sept. 1841 (PC 2/221 p. 440); 22 July 1847–27 Feb. 1852 (PC 2/230 p. 463).

President of Railway Commission 10 April 1848–10 Oct. 1851 (*London Gazette* no. 20845). Office abolished 10 Oct. 1851 (14 & 15 Vict., c 64, s 1).

Lack, Edward John   *Clerk* 4 April 1816–25 March 1822 (BT 5/24 p. 428). *Junior Clerk* 25 March 1822–3 June 1834 (BT 5/30 pp. 182–4). *Senior Clerk* 3 June 1834–5 Jan. 1842 (BT 5/42 p. 108). *Deputy Comptroller of Corn Returns* 5 Jan. 1842–11 May 1843 (BT 5/50). Res. 11 May 1843 (BT 5/51). *Clerk (Corn Department)* 10 Aug. 1843–5 Jan. 1848 (ibid.). Removed from office 5 Jan. 1848 (BT 5/57· BT 3/45 pp. 37–9).

Private Secretary: to President (Auckland) probably app. Nov. 1830; occ. from 1831 to 1834 (*Royal Kal.* (1831), 136; ibid. (1834), 136); to *Vice President* (Labouchere, Sheil, Maule) 6 May 1835–Sept. 1841 (BT 5/43 p. 55; BT 5/44 p. 203; BT 5/45 p. 115; BT 5/47, 26 March 1839; BT 5/48, 26 Dec. 1840).

Lack, Frederick   *Clerk (Corn Department)* 26 Jan. 1825–5 Jan. 1842 (BT 5/33 p. 300). *Senior Clerk* 5 Jan. 1842–April 1853 (BT 5/50). *Old Senior Clerk* April 1853–30 July 1863 ([Cd. 1713] pp. 142, 157 HC (1854) xxvii, 174, 189; BT 5/65, 30 April 1857). Res. 30 July 1863 (BT 3/64 no. 413).

Private Secretary to Secretary (MacGregor, Porter) 16 March 1842–c. 1848 (BT 5/50). Last occ. 1848 (*Royal Kal.* (1848), 162).

Lack, Henry Reader   *Copyist* 1853–4 (BT 5/67, 10 Feb. 1859; *Royal Kal.* (1854), 160). *Senior Supplementary Clerk* 1854–29 Jan. 1855 (BT 3/47 pp. 270–2; *Royal Kal.* (1855), 159). *Junior Clerk* 29 Jan. 1855–30 April 1857 (BT 5/63). *Second Class Clerk* 30 April 1857–July 1863 (BT 5/65). *Senior Clerk* July 1863 (BT 3/64 no. 379; *Royal Kal.* (1864), 164).

Lack, Richard William   *Junior Clerk* 22 Nov. 1827–5 Jan. 1842 (BT 5/36 pp. 446–7). *Senior Clerk* 5 Jan. 1842–April 1853 (BT 5/50). *Old Senior Clerk* April 1853–July 1863 ([Cd. 1713] pp. 142, 157 HC (1854) xxvii, 174, 189; BT 5/65, 30 April 1857). *Senior Clerk* July 1863–2 Jan. 1867 (BT 3/64 no. 379; *Royal Kal.* (1864), 164). Ret. 2 Jan. 1867 (HC 47 p. 16 (1867) xxxix, 228; BT 5/75).

Lack, Thomas   *Clerk* 25 Aug. 1786–25 March 1822 (BT 5/4 p. 15). Left office 25 March 1822 (BT 5/30 pp. 182–4).

Secretary 25 Aug. 1810–14 Jan. 1836 (BT 5/20 pp. 95–6). Ret. 14 Jan. 1836 (BT 5/43 pp. 248–9).

Laffan, Robert Michael   *Inspector of Railways* 24 Aug. 1847–6 Nov. 1852 (MT 13/7 pp. 557, 561–3). Res. 6 Nov. 1852 on election as M.P. (BT 5/60; BT 3/43 pp. 225–7).

Laing, Samuel   *Private Secretary to President* (Labouchere) 8 Oct. 1839–Sept. 1841 (BT 5/47).

Law and Corresponding Clerk (Railway Department) 11 Aug. 1840–6 Aug. 1844 (BT 5/49, 18 Oct. 1841). *Secretary (Railway Department)* 6 Aug. 1844–22 July 1845 (BT 5/52). Res. 22 July 1845 (BT 5/54).

Lamb, Matthew (cr. Bart. 17 Jan. 1755)   *Counsel* 12 Nov. 1746–5 Nov. 1768 (C 66/3620, 3674; *JCTP 1742–9*, 214–15). D. 5 Nov. 1768.

Lambert, Charles   *Clerk (Railway Department)* 5 Oct. 1844–18 Feb. 1848 (BT 5/52). *Senior Clerk (Railway Department)* 18 Feb. 1848–April 1853 (MT 13/9 p. 161). *Old Senior Clerk* April 1853–30 April 1857 ([Cd. 1713] pp. 142, 157 HC (1854) xxvii, 174, 189; BT 5/65, 30 April 1857). *Second Class Clerk* 30 April 1857–30 July 1863 (BT 5/65). Ret. 30 July 1863 (BT 3/64 no. 414).

Langlois, Benjamin   *Commissioner* 16 Sept. 1780–2 Jan. 1782.

Lanham, Richard   *Clerk* 18 April 1727–c. 30 March 1736 (*JCTP 1732–8*, 323–4). D. by 30 March 1736 (*JCTP 1735–41*, 98).

Larkins, Walter F.   *Junior Clerk* 5 Jan. 1842–4 July 1849 (BT 5/50). *Senior Clerk* 4 July 1849–30 April 1857 (BT 5/58; [Cd. 1713] p. 157 HC (1854) xxvii, 189). *First Class Clerk* 30 April 1857–July 1863 (BT 5/65). *Assistant* July 1863–1 April 1870 (BT 3/64 no. 379; *Royal Kal.* (1864), 164). Ret. 1 April 1870 (BT 20/2 no. 750).
    Private Secretary to Vice President (Colchester) probably app. Feb. 1852; occ. 1853 (*Royal Kal.* (1853), 160).

Latimer, Viscount *see* **Osborne,** Sir Thomas

Lauderdale, John (Maitland) 2nd Earl of (cr. Duke of **Lauderdale** 26 May 1672)   *Commissioner* (*Trade*) 20 Oct. 1668, 16 April 1669.
    Commissioner (*Plantations*) 4 April 1671. *Commissioner* 27 Sept. 1672.
    Member 12 March 1675 (PC 2/64 p. 395), 22 April 1679 (PC 2/68 p. 6).

Laws, Robert   *Junior Supplementary Clerk* 1854–23 March 1859 (BT 5/67, 10 Feb. 1859; *Royal Kal.* (1855), 159). *Senior Supplementary Clerk* 23 March 1859 (BT 5/67).

Leaker, William Wilder   *Junior Supplementary Clerk* 29 Jan. 1855–30 April 1857 (BT 5/63). *Senior Supplementary Clerk* 30 April 1857–29 Feb. 1864 (BT 5/65). *Junior Clerk* 29 Feb. 1864 (BT 5/72).

Lee, Nicholas   *Junior Supplementary Clerk* 29 Jan. 1855–30 April 1857 (BT 5/63). *Senior Supplementary Clerk* 30 April 1857–July 1863 (BT 5/65). *Junior Clerk* July 1863–7 May 1868 (BT 3/64 no. 379; *Royal Kal.* (1864), 164). *Senior Clerk* 7 May 1868 (BT 5/76).

Leere, Sir Peter, kt.   *Commissioner* (*Plantations*) 1 Dec. 1660.

Leeves, Edward   *Junior Clerk* 3 July 1823–13 Nov. 1830 (BT 5/31 pp. 337–8). Res. 13 Nov. 1830 (BT 5/39 p. 500).
    Private Secretary to President (Huskisson) 3 July 1823–Sept. 1827 (BT 5/31 pp. 337–8).

Lefevre *see* **Shaw Lefevre**

Le Marchant, Denis (cr. Bart. 14 Oct. 1841)   *Secretary* 8 Feb. 1836–19 June 1841 (BT 5/43 p. 284). Left office 19 June 1841 on app. as Secretary, Treasury (T 29/438 p. 381); reapp. 15 May 1848 (BT 5/57). Left office 10 Oct. 1850 on app. as Clerk, House of Commons (BT 5/59; *London Gazette* no. 21140).

Leveson Gower, Hon. Baptist   *Commissioner* 24 May 1745–23 June 1749.

Lewis, John   *Commissioner* (*Trade*) 7 Nov. 1660.
    Commissioner (*Plantations*) 1 Dec. 1660.

Lewis, John   *Clerk* 4 July 1764–29 June 1769 (*JCTP 1764–7*, 91). Dis. 29 June 1769 (*JCTP 1768–75*, 101).

Lewis, Thomas Frankland   *Vice President* 5 Feb.–30 May 1828 (PC 2/209 p. 73).

Lexington, Robert (Sutton) 2nd Lord   *Commissioner* 9 June 1699–19 June 1702.

Lidcot, Giles   *Commissioner* (*Trade*) 7 Nov. 1660.

Limbrey, John   *Commissioner* (*Plantations*) 1 Dec. 1660.

Lincoln, Theophilus (Clinton) 4th Earl of   *Commissioner* (*Plantations*) 1 Dec. 1660.

Lisburne, Wilmot (Vaughan) 4th Viscount   *Commissioner* 30 Dec. 1768–25 April 1770.

Littleton, Sir Thomas, 2nd Bart.   *Commissioner* (*Trade*) 20 Oct. 1668, 16 April 1669.

Liverpool, Earl of *see* **Jenkinson,** Charles

Lloyd, Frederick *Extra Messenger* June 1866 (*Staff Lists,* 392).

Lloyd, William *Clerk* 24 Jan. 1770–2 May 1782 (*JCTP 1768–75,* 164). Office abolished 2 May 1782 (*JCTP 1776–82,* 472; T 1/579 Schedule 3).

Locke, John *Secretary* 14 Oct. 1673–21 Dec. 1674 (*CSPD 1673,* 578). Remained in office until abolition of Council 21 Dec. 1674 (Journal (Trade and Plantations) 1672–4, 105).
    Commissioner 15 May 1696–11 July 1700.

Loggan, Justinian *Clerk* 4 Nov. 1701–22 March 1717 (CO 389/36 pp. 136–8). Res. 22 March 1717 on app. to commission in Guards (*JCTP 1715–18,* 219–20).

London, Beilby (Porteus) Bishop of *Member* 25 Jan. 1788 (PC 2/133 p. 25).

London, Henry (Compton) Bishop of *Member* 22 April 1679 (PC 2/68 p. 6), 16 Feb. 1689 (PC 2/73 p. 8).

London, Humphrey (Henchman) Bishop of *Member* 20 Oct. 1676 (PC 2/65 p. 357).

London, John (Randolph) Bishop of *Member* 11 Oct. 1809 (PC 2/183 p. 327).

London, Robert (Lowth) Bishop of *Member* 5 March 1784 (PC 2/129 p. 56), 23 Aug. 1786 (PC 2/131 pp. 403–4).

London, William (Howley) Bishop of *Member* 30 Nov. 1813 (PC 2/195 p. 208).

Long, Charles *Member* 17 Feb. 1802 (PC 2/160 p. 220).

Long, Sir Robert, 1st Bart. *Commissioner* 27 Sept. 1672.

Lousada *see* de Lousada

Lovaine, Algernon George (Percy) *styled* Lord *Vice President* 3 March–18 June 1859 (PC 2/249 p. 169).

Love, William *Commissioner* (*Trade*) 20 Oct. 1668, 16 April 1669.

Lowe, Robert *Vice President* 13 Aug. 1855–6 April 1858 (PC 2/242 p. 120).

Lowrie, William *Senior Clerk* July 1863–28 Aug. 1865 (BT 3/62 no. 676; BT 3/64 no. 379; *Royal Kal.* (1864), 164). D. 28 Aug. 1865 (death certificate).

Lowther, William (Lowther) *styled* Viscount *Vice President* 20 Dec. 1834–6 May 1835 (PC 2/215 p. 886).

Lumley, Richard (Lumley) 2nd Viscount *Member* 26 Feb. 1689 (PC 2/73 p. 8).

Lyons, Wilson Dobie Wilson *Junior Supplementary Clerk* Jan. 1861–Nov. 1863 (BT 3/59 no. 18). *Junior Clerk* Nov. 1863 (BT 3/64 no. 624).

McCullagh, William Torrens *Private Secretary to President* (Labouchere) 6 Aug. 1847–17 March 1848 (BT 5/56). Res. 17 March 1848 (BT 5/57, 20 March 1848).

Macdonald, Kenneth *Messenger* May 1858–1867 (*Staff Lists,* 392; *Royal Kal.* (1867), 166). *Assistant Office Keeper* probably app. 1867; first occ. 1868 (*Royal Kal.* (1868), 167).

MacGregor, Duncan *Registrar* (*Railway Department*) 13 July 1842–April 1853 (BT 5/50; BT 5/51, 7 Jan. 1843; *Royal Kal.* (1844), 163). *Senior Clerk* April 1853–30 April 1857 ([Cd. 1713] p. 157 HC (1854) xxvii, 189). *First Class Clerk* 30 April 1857–July 1863 (BT 5/65). *Assistant* July 1863 (BT 3/64 no. 379; *Royal Kal.* (1864), 164).

MacGregor, John *Secretary* 24 Jan. 1840–6 Aug. 1847 (BT 5/48). Left office 6 Aug. 1847 on election as M.P. (BT 5/56; *London Gazette* no. 20762).

McKenzie, Finlay *Clerk* (*Railway Department*) 5 Jan. 1842–18 Feb. 1848 (BT 5/50). *Senior Clerk* (*Railway Department*) 18 Feb. 1848–April 1853 (MT 13/9 p. 161). *Old Senior Clerk* April 1853–30 April 1857 ([Cd. 1713] pp. 142, 157 HC (1854) xxvii, 174, 189; BT 5/65, 30 April 1857). *Second Class Clerk* 30 April 1857–14 Nov. 1862 (BT 5/65). *First Class Clerk* 14 Nov. 1862–July 1863 (BT 5/70). *Draftsman* July 1863 (BT 3/64 no. 379).

Mackett, Thomas *Messenger* 15 June 1803–c. 1 Jan. 1815 (BT 5/14 p. 81; *Royal Kal.* (1815), 145–6). Res. by 1 Jan. 1815 (BT 5/24 p. 9).

Madox, Philip *Clerk* pd. 11 July 1676 for period from 25 Dec. 1674 to 26 March 1676 (BM Add. MS 9767 p. 14); no further occ.

Maguire, James *Messenger* 4 Dec. 1838–c. 1854 (BT 5/46 p. 117). Last occ. 1854 (*Royal Kal.* (1854), 160).

Malan, Henry Noel de Merindol *Junior Clerk* 25 Nov. 1868 (BT 5/76).

Malcolm, William Rolle *Assistant Secretary (Railways)* 1 Feb. 1870 (BT 5/78).

Mallet, Louis (ktd. 9 Dec. 1868) *Junior Clerk (Statistical Department)* 8 Nov. 1847–24 Feb. 1848 (BT 5/56). *Junior Clerk* 24 Feb. 1848–April 1853 (BT 5/57). *Senior Clerk* April 1853–30 April 1857 ([Cd. 1713] p. 157 HC (1854) xxvii, 189; BT 5/65, 30 April 1857). *First Class Clerk* 30 April 1857–July 1863 (BT 5/65). *Assistant* July 1863–2 Jan. 1867 (BT 3/64 no. 379). *Assistant Secretary (Commercial)* 2 Jan. 1867 (BT 5/75).

　Private Secretary : to President (Labouchere) 20 March–10 May 1848 (BT 5/57); probably reapp. 1851; occ. 1852 (*Royal Kal.* (1852), 160); *to Vice President* (Stanley of Alderley) 28 Feb.–March 1855 (BT 5/63); *to President* (Stanley of Alderley) probably app. March 1855; occ. from 1856 to 1858 (*Royal Kal.* (1856), 161; ibid. (1858), 161).

Mallett, William *Messenger* 2 July 1850–1858 (BT 5/59; *Royal Kal.* (1858), 161). *Office Keeper* probably app. 1858; occ. from 1859 to 1867 (*Royal Kal.* (1859), 165; ibid. (1867), 166). D. by 28 March 1867 (BT 20/1 no. 363).

Manchester, Edward (Montagu) 2nd Earl of *Commissioner (Trade)* 7 Nov. 1660.
　Commissioner (Plantations) 1 Dec. 1660.

Manning, Edmund *Extra Messenger* 23 Feb. 1841–2 Aug. 1843 (BT 5/49). *Messenger* 2 Aug. 1843–30 April 1844 (BT 5/51). Suspended from office 30 April 1844 (BT 5/52).

Marchant *see* **Le Marchant**

Marlborough, James (Ley) 3rd Earl of *Commissioner (Trade)* 7 Nov. 1660.
　Commissioner (Plantations) 1 Dec. 1660.

Martyn, John Waddon *Junior Clerk* 6 Feb. 1867 (BT 5/75).

Matthias, Gabriel *Clerk* 5 June 1735–23 May 1749 (*JCTP 1735–41*, 19). Res. 23 May 1749 (*JCTP 1742–9*, 415).

Maude, Ashley Henry *Junior Clerk* 2 Sept. 1868 (BT 5/76).

Maule, Hon. Fox *Vice President* 28 June–3 Sept. 1841 (PC 2/223 p. 313).

Maxwell *see* **Heron Maxwell**

Mayo, John Joseph *Junior Clerk* 22 April 1854–10 Nov. 1855 (Ind. 20457 no. 787). *Deputy Accountant* 10 Nov. 1855–30 April 1857 (BT 5/63). *First Class Clerk* 30 April 1857–3 Nov. 1862 (BT 5/65). Left office 3 Nov. 1862 on app. as Registrar of Seamen (BT 5/70).

Meadows, Sir Philip, kt. *Commissioner* 15 May 1696–13 Dec. 1714.

Methuen, John *Commissioner* 15 May 1696–6 July 1697.

Michelsen, Edward Henry *Senior Supplementary Clerk* June 1854–1 April 1870 (BT 3/47 pp. 271–2). Ret. 1 April 1870 (BT 20/2 no. 750).

Middleton, Thomas *Commissioner (Plantations)* 1 Dec. 1660.

Mills, John *Messenger* 25 Aug. 1786–15 June 1803 (BT 5/4 p. 15). Left office 15 June 1803 on app. as Messenger to Secretaries of State (BT 5/14 p. 81).

Milne, Alexander *Supernumerary Clerk* 26 July 1802–14 March 1809 (BT 5/13 pp. 146–7). Res. 14 March 1809 (BT 5/18 p. 471).

Milner Gibson, Thomas *Vice President* 8 July 1846–8 May 1848 (PC 2/229 p. 1). *President* 6 July 1859–6 July 1866 (PC 2/250 p. 2).

Minnes, Sir John, kt. *Commissioner (Plantations)* 1 Dec. 1660.

Miro, Samuel *Commissioner (Trade)* 7 Nov. 1660.

Mitchell, George *Messenger* 11 Jan. 1827–2 Aug. 1843 (BT 5/35 p. 387). *Office Keeper* 2 Aug. 1843–30 June 1858 (BT 5/51). Res. 30 June 1858 (BT 3/53 no. 345).

Mitchell, Thomas *Messenger* 9 Dec. 1816–10 Jan. 1827 (BT 5/25 p. 200). Ret. 10 Jan. 1827 (BT 5/35 p. 380).

Mitchell, Thomas *Porter (Railway Department)* probably app. Dec. 1846 (MT 13/6 p. 53); occ. from 8 July 1847 to 1853 (MT 13/7 pp. 404–5; *Royal Kal.* (1853), 160). *Messenger* April 1853 ([Cd. 1713] pp. 147, 157 HC (1854) xxvii, 179, 189; *Royal Kal.* (1854), 160).

Molesworth, John *(styled* Hon. 16 July 1716*) Commissioner* 5 Jan. 1716–24 June 1720.

Molesworth, Robert *Commissioner* 13 Dec. 1714–5 Jan. 1716.

Monckton, Robert *Commissioner* 25 April 1707–13 Dec. 1714.

Monkhouse, William Cosmo *Junior Supplementary Clerk* Oct. 1857–Nov. 1863 (BT 3/52 nos. 626, 640; Ind. 20461 no. 1622). *Junior Clerk* Nov. 1863–7 May 1868 (BT 3/64 no. 624). *Senior Clerk* 7 May 1868 (BT 5/76).

Monsell, William *Vice President* 12 March–10 July 1866 (PC 2/263 p. 241).

Monson, John (Monson) 1st Lord *First Lord* 27 June 1737–18 July 1748. D. 18 July 1748.

Montrose, Duke of *see* **Graham**, Marquess of

Moore, Arthur *Commissioner* 4 Oct. 1710–13 Dec. 1714.

Moorhead, William Hipkin *Junior Supplementary Clerk* June 1857–Nov. 1863 (BT 3/51 nos. 285, 361; Ind. 20461 no. 901). *Junior Clerk* probably app. Nov. 1863 (BT 3/64 nos. 379, 624; *Royal Kal.* (1864), 164). Res. 28 Dec. 1863 (BT 12/1 no. 16).

Mordaunt, Charles (Mordaunt) 2nd Viscount *Member* 16 Feb. 1689 (PC 2/73 p. 8).

Morland, Henry *Assistant Secretary (Railway Department)* 6 Nov. 1852–April 1853 (BT 5/60). *Assistant (Railways)* April 1853–8 Aug. 1855 ([Cd. 1713] pp. 134–5, 157 HC (1854) xxvii, 166–7, 189; *Royal Kal.* (1854), 160). Res. 8 Aug. 1855 (BT 3/49 no. 474).

Morrice, Sir William, kt. *Commissioner (Trade)* 7 Nov. 1660, 20 Oct. 1668, 16 April 1669.
    Commissioner (Plantations) 1 Dec. 1660.

Moulin *see* **du Moulin**

Mulgrave, Constantine John (Phipps) 2nd Lord *Member* 11 June 1784 (PC 2/129 p. 183).

Nailer, Robert *Junior Clerk* 13 Nov. 1830–4 July 1849 (BT 5/39 p. 500). *Senior Clerk* 4 July 1849–April 1853 (BT 5/58). *Old Senior Clerk* April 1853–21 Dec. 1854 ([Cd. 1713] pp. 142, 157 HC (1854) xxvii, 174, 189; BT 5/63, 29 Jan. 1855). Res. 21 Dec. 1854 (Ind. 20457 no. 2270).

Napier, Walter Edward *Junior Clerk* 17 Feb. 1868 (BT 5/76).

Nedham, William Thomas *Clerk (Corn Department)* probably app. 1822 (BT 5/30 pp. 60, 182–4); occ. 1824 (*Royal Kal.* (1824), 135). D. 9 Dec. 1824 (*Gent. Mag.* (1824), xc (2), 645).

Nelme, Lemuel Dole *Clerk* 29 Nov. 1764–2 May 1782 (*JCTP 1764–7*, 117). Office abolished 2 May 1782 (*JCTP 1776–82*, 472; T 1/579 Schedule 3).

Newport, Henry R. *Junior Clerk* 2 March 1867 (BT 5/75).

Nicholas, Sir Edward, kt. *Commissioner (Trade)* 7 Nov. 1660.
Commissioner (Plantations) 1 Dec. 1660.

Nicholl, Sir John, kt. *Member* 6 Feb. 1809 (PC 2/179 p. 426).

Nicholl, John *Member* 21 Jan. 1846 (PC 2/228 p. 4).

Noel, Martin *Commissioner (Trade)* 7 Nov. 1660.
Commissioner (Plantations) 1 Dec. 1660.

Northampton, Spencer (Compton) 3rd Earl of *Member* 22 Dec. 1677 (PC 2/66 p. 219).

Northcote, Stafford Henry (succ. as 8th Bart. 17 March 1851) *Private Secretary: to Vice President* (Gladstone) 1842–June 1843 (BT 5/50, 21 Dec. 1842); *to President* (Gladstone) probably app. June 1843; occ. from 1844 to 1845 (*Royal Kal.* (1844), 163; ibid. (1845), 162). *Legal Assistant* 22 March 1845–1850 (BT 5/53). Office abolished 1850 (BT 3/43 p. 258). *President* 6 July 1866–8 March 1867 (PC 2/264 p. 37).

Northey, William *Commissioner* 25 April–24 Dec. 1770. D. 24 Dec. 1770 (T 53/52 p. 160).

Norwich, George (Goring) 1st Earl of *Commissioner (Trade)* 7 Nov. 1660.

Nottingham, Daniel (Finch) 2nd Earl of *Member* 16 Feb. 1689 (PC 2/73 p. 8).

Noyes, Charles *Supernumerary Clerk* 14 March 1809–24 Sept. 1811 (BT 5/18 p. 471). *Clerk* 24 Sept. 1811–25 March 1822 (BT 5/20 pp. 521–2). *Junior Clerk* 25 March 1822–3 July 1823 (BT 5/30 pp. 182–4). *Senior Clerk* 3 July 1823–5 Jan. 1842 (BT 5/31 pp. 337–8). *Registrar* 5 Jan. 1842–April 1853 (BT 5/50). *Senior Clerk* April 1853–30 April 1857 ([Cd. 1713] p. 157 HC (1854) xxvii, 189). *First Class Clerk* 30 April 1857–23 March 1859 (BT 5/65). Ret. 23 March 1859 (BT 5/67).

Noyes, William *Messenger* 3 Dec. 1795–17 Oct. 1807 (BT 5/10 p. 144). *Office Keeper* 17 Oct. 1807–c. 24 July 1826 (BT 5/17 p. 447). D. by 24 July 1826 (BT 5/35 p. 160).

Nugent, Robert (cr. Viscount **Clare** 19 Jan. 1767) *First Lord* 18 Dec. 1766–12 July 1768.

O'Brien, Donatus *Secretary (Railway Department)* 6 Aug. 1844–Nov. 1846 (BT 5/52). Left office Nov. 1846 (MT 13/6 pp. 1–2, 5; MT 13/7 pp. 403–4).

O'Neill, Daniel *Commissioner (Trade)* 7 Nov. 1660.
Commissioner (Plantations) 1 Dec. 1660.

Orde, Thomas *Member* 23 Aug. 1786 (PC 2/131 pp. 403–4).

Ormond, James (Butler) 1st Duke of *Commissioner (Trade)* 20 Oct. 1668, 16 April 1669.
Commissioner (Plantations) 4 April 1671. *Commissioner* 27 Sept. 1672.
Member 12 March 1675 (PC 2/64 p. 395), 22 April 1679 (PC 2/68 p. 6).

Orwell, Francis (Vernon) 1st Lord *Commissioner* 5 Jan. 1763–12 Aug. 1765.

Osborne, Hon. George Godolphin (succ. as 2nd Lord **Godolphin** 15 Feb. 1850) *Assistant Secretary (Railway Department)* 9 July 1847–18 Feb. 1850 (MT 13/7 p. 408). Res. 18 Feb. 1850 (MT 13/12 p. 75).

Osborne, Sir Thomas, 2nd Bart. (cr. Viscount **Osborne** 2 Feb. 1673; Viscount **Latimer** 15 Aug. 1673; Earl of **Danby** 27 June 1674) *Commissioner (Trade)* 20 Oct. 1668, 16 April 1669. *Commissioner* 27 Sept. 1672.

Member 12 March 1675 (PC 2/64 p. 395), 16 Feb. 1689 (PC 2/73 p. 8).

Ossory, Thomas (Butler) *styled* Earl of *Commissioner (Trade)* 20 Oct. 1668, 16 April 1669.

Member 12 March 1675 (PC 2/64 p. 395).

Oswald, James *Commissioner* 6 Jan. 1752–14 Jan. 1760.

Oswald, William Drummond *Junior Clerk (Statistical Department)* 11 Nov. 1834–Aug. 1840 (BT 5/42 p. 267). *Clerk (Railway Department)* probably app. Aug. 1840 (BT 3/29 pp. 535–8); occ. from 1841 to 1842 (*Royal Kal.* (1841), 135; ibid. (1842), 135). *Registrar (Railway Department)* 5 Jan.–13 July 1842 (BT 5/50; BT 5/51, 7 Jan. 1843). *Assistant (Statistical Department)* 13 July 1842–1854 (BT 5/50; HC 172 p. 12 (1854), xl, 364; HC 140 p. 11 (1854–5) xxxi, 417; *Royal Kal.* (1854), 160). (?) *Deputy Accountant* position obscure; possibly app. 1854; occ. as 'Assistant Accountant' 1855 (*Royal Kal.* (1855), 159). *Old Senior Clerk* probably app. 1855; occ. as 'Senior Clerk' from 1856 to 1857 (ibid. (1856), 160; ibid. (1857), 160); described as 'Old Senior Clerk' 30 April 1857 (BT 5/65). D. 3 Oct. 1857 (*Gent. Mag.* (1857), cxli, 573).

Ough, George Neal *Junior Supplementary Clerk* May 1857–Nov. 1863 (BT 3/51 no. 285; Ind. 20461 no. 824). *Junior Clerk* Nov. 1863 (BT 3/64 no. 624).

Owen, Hugh *Junior Clerk (Railway Department)* 18 Feb. 1848–April 1853 (MT 13/9 p. 161). *Junior Clerk* April 1853–30 April 1857 ([Cd. 1713] p. 157 HC (1854) xxvii, 189; *Royal Kal.* (1854), 160). *Second Class Clerk* 30 April 1857–July 1863 (BT 5/65). *Deputy Accountant* July 1863–12 Oct. 1869 (BT 3/64 no. 379; *Royal Kal.* (1864), 164). *Senior Clerk* 8 Dec. 1869 (BT 5/77).

Owens, Edward *Clerk* 22 April 1765–c. 31 July 1766 (*JCTP 1764–7*, 168). D. by 31 July 1766 (ibid. 317).

Pace, Samuel *Messenger* July 1865 (BT 20/1 nos. 87, 99).

Page, John *Commissioner (Trade)* 20 Oct. 1668, 16 April 1669.

Pallett, George W. *Extra Messenger* April 1866–1867 (BT 20/1 no. 242; *Royal Kal.* (1867), 166). *Messenger* probably app. 1867; occ. from 1868 to 1869 (*Royal Kal.* (1868), 167; ibid. (1869), 167). D. c. 6 Feb. 1869 (Ind. 20474 no. 1028).

Palmer, John Sharpe *Clerk* 16 Feb. 1758–26 Dec. 1777 (*JCTP 1754–8*, 376). Ret. 26 Dec. 1777 (*JCTP 1776–82*, 125).

Acting Solicitor and Clerk of Reports 21 May 1776–26 Dec. 1777 (ibid. 28).

Palmerston, Henry (Temple) 2nd Viscount *Commissioner* 3 Jan.–22 Oct. 1766.

Papillon, Thomas *Commissioner (Trade)* 20 Oct. 1668, 16 April 1669.

Parker, John *Commissioner (Trade)* 7 Nov. 1660.

Parsley, James Whiting *Copyist* 1853–4 (BT 5/67, 10 Feb. 1859; *Royal Kal.* (1854), 160). *Junior Supplementary Clerk* 1854–29 Jan. 1855 (BT 3/47 pp. 270–2; *Royal Kal.* (1855), 159). *Senior Supplementary Clerk* 29 Jan. 1855–2 Jan. 1867 (BT 5/63). *Registrar* 2 Jan. 1867 (BT 5/75).

Parsons, W. J. *Extra Messenger* probably app. 1861; occ. from 1862 to 1864 (*Royal Kal.* (1862), 164; ibid. (1864), 165). *Messenger* probably app. 1864; first occ. 1865 (ibid. (1865), 164).

Paskin, Charles Seymour *Junior Supplementary Clerk* 1856–14 Nov. 1862 (BT 5/67, 10 Feb. 1859; BT 3/58 no. 800). *Third Class Clerk* 14 Nov. 1862–July 1863

(BT 5/70). *Junior Clerk* July 1863–5 June 1864 (BT 3/64 no. 379; *Royal Kal.* (1864), 164). D. 5 June 1864 (death certificate).

Pasley, Charles William *Inspector General of Railways* 5 Jan. 1842–Nov. 1846 (BT 5/50). Left office Nov. 1846 on app. of Railway Commission (MT 13/6 pp. 1–2, 19).

Pattrickson, William *Copyist* 1853–4 (BT 5/67, 10 Feb. 1859; *Royal Kal.* (1854), 160). *Junior Supplementary Clerk* 1854–29 Jan. 1855 (BT 3/47 pp. 270–2; *Royal Kal.* (1855), 159). *Senior Supplementary Clerk* 29 Jan. 1855–July 1863 (BT 5/63). *Junior Clerk* July 1863–2 Jan. 1867 (BT 3/64 no. 379; *Royal Kal.* (1864), 164). *Senior Clerk* 2 Jan. 1867 (BT 5/75).

Peacock, John *Clerk* 5 Dec. 1752–4 July 1764 (*JCTP 1750–3*, 370). Ret. 4 July 1764 (*JCTP 1764–7*, 89).

Pearson, Alexander Edwin *Junior Clerk* 12 May 1865 (BT 5/73).
   Private Secretary to Parliamentary Secretary (Shaw Lefevre) probably app. Dec. 1868; first occ. Oct. 1869 (*Staff Lists*, 25).

Pearson, Edwin James *Junior Clerk* Jan. 1865 (BT 20/1 no. 1).

Peel, Charles Lennox *Private Secretary to President* (Richmond) 13 March 1867–Dec. 1868 (BT 5/75).
   Corresponding Clerk (*Railway Department*) 27 Nov. 1868 (BT 5/76).

Pelham, Thomas *Commissioner* 13 July 1717–5 May 1741.

Pelham, Thomas *Commissioner* 5 May 1741–30 July 1743. D. 30 July 1743 (T 53/41 p. 435).

Pelham, Thomas *Commissioner* 6 April 1754–21 March 1761.

Pembroke, Philip (Herbert) 5th Earl of *Commissioner* (*Trade*) 7 Nov. 1660.

Penny, Richard *Supernumerary Clerk* 6 Aug. 1800–15 July 1801 (BT 5/12 p. 49). *Clerk* 15 July 1801–25 March 1822 (ibid. pp. 320–1). *Senior Clerk* 25 March 1822–18 Dec. 1841 (BT 5/30 pp. 182–4). Ret. 18 Dec. 1841 (BT 5/49).

Pettet, Charles *Junior Supplementary Clerk* 1854–30 April 1857 (BT 5/67, 10 Feb. 1859). *Senior Supplementary Clerk* 30 April 1857–29 Feb. 1864 (BT 5/65). *Junior Clerk* 29 Feb. 1864 (BT 5/72).

Phillips, Sir John, 6th Bart. *Commissioner* 5 Jan.–24 May 1745.

Pillet, Enesmont Jean Baptiste *Messenger* 29 Nov. 1792–29 March 1816 (BT 5/8 p. 326). Res. 29 March 1816 (BT 5/24 pp. 415–16).

Pitt, John *Commissioner* 5 Jan. 1745–29 Dec. 1755.

Pitt, Hon. William *Member* 13 Jan. 1786 (PC 2/131 p. 8).

Pleydell Bouverie, Hon. Edward *Vice President* 31 March–13 Aug. 1855 (PC 2/241 p. 322).

Plumer, Richard *Commissioner* 4 Sept. 1721–8 Aug. 1727; 22 May 1735–30 Dec. 1748.

Pocklington, Roger *Junior Clerk* 4 July 1849–30 April 1857 (BT 5/58). *Third Class Clerk* 30 April 1857–July 1863 (BT 5/65). *Senior Clerk* July 1863 (BT 3/64 no. 379; *Royal Kal.* (1864), 164).

Pole Carew, Reginald *Member* 1 May 1805 (PC 2/167 p. 360).

Pollexfen, John *Commissioner* 15 May 1696–25 April 1707.

Popple, Alured *Clerk* 22 March 1717–17 May 1722 (*JCTP 1715–18*, 219–20). *Secretary* 17 May 1722–19 Oct. 1737 (*JCTP 1718–22*, 359; *JCTP 1723–8*, 346). Res. 19 Oct. 1737 on app. as Governor, Bermuda (*JCTP 1735–41*, 215).

Popple, Henry *Clerk* 18 April–12 Aug. 1727 (*JCTP 1718–22*, 327). Res. 12 Aug. 1727 (ibid. 346).

Popple, William *Secretary* 25 June 1696–19 May 1707 (CO 391/9 p. 7; CO 391/15 pp. 103–4). Res. 19 May 1707 (*JCTP 1704–9*, 356).

Popple, William *Deputy Secretary* 1696–19 May 1707 (CO 389/36 pp. 136–8). *Secretary* 19 May 1707–15 May 1722 (*JCTP 1704–9*, 356; *JCTP 1709–15*, 575). D. 15 May 1722 (*Hist. Reg. Chron.* (1722), vii, 28).

Popple, William *Solicitor and Clerk of Reports* 3 June 1737–1 May 1745 (*JCTP 1735–41*, 189). Res. 1 May 1745 on app. as Governor, Bermuda (*JCTP 1742–9*, 163).

Porter, David *Mechanic* (*Standard Department*) 20 Aug. 1866 (BT 5/74).

Porter, George Richardson *Superintendent* (*Statistical Department*) 31 Jan. 1834–6 Aug. 1847 (BT 5/41 pp. 543–4). *Secretary* 6 Aug. 1847–3 Sept. 1852 (BT 5/56). D. 3 Sept. 1852 (*Gent. Mag.* (1852), cxxxi, 427).
  Superintendent (*Railway Department*) 11 Aug. 1840–6 Aug. 1844 (MT 13/1 pp. 1–2). *Senior Member of Railway Board* 6 Aug. 1844–10 July 1845 (BT 5/52, 6 and 11 Aug. 1844). Left office 10 July 1845 on abolition of Railway Board (BT 5/54; BT 5/55, 19 Nov. 1846).

Porter, John *Clerk* 25 Aug. 1786–25 March 1822 (BT 5/4 p. 15). *First Class Clerk* 25 March 1822–5 May 1829 (BT 5/30 pp. 182–4). Ret. 5 May 1829 (BT 5/38 pp. 143–4).

Portland, Jerome (Weston) 2nd Earl of *Commissioner* (*Trade*) 7 Nov. 1660.
  Commissioner (*Plantations*) 1 Dec. 1660.

Pottle, William *Clerk* app. by 13 Nov. 1672 (Journal (Trade and Plantations) 1672–4, 10); pd. to 25 Dec. 1673 (CO 389/5 p. 117).

Poulett Thomson, Charles *Vice President* 22 Nov. 1830–5 June 1834 (PC 2/211A p. 413). *President* 5 June–15 Dec. 1834 (PC 2/215 p. 208); 18 April 1835–29 Aug. 1839 (PC 2/216 p. 347).

Povey, John *Clerk* probably app. c. 1684 (BM Add. MS 38703 f. 43). *Assistant Secretary* 1 March 1692–15 May 1696 (PC 2/74 p. 340). Remained in office until app. of Council 15 May 1696 (*CTB*, xxi, 222).

Povey, Thomas *Commissioner* (*Trade*) 7 Nov. 1660.
  Commissioner (*Plantations*) 1 Dec. 1660.

Powell, John Joseph *Clerk* 24 Jan. 1770–2 May 1782 (*JCTP 1768–75*, 164). Office abolished 2 May 1782 (*JCTP 1776–82*, 472; T 1/579 Schedule 3).

Powle, Henry *Member* 22 April 1679 (PC 2/68 p. 6), 16 Feb. 1689 (PC 2/73 p. 8).

Pownall, George *Clerk* 21 Dec. 1772–11 April 1775 (*JCTP 1768–75*, 330). Res. 11 April 1775 (ibid. 421).

Pownall, John *Clerk* 24 June 1741–1 May 1745 (*JCTP 1735–41*, 390). *Solicitor and Clerk of Reports* 1 May 1745–6 June 1753 (*JCTP 1742–9*, 163). *Secretary* 6 June 1753–23 Jan. 1776 (*JCTP 1750–3*, 430–1; *JCTP 1754–8*, 416; *JCTP 1759–63*, 165). Res. 23 Jan. 1776 (*JCTP 1776–82*, 2).

Pownall, John Lillingston *Clerk* 24 Jan. 1770–21 Dec. 1772 (*JCTP 1768–75*, 164). Res. 21 Dec. 1772 (ibid. 330).

Price, Thomas Edward *Junior Clerk* 6 Feb. 1867 (BT 5/75).

Prior, Matthew *Commissioner* 11 July 1700–25 April 1707.

Pulteney, Daniel *Commissioner* 13 July 1717–14 Oct. 1721.

Pulteney, John *Commissioner* 25 April 1707–12 June 1711.

Pym, Charles *Commissioner* (*Plantations*) 1 Dec. 1660.

Pytts, Samuel *Commissioner* 15 Sept. 1713–13 Dec. 1714.

Quelch, Frederick *Porter* 22 June 1850–1854 (BT 5/59; *Royal Kal.* (1854), 160). *Messenger* probably app. 1854; first occ. 1855 (*Royal Kal.* (1855), 160).

Rawson, Rawson William *Clerk* (*Corn Department*) 26 Jan. 1829–31 Jan. 1834 (BT 5/38 p. 43). *Junior Clerk* (*Statistical Department*) 31 Jan. 1834–3 July 1838 (BT 5/41 pp. 543–4). *Senior Clerk* (*Statistical Department*) 3 July 1838–5 Jan. 1842 (BT 5/45 pp. 412–13). *Assistant* (*Statistical Department*) 5 Jan.–13 July 1842 (BT 5/50). Left office 13 July 1842 on app. as Civil Secretary to Governor of Canada (ibid.; *London Gazette* no. 20122).

 Private Secretary: to Vice President (Poulett Thomson) probably app. Nov. 1830 (BT 5/40 p. 131); occ. from 3 Feb. 1832 to 14 June 1833 (ibid. p. 430; BT 5/41 p. 328); to President (Baring) probably app. Dec. 1834; occ. 1835 (*Royal Kal.* (1835), 136); to Vice President (Gladstone) 4 Sept. 1841–13 July 1842 (BT 5/49).

Redesdale, John (Mitford) 1st Lord *Member* 30 March 1808 (PC 2/176 p. 240).

Reed, J. Murray *Junior Supplementary Clerk* April 1859–29 Feb. 1864 (BT 3/55 no. 159; Ind. 20463 no. 490). *Junior Clerk* 29 Feb. 1864 (BT 5/72).

Reeves, John *Law Clerk* 10 Aug. 1787–31 March 1823 (BT 5/4 pp. 319, 331–3). Res. 31 March 1823 (BT 5/31 pp. 227–9).

Riccard, Sir Andrew, kt. *Commissioner* (*Trade*) 7 Nov. 1660, 20 Oct. 1668, 16 April 1669.

 Commissioner (*Plantations*) 1 Dec. 1660.

Rice, George *Commissioner* 21 March 1761–25 April 1770.

Rich, Frederick Henry *Inspector of Railways* 1 April 1861 (BT 5/69).

Richards, John *Clerk* 20 March–21 Dec. 1674 (Journal (Trade and Plantations) 1672–4, 78). Remained in office until abolition of Council 21 Dec. 1674 (*CTB*, v, 308).

Richbell, Robert *Commissioner* (*Trade*) 7 Nov. 1660.

Richmond, Charles Henry (Gordon Lennox) 6th Duke of *President* 8 March 1867–9 Dec. 1868 (PC 2/265 p. 407).

Ridler, Thomas *Messenger* probably app. 1849; occ. from 1850 to 1857 (BT 5/59, 2 July 1850; *Royal Kal.* (1850), 161; ibid. (1857), 161).

Rigby, Richard *Commissioner* 29 Dec. 1755–14 Jan. 1760.

Ripon, Earl of *see* **Robinson**, Hon. Frederick John

Robartes, John (Robartes) 2nd Lord *Commissioner* (*Trade*) 7 Nov. 1660, 20 Oct. 1668, 16 April 1669.

 Commissioner (*Plantations*) 1 Dec. 1660.

 Member 27 June 1679 (PC 2/68 p. 6).

Roberts, John *Commissioner* 4 Dec. 1761–5 Jan. 1763; 12 Aug. 1765–13 July 1772. D. 13 July 1772 (T 53/52 p. 368).

Roberts, William *Clerk* 22 April 1765–4 Dec. 1781 (*JCTP 1764–7*, 168). *Deputy Secretary* 4 Dec. 1781–2 May 1782 (*JCTP 1776–82*, 442). Office abolished 2 May 1782 (ibid. 472; T 1/579 Schedule 3).

Robertson, Robert *Surveyor General of Steam Ships* 17 Aug. 1854 (BT 5/63, 1 May 1855).

Robinson, Hon. Frederick John (cr. Viscount **Goderich** 28 April 1827; Earl of **Ripon** 13 April 1833) *Member* 13 Aug. 1812 (PC 2/193 p. 391). *Vice President* 29 Sept. 1812–24 Jan. 1818 (ibid. p. 434). *President* 24 Jan. 1818–21 Feb. 1823 (PC 2/200 pp. 16–17); 3 Sept. 1841–10 June 1843 (PC 2/223 p. 466).

Robinson, Sir Thomas, kt. *Commissioner* 30 Dec. 1748–21 Dec. 1749.

Robinson, Hon. Thomas (succ. as 2nd Lord **Grantham** 30 Sept. 1770) *Commissioner* 22 Oct. 1766–25 April 1770. *First Lord* 12 Dec. 1780–2 May 1782. *Member* 5 March 1784 (PC 2/129 p. 56).

Roe, Thomas *Doorkeeper* (*Plantations*) 12 Aug. 1670–27 Sept. 1672 (Journal (Plantations) 1670–2, 4). *Doorkeeper* app. by 13 Nov. 1672 (Journal (Trade and Plantations) 1672–4, 10). Remained in office until abolition of Council 21 Dec. 1674 (*CTB*, v, 308).

Rogers, Richard *Clerk* 10 May 1727–12 April 1758 (*JCTP 1723–8*, 331). *Deputy Secretary* 12 April 1758–4 July 1764 (*JCTP 1754–8*, 396). Res. 4 July 1764 (*JCTP 1764–7*, 89).

Roscoe, Edward *Junior Supplementary Clerk* April 1859–Nov. 1863 (BT 3/55 no. 165; Ind. 20463 no. 507). *Junior Clerk* Nov. 1863 (BT 3/64 no. 624).

Rose, George *Member* 17 Feb. 1802 (PC 2/160 p. 220). *Vice President* 6 June 1804–5 Feb. 1806 (PC 2/165 p. 319); 30 March 1807–29 Sept. 1812 (PC 2/172 p. 404).

Ross, George *Inspector of Railways* 28 April 1858–17 Dec. 1860 (BT 5/66). Res. 17 Dec. 1860 (BT 3/59 no. 47).

Rossiter, William Henry *Extra Messenger* Sept. 1869 (BT 20/2 no. 695; Ind. 20470 no. 1159).

Rowe, Joshua L. *Junior Supplementary Clerk* 1854–Jan. 1861 (BT 5/67, 10 Feb. 1859). *Senior Supplementary Clerk* Jan. 1861 (BT 3/59 no. 49).

Rupert, Prince *Commissioner* (*Trade*) 20 Oct. 1668, 16 April 1669. *Commissioner* (*Plantations*) 4 April 1671. *Commissioner* 27 Sept. 1672.

Russell, Edward *Member* 16 Feb. 1689 (PC 2/73 p. 8).

Russell, William (Russell) *styled* Lord *Member* 22 April 1679 (PC 2/68 p. 6).

Ryan, Sir Edward, kt. *Commissioner of Railways* 4 Nov. 1846–10 Oct. 1851 (*London Gazette* no. 20657). Office abolished 10 Oct. 1851 (14 & 15 Vict., c 64, s 1). *Member* 15 April 1848 (PC 2/231 p. 192).

Ryder, Hon. Dudley *Member* 3 March 1790 (PC 2/134 p. 534). *Vice President* 20 Oct. 1790–18 Nov. 1801 (PC 2/135 p. 291).

Samber, James Selwyn *Clerk* 22 April 1765–c. 24 Jan. 1770 (*JCTP 1764–7*, 168). D. by 24 Jan. 1770 (*JCTP 1768–75*, 164).

Sampson, John *Messenger* (*Plantations*) 12 Aug. 1670–27 Sept. 1672 (Journal (Plantations) 1670–2, 4). *Messenger* app. by 13 Nov. 1672 (Journal (Trade and Plantations) 1672–4, 10). Remained in office until abolition of Council 21 Dec. 1674 (*CTB*, v, 308).

Sanders, Joseph *Messenger* (*Railway Department*) 23 Dec. 1846–April 1853 (MT 13/6 p. 77). *Messenger* April 1853–1865 ([Cd. 1713] pp. 147, 157 HC (1854) xxvii, 179, 189; *Royal Kal.* (1854), 160). Last occ. 1865 (*Royal Kal.* (1865), 164).

Sanderson, Anthony *Clerk* first occ. 20 Dec. 1714 (*JCTP 1709–15*, 575). D. by 5 June 1735 (*JCTP 1735–41*, 19).

Sandwich, Edward (Montagu) 1st Earl of *Commissioner* (*Trade*) 7 Nov. 1660, 16 April 1669. *President* (*Plantations*) 30 July 1670–28 May 1672. D. 28 May 1672.

Sandys, Samuel (Sandys) 1st Lord *First Lord* 21 March 1761–1 March 1763.

Savile, Henry *Member* 12 March 1675 (PC 2/64 p. 395).

Saye and Sele, William (Fiennes) 1st Viscount *Commissioner (Plantations)* 1 Dec. 1660.

Scarrott, George *Messenger* probably app. 1858; first occ. 1859 (*Royal Kal.* (1859), 165).

Schebenmeyer, Carl Friedrich August *Translator* 9 Jan. 1868 (BT 5/76).

Scoons, William Bailey *Messenger (Railway Department)* 23 Dec. 1846–April 1853 (MT 13/6 p. 77). *Messenger* April 1853–20 Feb. 1858 ([Cd. 1713] pp. 147, 157 HC (1854) xxvii, 179, 189; *Royal Kal.* (1854), 160). Dis. 20 Feb. 1858 (BT 5/66).

Scott, Charles *Junior Supplementary Clerk* 30 April 1857–27 Aug. 1864 (BT 5/65). *Senior Supplementary Clerk* 27 Aug. 1864 (BT 5/72).

Scott, Sir John, kt. *Member* 17 July 1799 (PC 2/153 p. 153).

Scott, Sir William, kt. *Member* 31 Oct. 1798 (PC 2/151 p. 601).

Scott, William *Porter* 5 Jan. 1816–21 May 1844 (BT 5/52, 21 May 1844). Ret. 21 May 1844 (ibid.).

Scott, William *Messenger* 22 March 1845–12 May 1865 (BT 5/63). Ret. 12 May 1865 (BT 20/1 no. 58).

Sedgwick, Edward *Clerk* 14 June 1738–16 Dec. 1755 (*JCTP 1735–41*, 243). Res. 16 Dec. 1755 (*JCTP 1754–8*, 195).
    Solicitor and Clerk of Reports 6 June 1753 28 Sept. 1763 (*JCTP 1750–3*, 430–1). Res. 28 Sept. 1763 on app. as Under Secretary of State (*JCTP 1759–63*, 381; *Calendar of Home Office Papers 1760–5*, 302–3).

Selby, W. C. *Messenger* May 1865 (BT 20/1 no. 70).

Sergeant, Beza *Clerk* pd. 11 July 1676 for period from 25 Dec. 1674 to 26 March 1676 (BM Add. MS 9767 p. 14); no further occ.

Serle, Ambrose *Solicitor and Clerk of Reports* 23 Jan. 1776–15 June 1779 (*JCTP 1776–82*, 2, 24–6, 28). Office declared vacant 15 June 1779 (ibid. 257).

Serle, Edward *Messenger* 19 Dec. 1749–2 May 1782 (*JCTP 1742–9*, 471). Office abolished 2 May 1782 (*JCTP 1776–82*, 472; T 1/579 Schedule 3).
    Porter 7 Oct. 1756–2 May 1782 (*JCTP 1754–8*, 258). Office abolished 2 May 1782 (*JCTP 1776–82*, 472; T 1/579 Schedule 3).

Serle, Mary *Necessary Woman* 29 April 1777–2 May 1782 (*JCTP 1776–82*, 2, 87) Office abolished 2 May 1782 (ibid. 472; T 1/579 Schedule 3).

Seton, Bertram W. *Junior Clerk* Feb.–4 March 1868 (BT 20/1 no. 495). Res. 4 March 1868 (Ind. 20470 no. 795).

Seymour, Edward *Member* 12 March 1675 (PC 2/64 p. 395).

Shaftesbury, Earl of *see* **Cooper,** Sir Anthony Ashley

Sharp, John *Commissioner* 15 Sept. 1713–13 Dec. 1714.

Shaw, Sir John, kt. *Commissioner (Trade)* 7 Nov. 1660.
    Commissioner (Plantations) 1 Dec. 1660.

Shaw Lefevre, George John *Parliamentary Secretary* 14 Dec. 1868 (BT 5/76).

Shaw Lefevre, John George *Secretary* 19 June 1841–10 May 1848 (BT 5/49; BT 5/56, 6 Aug. 1847). Left office 10 May 1848 on app. as Clerk Assistant, House of Lords (BT 5/57; *London Gazette* no. 20843).

Sheffield, John (Baker Holroyd) 1st Lord *Member* 20 Dec. 1809 (PC 2/184 p. 175).

Sheil, Richard Lalor *Vice President* 29 Aug. 1839–28 June 1841 (PC 2/221 p. 440).

Shelburne, William (Petty) 2nd Earl of *First Lord* 23 April–17 Sept. 1763.

Shergold, James *Messenger* 17 Oct. 1807–7 March 1810 (BT 5/17 p. 447). Res. 7 March 1810 (BT 5/19 p. 426).

Shorter, John   *Commissioner (Trade)* 20 Oct. 1668, 16 April 1669.

Shrewsbury, Charles (Talbot) 12th Earl of   *Member* 16 Feb. 1689 (PC 2/73 p. 8).

Silvester, Eusebius   *Solicitor and Clerk of Reports* 4 July 1764–31 May 1765 (*JCTP 1764–7*, 89). Res. 31 May 1765 on app. as Agent for West Africa (ibid. 175).

Simkins, Anthony L.   *Copyist* 1853–4 (BT 5/67, 10 Feb. 1859; *Royal Kal.* (1854), 160). *Senior Supplementary Clerk* 1854–30 July 1856 (BT 3/47 pp. 270–2; *Royal Kal.* (1855), 159). Left office 30 July 1856 on app. as Senior Clerk and Financial Officer, Department of Science and Art (BT 5/64).

Simmonds, George Harvey   *Extra Clerk* 30 April 1864–1868 (BT 5/72). *Supplementary Clerk* 1868 (*Staff Lists*, 18; *Royal Kal.* (1869), 166).

Simmons, John Lintorn Arabin   *Inspector of Railways* 28 Jan. 1847–3 April 1850 (MT 13/7 p. 44). *Secretary (Railway Department)* 3 April 1850–April 1853 (MT 13/12 p. 152). *Assistant Secretary (Railways)* April 1853–29 June 1854 ([Cd. 1713] pp. 135, 156–7 HC (1854) xxvii, 167, 188–9; *Royal Kal.* (1854), 160). Left office 29 June 1854 (MT 13/20 no. 147).

Simmons, Thomas   *Extra Messenger* probably app. 1859; occ. from 1860 to 1862 (*Royal Kal.* (1860), 165; ibid. (1862), 165). *Messenger* Oct. 1862 (BT 3/62 no. 575).

Simpson, Samuel   *Office Keeper* 7 Oct. 1740–c. 8 July 1742 (*JCTP 1735–41*, 347). D. by 8 July 1742 (*JCTP 1742–9*, 27).

Sivrac, Charles Anthony George   *Junior Clerk (Statistical Department)* 4 Dec. 1838–Jan. 1851 (BT 5/46 p. 117). *Senior Clerk* Jan. 1851–April 1853 (BT 3/41 pp. 89–93). *Old Senior Clerk* April 1853–16 May 1856 ([Cd. 1713] pp. 142, 157 HC (1854) xxvii, 174, 189). D. 16 May 1856 (*Gent. Mag.* (1856), cxxxviii, 667).

Skynner, Cyriacus   *Clerk* probably app. 1696 (CO 389/36 p. 106). D. 6 Aug. 1700 (ibid.; Prob 6/76 f. 168).

Slingsby, Henry   *Commissioner (Trade)* 7 Nov. 1660, 20 Oct. 1668, 16 April 1669. *Commissioner and Secretary (Plantations)* 30 July 1670–27 Sept. 1672. *Commissioner* 27 Sept. 1672–21 Dec. 1674.

Sloane, Hans   *Commissioner* 16 Sept. 1780–2 May 1782.

Sloper, William   *Commissioner* 13 Dec. 1756–21 March 1761.

Smith, Sir John Mark Frederick, kt.   *Inspector General of Railways* 2 Dec. 1840–5 Jan. 1842 (BT 5/48). Left office 5 Jan. 1842 on app. as Director of Field Works, Chatham (BT 5/50).

Smyth, John   *Member* 1 May 1805 (PC 2/167 p. 360).

Southampton, Thomas (Wriothesley) 4th Earl of   *Commissioner (Trade)* 7 Nov. 1660. *Commissioner (Plantations)* 1 Dec. 1660.

Sowerby, John   *Clerk* 25 Aug. 1786–25 March 1822 (BT 5/4 p. 15). *Senior Clerk* 25 March 1822–5 Nov. 1827 (BT 5/30 pp. 182–4). Ret. 5 Nov. 1827 (BT 5/36 pp. 399–400).

Sowerby, John   *Supernumerary Clerk* 15 July 1801–16 Oct. 1805 (BT 5/12 pp. 320–1). *Clerk* 16 Oct. 1805–24 Sept. 1811 (BT 5/15 pp. 315–22, 346). Dis. 24 Sept. 1811 (BT 5/20 pp. 521–2).

Spence, Henry Donald Maurice   *Junior Supplementary Clerk* 29 Jan. 1855–30 April 1857 (BT 5/63). *Third Class Clerk* 30 April 1857–27 Jan. 1860 (BT 5/65). Res. 27 Jan. 1860 (BT 3/57 nos. 53, 68).

Spence, Lancelot Molyneux Dalrymple   *Junior Supplementary Clerk* Nov. 1855–28 Jan. 1860 (BT 3/49 no. 686; Ind. 20458 no. 2085). *Third Class Clerk* 28 Jan.

1860–July 1863 (BT 3/57 no. 53). *Junior Clerk* July 1863–4 July 1865 (BT 3/64 no. 379; *Royal Kal.* (1864), 164). D. 4 July 1865 (*Record of Old Westminsters*, ed. G. F. R. Barker and A. H. Stenning (London 1928), ii, 872).

Private Secretary to Secretary (Booth) probably app. 1863; occ. from 1864 to 1865 (*Royal Kal.* (1864), 164; ibid. (1865), 164).

Spencer, John   *Clerk* 7 Nov. 1721–10 May 1727 (*JCTP 1718–22*, 327). Dis. 10 May 1727 (*JCTP 1723–8*, 331).

Spencer, Lord Robert   *Commissioner* 25 April 1770–2 Jan. 1782.

Stacey, Elizabeth   *Housekeeper* 25 Aug. 1786–c. 5 Jan. 1838 (BT 5/4 p. 15). D. by 5 Jan. 1838 (BT 5/45 p. 135).

Stacey, William   *Supernumerary Clerk* 20 Feb. 1792–10 Dec. 1794 (BT 5/9 p. 90). *Clerk* 10 Dec. 1794–10 Oct. 1795 (ibid. p. 301). Res. 10 Oct. 1795 on app. as Assistant Commissary to Superintendent and Director of Forage, St. Domingo (BT 5/10 p. 115).

Stamford, Thomas (Grey) 2nd Earl of   *First Lord* 9 June 1699–19 June 1702; 25 April 1707–12 June 1711.

Stanley of Alderley, Edward John (Stanley) 2nd Lord   *Vice President* 11–27 Feb. 1852 (PC 2/235 p. 102); 4 Jan. 1853–31 March 1855 (PC 2/237 p. 32). *President* 31 March 1855–26 Feb. 1858 (PC 2/241 p. 322).

Stephen, James   *Law Clerk* 30 July 1825–14 Jan. 1836 (BT 5/34 pp. 67–70). Office discontinued 14 Jan. 1836 (BT 5/43 pp. 248–9). *Member* 15 April 1848 (PC 2/231 p. 192).

Stepney, George   *Commissioner* 6 July 1697–15 Sept. 1707. D. 15 Sept. 1707 (*CTB*, xxii, 150).

Stokes, James   *Messenger* 6 Jan. 1794–3 Dec. 1795 (BT 5/9 p. 131). *Office Keeper* 3 Dec. 1795–c. 17 Oct. 1807 (BT 5/10 p. 144). D. by 17 Oct. 1807 (BT 5/17 p. 447).

Stone, Andrew   *Commissioner* 21 Dec. 1749–4 Dec. 1761.

Stoneham, Allen   *Junior Supplementary Clerk* 29 Jan. 1855–30 July 1856 (BT 5/63). *Senior Supplementary Clerk* 30 July 1856–July 1863 (BT 5/64). *Bookkeeper* July 1863–2 Jan. 1867 (BT 3/64 no. 379; *Royal Kal.* (1864), 164). *Senior Clerk* 2 Jan. 1867–12 Oct. 1869 (BT 5/75). *Deputy Accountant* 12 Oct. 1869 (BT 5/77).

Storer, Anthony Morris   *Commissioner* 2 Jan.–2 May 1782.

Straton, J. Ward   *Private Secretary to Vice President* (Donoughmore) probably app. April 1858; occ. 1859 (*Royal Kal.* (1859), 165).

Strutt, Edward   *President of Railway Commission* 29 Aug. 1846–c. 10 April 1848 (*London Gazette* no. 20637). Left office by 10 April 1848 (app. of Labouchere).

Stuart, Andrew   *Commissioner* 14 July 1779–2 May 1782.

Suffolk, Henry (Howard) 6th Earl of   *First Lord* 12 May 1715–31 Jan. 1718.

Suft, Herbert Manson   *Clerk (Railway Department)* 8 Dec. 1846–18 Feb. 1848 (MT 13/6 pp. 53, 65). *Junior Clerk (Railway Department)* 18 Feb. 1848–April 1853 (MT 13/9 p. 191). *Junior Clerk* April 1853–30 July 1856 ([Cd. 1713] p. 157 HC (1854) xxvii, 189; *Royal Kal.* (1854), 160). *Senior Clerk* 30 July 1856–30 April 1857 (BT 5/64). *First Class Clerk* 30 April 1857–30 July 1860 (BT 5/65). Left office 30 July 1860 on app. as Clerk, Privy Council Office (BT 3/58 no. 529).

Suft, Robert Francis   *Clerk* 24 Sept. 1806–25 March 1822 (BT 5/16 p. 348). *Senior Clerk* 25 March 1822–21 June 1849 (BT 5/30 pp. 182–4). D. 21 June 1849 (death certificate).

Sulivan, Bartholomew James *Professional Member (Marine Department)* 26 March 1857–29 May 1865 (BT 5/65). Res. 29 May 1865 (BT 5/73).

Sullivan, John *Member* 1 May 1805 (PC 2/167 p. 360).

Sunderland, Robert (Spencer) 2nd Earl of *Member* 22 April 1679 (PC 2/68 p. 6).

Swan, William *Clerk* app. by 13 Nov. 1672 (Journal (Trade and Plantations) 1672–4, 10); pd. to 25 Dec. 1673 (CO 389/5 p. 119). Left office by 20 March 1674 (Journal (Trade and Plantations) 1672–4, 78).

Swanston, George John *Supernumerary Clerk (Railway Department)* 26 July 1849–6 Sept. 1851 (MT 13/11 p. 443). *Junior Clerk (Railway Department)* 6 Sept. 1851–April 1853 (MT 13/15 p. 490). *Junior Clerk* April 1853–30 April 1857 ([Cd. 1713] p. 157 HC (1854) xxvii, 189; *Royal Kal.* (1854), 160). *Second Class Clerk* 30 April 1857–July 1863 (BT 5/65). *Senior Clerk* July 1863 (BT 3/64 no. 379; *Royal Kal.* (1864), 164).

    Private Secretary to Vice President (Lowe) probably app. Aug. 1855; occ. from 1856 to 1857 (*Royal Kal.* (1856), 161; ibid. (1857), 161).

Sydney, Thomas (Townshend) 1st Lord (cr. Viscount **Sydney** 11 June 1789) *Member* 5 March 1784 (PC 2/129 p. 56), 8 Aug. 1789 (PC 2/134 p. 200).

Symonds, Arthur *Private Secretary to President* (Poulett Thomson) 2 May 1835–Aug. 1839 (BT 5/43 p. 2).

Talbot, Hon. John *Commissioner* 29 Dec. 1755–23 Sept. 1756. D. 23 Sept. 1756 (*Gent. Mag.* (1756), xxvi, 451).

Talbot, John Chetwynd (succ. as 3rd Lord **Talbot** 27 April 1782) *Commissioner* 2 Jan.–2 May 1782.

Tankerville, Ford (Grey) 1st Earl of *Commissioner* 15 May 1696–9 June 1699.

Taylor, John *Junior Clerk* March 1868 (BT 20/1 no. 511).

Temple, Sir Richard, 3rd Bart. *Commissioner (Plantations)* 19 June 1671, 15 Aug. 1671.

Temple, Richard (Temple Nugent Brydges Chandos Grenville) *styled* Earl *Vice President* 5 Feb. 1806–30 March 1807 (PC 2/169 pp. 286, 472).

Temple, Sir William, 1st Bart. *Member* 22 April 1679 (PC 2/68 p. 6).

Tennent *see* **Emerson Tennent**

Terrie, Thomas *Office Keeper* 19 Dec. 1758–27 Feb. 1767 (*JCTP 1754–8*, 437). Dis. 27 Feb. 1767 (*JCTP 1764–7*, 371).

Thomas, Sir Edmund, 3rd Bart. *Commissioner* 21 March 1761–23 April 1763.

Thompson, Sir William, kt. *Commissioner (Trade)* 7 Nov. 1660, 20 Oct. 1668, 16 April 1669.

Thomson *see* **Poulett Thomson**

Thynne, Lord George *Member* 1 May 1805 (PC 2/167 p. 360).

Thynne, Lord John *Member* 1 May 1805 (PC 2/167 p. 360).

Titus, Silas *Commissioner (Trade)* 20 Oct. 1668, 16 April 1669.
    Commissioner (Plantations) 30 July 1670–27 Sept. 1672. *Commissioner* 27 Sept. 1672–21 Dec. 1674.

Torriano, George *Commissioner (Trade)* 7 Nov. 1660.

Townsend, Richard *Junior Supplementary Clerk* 29 Jan. 1855–25 Nov. 1858 (BT 5/63). Res. 25 Nov. 1858 (Ind. 20462 no. 1756).

Townshend, Hon. Charles *Commissioner* 23 June 1749–6 April 1754. *First Lord* 1 March–23 April 1763.

Travers *see* **Clarke Travers**

Tregonning, Richard *Office Keeper* 7 March 1721–c. 27 Feb. 1733 (*JCTP 1718–22*, 253; *JCTP 1723–8*, 425). D. by 27 Feb. 1733 (*JCTP 1729–34*, 335).

Trevor, Charles Cecil *Assistant Secretary (Harbours)* 2 Jan. 1867 (BT 5/75).

Trevor, Sir John, kt. *Commissioner (Trade)* 20 Oct. 1668, 16 April 1669.

Turner, Sir Charles, kt. *Commissioner* 4 May 1708–7 July 1712.

Turner, H. *Messenger* May 1865 (*Staff Lists*, 392).

Tutté, John *Clerk* 14 June 1738–21 June 1775 (*JCTP 1735–41*, 243). D. 21 June 1775 (*Gent. Mag.* (1775), xlv, 304).

Tyler, Henry Whatley *Inspector of Railways* 15 April 1853 (BT 3/50 no. 778).

Tyte, Thomas *Commissioner (Trade)* 7 Nov. 1660, 20 Oct. 1668, 16 April 1669.

Underdown, James *Messenger* 29 March 1816–4 Nov. 1820 (BT 5/24 pp. 415–16). D. 4 Nov. 1820 (BT 5/29 p. 237).

Valpy, Richard *Assistant (Statistical Department)* 5 Jan. 1842–April 1853 (BT 5/50). *Senior Clerk* April 1853–30 April 1857 ([Cd. 1713] p. 157 HC (1854) xxvii, 189; *Royal Kal.* (1854), 160). *First Class Clerk* 30 April 1857–10 Feb. 1859 (BT 5/65). *Assistant (Statistical Department)* 10 Feb. 1859–July 1863 (BT 5/67). *Assistant* July 1863 (BT 3/64 no. 379).

Venables, Robert *Commissioner (Plantations)* 1 Dec. 1660.

Vereker, Hon. Henry Prendergast *Supernumerary Clerk (Railway Department)* 8 Sept. 1848–6 Sept. 1851 (MT 13/10 p. 304). *Junior Clerk (Railway Department)* 6 Sept. 1851–21 Feb. 1852 (MT 13/15 p. 490). Left office 21 Feb. 1852 on app. as Consul, Rio Grande do Sul (*London Gazette* no. 21297).

Vernon, Edward *Commissioner (Plantations)* 1 Dec. 1660.

Vernon, Thomas *Commissioner* 15 Sept. 1713–13 Dec. 1714.

Vesey Fitzgerald, William *President* 11 June 1828–2 Feb. 1830 (PC 2/209 p. 441).

Villiers, Hon. John Charles *Member* 24 Feb. 1790 (PC 2/134 pp. 522–3).

Vodoz, Charlotte *Housekeeper* 5 Jan. 1838–21 Feb. 1863 (BT 5/45 p. 135). Res. 21 Feb. 1863 (BT 3/63 no. 88).

Waddington, Samuel *Junior Clerk* 17 Feb. 1868 (BT 5/76).

Waldrond, Edward *Commissioner (Plantations)* 1 Dec. 1660.

Walker, Ingram Bathurst *Junior Clerk* 6 Feb. 1867 (BT 5/75).

Walker, William *Commissioner (Trade)* 7 Nov. 1660.

Walker, William Harrison *Professional Member (Marine Department)* 15 Aug. 1850 (BT 5/59, 23 Dec. 1850).

Wallace, Thomas *Vice President* 24 Jan. 1818–3 April 1823 (PC 2/200 pp. 16–17).

Waller, Edmund *Commissioner (Plantations)* 30 July 1670–27 Sept. 1672. *Commissioner* 27 Sept. 1672–21 Dec. 1674.

Waller, Edward *Commissioner (Trade)* 7 Nov. 1660. *Commissioner (Plantations)* 1 Dec. 1660.

Walsh, John *Junior Supplementary Clerk* 29 Jan. 1855–30 April 1857 (BT 5/63). *Senior Supplementary Clerk* 30 April 1857–c. 2 Dec. 1861 (BT 5/65). D. by 2 Dec. 1861 (BT 5/69).

Walsingham, Lord *see* **de Grey**, Thomas

Ward, Thomas Poole *Junior Clerk (Statistical Department)* 6 July 1841–Jan. 1851 (BT 5/49). *Senior Clerk* Jan. 1851–April 1853 (BT 3/41 pp. 89–93). *Old Senior Clerk* April 1853–July 1863 ([Cd. 1713] pp. 142, 157 HC (1854) xxvii, 174, 189; BT 5/65, 30 April 1857). *Senior Clerk* July 1863–2 Jan. 1867 (BT 3/64 no. 379;

Royal Kal. (1864), 164). Ret. 2 Jan. 1867 (HC 47 p. 16 (1867) xxxix, 228; BT 5/75).

Private Secretary to Vice President (Milner Gibson) Sept. 1846–May 1848 (*Gent. Mag.* (1846), cxix, 312).

Warwick, Earl of *see* **Greville, Lord**

Watton, Charles *Extra Messenger* May 1868 (Ind. 20470 no. 594).

Watts, Henry *Supernumerary Clerk* 22 Feb. 1798–6 Aug. 1800 (BT 5/11 p. 87). Res. 6 Aug. 1800 on app. as Clerk, Customs (BT 5/12 p. 49).

Watts, William *Commissioner (Plantations)* 1 Dec. 1660.

Webb, Samuel *Supernumerary Clerk* 24 Sept. 1811–16 July 1812 (BT 5/20 pp. 521–2). *Clerk* 16 July 1812–25 March 1822 (BT 5/21 pp. 349-51, 470). *Junior Clerk* 25 March 1822–22 Nov. 1827 (BT 5/30 pp. 182–4). *Senior Clerk* 22 Nov. 1827–12 Aug. 1846 (BT 5/36 pp. 446–7). D. 12 Aug. 1846 (*Gent. Mag.* (1846), cix, 440).

West, Richard *Counsel* 23 April 1718–19 Aug. 1725 (*JCTP 1715–18*, 369). Left office by 19 Aug. 1725 on app. as Lord Chancellor, Ireland (app. of F. Fane; *JCTP 1723–8*, 195–6; *CSPC (America & West Indies) 1724-5*, 401).

Westley, John *Messenger* 22 July–c. 21 Nov. 1845 (BT 5/54). D. by 21 Nov. 1845 (ibid.).

Westmorland, Thomas (Fane) 6th Earl of *First Lord* 11 May 1719–22 May 1735.

Weymouth, Thomas (Thynne) 1st Viscount *First Lord* 19 June 1702–25 April 1707.

Whately, Thomas *Commissioner* 2 Feb. 1771–10 Feb. 1772.

Wheelock, Bryan *Clerk* 6 Aug. 1700–13 July 1714 (CO 389/36 pp. 106–7, 136–8). Dis. 13 July 1714 (*JCTP 1709–15*, 551). *Deputy Secretary* 20 Dec. 1714–20 July 1735 (ibid. 575). D. 20 July 1735 (*Gent. Mag.* (1735), v, 388).

Whitworth, Charles *Clerk* probably app. 1696 (CO 389/36 p. 107). Left office 11 March 1701 (ibid. pp. 107, 136–8).

Whitworth, Charles (Whitworth) 1st Lord *Member* 15 April 1807 (PC 2/172 p. 449).

Wickham, William *Member* 17 Feb. 1802 (PC 2/160 p. 220).

Wilks, Samuel *Clerk* 31 July 1766–24 Jan. 1770 (*JCTP 1764–7*, 317). Res. 24 Jan. 1770 (*JCTP 1768–75*, 164).

Williams, Henry Richard *Accountant* 8 Aug. 1851–19 June 1869 (BT 13/4 pt. i, 19 April 1869). Res. 19 June 1869 (BT 5/77).

Williams, William *Commissioner (Trade)* 7 Nov. 1660.
Commissioner (Plantations) 1 Dec. 1660.

Williamson, Sir Joseph, kt. *Member* 12 March 1675 (PC 2/64 p. 395).

Willis, Robert *Office Keeper* 8 May 1745–19 Dec. 1758 (*JCTP 1742–9*, 164). Ret. 19 Dec. 1758 (*JCTP 1754–8*, 437).

Willoughby, William *Commissioner (Plantations)* 1 Dec. 1660.

Willoughby of Parham, Francis (Willoughby) 5th Lord *Commissioner (Trade)* 7 Nov. 1660.
Commissioner (Plantations) 1 Dec. 1660.

Wilson, Gawyn *Clerk* 27 Oct. 1673–21 Dec. 1674 (Journal (Trade and Plantations) 1672-4, 51–2). Remained in office until abolition of Council 21 Dec. 1674 (*CTB*, v, 308).

Wilson, James *Vice President* 18 June–12 Aug. 1859 (PC 2/249 p. 422).

Wilson, John *Messenger* 10 Jan. 1723–c. 19 Dec. 1749 (*JCTP 1723–8*, 1). D. by 19 Dec. 1749 (*JCTP 1742–9*, 471).

Winch, Sir Humphrey, 1st Bart. *Commissioner* (*Plantations*) 30 July 1670–27 Sept. 1672. *Commissioner* 27 Sept. 1672–21 Dec. 1674.

Winchester, Charles (Powlett) 6th Marquess of *Member* 22 April 1679 (PC 2/68 p. 6).

Winchilsea, Charles (Finch) 4th Earl of *First Lord* 12 June 1711–5/16 Aug. 1712. D. 5 or 16 Aug. 1712.

Windsor, Thomas (Windsor) 7th Lord *Commissioner* (*Plantations*) 1 Dec. 1660.

Wolstenholme, Sir John, kt. *Commissioner* (*Trade*) 7 Nov. 1660.

Wood, George *Clerk* 22 Sept. 1786–4 Jan. 1798 (BT 5/4 p. 42). Res. 4 Jan. 1798 (BT 5/11 pp. 48–9).

Wood, Margaret *Necessary Woman* 6 July 1696–25 March 1701 (CO 391/9 p. 11). Left office 25 March 1701 (ibid. p. 107).

Worcester, Henry (Somerset) 3rd Marquess of *Member* 12 March 1675 (PC 2/64 p. 395), 22 April 1679 (PC 2/68 p. 6).

Worsley, Benjamin *Commissioner* (*Trade*) 20 Oct. 1668, 16 April 1669.
 Assistant (*Plantations*) probably app. following creation of Council 30 July 1670; salary authorised 2 Dec. 1670 from 24 June 1670 (*CSPD 1670*, 538–9; C 66/3121). *Secretary* 27 Sept. 1672–13 Sept. 1673 (C 66/3137). Res. 13 Sept. 1673 (Journal (Trade and Plantations) 1672–4, 45–7).

Wright, Anne *Necessary Woman* 5 Nov. 1760–c. 29 April 1777 (*JCTP 1759–63*, 134). D. by 29 April 1777 (*JCTP 1776–82*, 2).

Wright, Mary *Necessary Woman* app. 25 March 1701 (CO 389/36 p. 107). Last occ. 21 Jan. 1708 (*JCTP 1704–9*, 451).

Wynne, George *Inspector of Railways* 19 Aug. 1847–28 April 1858 (MT 13/7 pp. 557, 561–3). Res. 28 April 1858 (BT 5/66).

Wynne, Sir William, kt. *Member* 3 March 1790 (PC 2/134 p. 534).

Yolland, William *Inspector of Railways* 19 July 1854 (BT 3/50 no. 778).

York, James (Stuart) 1st Duke of *Commissioner* (*Trade*) 20 Oct. 1668, 16 April 1669.
 Commissioner (*Plantations*) 4 April 1671. *Commissioner* 27 Sept. 1672.

Yorke, Hon. John *Commissioner* 21 March 1761–2 May 1764; 12 Aug. 1765–3 Jan. 1766.

Yorke, Hon. Sir Joseph, kt. *Member* 5 March 1784 (PC 2/129 p. 56), 23 Aug. 1786 (PC 2/131 pp. 403–4).

Youde, Thomas *Porter* 11 June 1844–1845 (BT 5/52). Last occ. 1845 (*Royal Kal.* (1845), 162).

Index of Offices and Departments